The Design Matrix:
A Consilience of Clues

The Design Matrix:
A Consilience of Clues

by

Mike Gene

ARBOR VITAE PRESS

ARBOR VITAE PRESS
http://arborvitaepress.com

Book Design: Robin P. Simonds

"Face on Mars" photos courtesy NASA.

Library of Congress Control Number: 2006937418
ISBN: 978-0-9786314-0-6

First Edition
Printed in the United States
12 11 10 09 08 07 - 1 2 3 4 5

To Mary—for always believing in me.

TABLE OF CONTENTS

INTRODUCTION

The decision to write this book was not an easy one, as arguments about Intelligent Design and evolution generate a great deal of anxiety and hostility in our culture. The vast majority of scientists do not view Intelligent Design as science and I happen to agree with them. Nevertheless, this scientific consensus has not stopped many people from trying to get Intelligent Design taught in the science classrooms of the public school systems. This creates an understandable resentment among those who highly value the place of science in our educational system.

Because of the socio-political current that is attached to this debate, some may start with a false impression about the purpose of this book. Therefore, I should make it explicitly clear from the start that I did not write this book to help those seeking to change the way we teach science to our kids. I do not argue that design deserves to be known as science. At best, Intelligent Design may only be a nascent proto-science and thus does not belong in the public school curriculum. Nor does this book argue that evolution is false and deserves to be criticized in the public school curriculum. If the truth is to be told, I oppose such actions. So, you may ask, for what purpose would I write this type of book?

It is my belief that there are people in the world like me—people who are tired of the heated debates, name-calling, innuendo, and political fights. Such people might find themselves in the middle ground and would rather focus on the hypotheses, the arguments, and the evidence. We might not be completely convinced that life was designed, yet we find the hypothesis to be tremendously intriguing. Rather than belaboring the concern as to whether the study of Intelligent Design should be labeled science, metaphysics, or religion, it is my belief that there are people who would rather just ponder the issues that are raised by design and evolution.

The most important reason for writing this book is that I, like most authors, believe I have something to say. If we push aside all the politics, rhetoric, and concerns about what we should and should not do with the concept of Intelligent Design, I remain intrigued by the concept and evidences and continue to ponder the topic. I do not come to you as one with a preconceived belief that life was, indeed, designed. I come to you with nagging suspicions that there may really be something solid behind the hypothesis that life was designed. These suspicions are like 'splinters in my mind' that will not go away if left unattended.

What you will find in this book is the beginning of a journey. Writing in the journal *Science* in 1977, Nobel Laureate Francois Jacob once offered some truly profound words that have been the inspiration of this book:

> To produce a valuable observation, one has first to have an idea of what to observe, a preconception of what is possible. Scientific advances often come from uncovering a hitherto unseen aspect of things as a result, not so much of using new instruments, but rather of looking at objects from a different angle. This look is necessarily guided by a certain idea of what this so-called reality might be. It always involves a certain conception about the unknown, that is, about what lies beyond that which one has logical or experimental reasons to believe.

This book is indeed about looking at objects from a different angle and having a certain conception about reality that is beyond current logical or experimental reasons to believe. It is the first step in an investigation. You are invited to join along.

The Design Matrix is broken into four parts. Part I is entitled "The Way," as we start our journey by pondering new ways to think about Intelligent Design. In Chapter 1, arguments about the existence of the Face on Mars are considered, as these arguments provide important lessons that will help guide our perspective. In Chapter 2, I explore the conventional ways of thinking about design and biology and suggest a somewhat different way of approaching these issues. The approach I raise is not radical or novel; it has just been neglected.

In Part II, "The Clues," I outline features of biology that can fuel our new approach as they point toward design. It will be crucial to remember that I offer such features only as clues and not proofs. I have personally found these clues to be haunting and worthy of closer examination. It will then be my goal to help the reader move beyond the level of merely having hunches backed up by clues.

But before we can get to this, we will confront the challenges that we face in Part III. In Chapter 6, we meet Darwin's Theory of Evolution, learning to respect it, as well as expand our way of thinking about this theory. Chapter 7 highlights the possibilities on ways that design and evolution can actually co-exist, opening new doors for thinking about design.

Finally, in Part IV, I progressively outline a method for tentatively inferring the existence of design and helping us move beyond the suspicions—the Design Matrix. It is an open-ended method that can be used by both sides of this dispute to assess a design inference and it is my hope that you will find it easy to understand and use. After explaining the Design Matrix, I take it for a test drive to see how it scores things that are known to be designed by humans, along with various biological features. In Volume 2 that is eventually to follow, I will use it, and more, to explore the living world.

I have come to find myself in the highly unusual position of writing a book about design and evolution while using a pseudonym. Why would I make such a choice? My interest in this topic is a function of the Internet and my chosen handle for the Internet has long been Mike Gene. Idly surfing the internet forums one day, I stumbled across many heated arguments on Intelligent Design approximately a year after Michael Behe's book, *Darwin's Black Box,* was published. I found this "buzz" interesting and intriguing, while also noting that the author was a reputable biochemist at a mainstream university, rather than a typical author of creationist literature. As I read through the exchanges, and explored the Internet to better familiarize myself with Behe and his new argument, I must admit that I admired him for having such temerity.

Having long had an affinity for the underdog, I decided to join the fray, since Behe's supporters on the forum seemed outgunned and outnumbered. My original intention had been to play the gadfly for a short time and walk away. But through the various arguments I had with many other people, a way of viewing things slowly began to open up and become clearer to me. I eventually became convinced that there could very well be something solid with this notion of Intelligent Design, and gradually came to envision what you now hold in your hands—this book.

My decision to stick with my pseudonym is about more than maintaining a sense of continuity with my Internet presence, but also because it pays tribute to a personal belief that I hold dear. As I have repeatedly argued on the Internet, I am not going to make any appeal to qualifications or training. If I have no qualifications or relevant training, this may cause some to dismiss or overlook a good argument for this reason alone. If I do have qualifications and relevant training, this may cause some to embrace a bad argument for this reason alone. I would rather let the arguments stand on their own to be evaluated without prejudice. The Internet functions in such a way that it allows us to strip most of the extraneous material from an argument (a person's reputation, degrees, popularity, etc.) and focus instead on the core of the argument and the data used to support it. It is my hope that this approach carries out of the Internet and into this book. Of course, since I make no appeal to qualifications or relevant training, you, the reader should not treat me as an authority. You must decide for yourself if the evidence and arguments make sense and if need be, track down the references that may support them.

I would like to further mention that this book was largely written as a late night hobby. While I have tried to be as careful as possible, it is likely that the book does contain some errors. However, I do not envision any possible error as being significant enough to overturn any of the major arguments in the book. If corrections or further commentary are needed, readers will find them on this book's blog at www.thedesignmatrix.com.

Because this book is largely an outcome of my Internet experience, I would like to publicly acknowledge some of the various people I have met in cyberspace over the years. The Internet can be an extremely hostile environment and their support with stimulating questions, commentary, and/or kind words has been greatly appreciated. These people include Guts, Krauze, The Deuce, Bipod, Steve Petermann, Joy, Jazzraptor, Jack, Leonard, Nobody, Bilbo, Rock, Bones, Mesk, Art, David, theforce, Salvador, DNAUnion, Ilion, Douglas, Teleologist, Mturner, Bertvan, Vividbleau, and jon_e.

I am sure there are many more and I hope those whom I have overlooked will forgive my oversight. I would also like to especially thank Krauze for reading over a few of the chapters and offering helpful suggestions and comments.

Finally, I must acknowledge the one person whose contributions to this book have come in so many forms that it would be hard to list—my wife. Her sacrifice and help have been so substantial that I can firmly say that this book would simply never have come into existence without her.

I hope this book will provide as exciting a journey for you as it has for me—a journey to new and stimulating ideas on this heavily debated topic.

PART I — THE WAY

CHAPTER 1

LESSONS FROM A VANISHING FACE

A s a boy, one of my favorite movies was George Pal's *War of the Worlds*, the big screen adaptation of H.G. Wells's popular book. In the movie, a hostile alien intelligence invades our planet with machines superior to anything that our science or military could match. As an avid fan of science fiction movies, this particular movie captured my imagination. Leaning forward in my seat, I watched the screen with dawning horror as I realized that the Martian invaders were determined to exterminate the human race. The military fought back valiantly, but with little success as the human population of the earth was systematically destroyed. Mentally urging the military on, I kept thinking "Drop the bomb! Drop the bomb!" When the military finally did make the decision to drop a nuclear bomb on the enemy Martian invaders, I cheered in boyish delight, believing the movie would end in a glorious victory. On the screen, the bomb exploded in a satisfying frenzy of glory. As the smoke cleared, my jubilation slowly turned to shocked amazement when I saw that the alien warship continued to cruise along, as if simply taking a morning stroll under that massive nuclear explosion. Realizing that the best of our doomsday machines could not put a dent in those alien war machines was even more terrifying. Questions arose in my young mind. Maybe we were not the most intelligent beings in the universe. Maybe somebody out there did not like us. Surprised at the conclusion of the movie, I collapsed in my seat in relief. We had beaten those Martian invaders after all, but not by our own intelligence.

In 1877, Italian astronomer Giovanni Schiaparelli observed markings on Mars and described them as *"canali"* which literally mean "channels." Due to a translation error, English-speaking people thought the astronomer had identified canals on Mars, leading to much speculation about life there. It is from this context of speculation that H.G. Wells originally got the inspiration for his story.

How is it that a novel originally created in 1898 lives on into the Twentieth Century and beyond? Stories such as *War of the Worlds* tap into our public angst over global events beyond our control. Orson Welles introduced the world to the real power of radio with his 1938 broadcast of this Wells's tale, during a time when many Americans feared the rise of Nazi Germany. There was much public chaos when many people mistakenly believed that the story was a news broadcast. The original movie version was released in 1953 during the Cold War with the Soviet Union. Since a doomsday machine called the atomic bomb now existed, many people were afraid the world could end at any moment because careless world leaders might usher in a nuclear holocaust. And it is interesting that the most recent re-telling of H.G. Wells's story, Stephen Spielberg's 2005 version of this movie, is concurrent with America's concern over the War on Terror. While these are factors to consider, I think the fundamental reason for the enduring popularity of this story is captured in the first paragraph of H.G. Wells's book:

> No one would have believed in the last years of the nineteenth century that this world was being watched keenly and closely by intelligences greater than man's and yet as mortal as his own; that as men busied themselves about their various concerns they were scrutinized and studied, perhaps almost as narrowly as a man with a microscope might scrutinize the transient creatures that swarm and multiply in a drop of water. With infinite complacency men went to and fro over this globe about their little affairs, serene in their assurance of their empire over matter. It is possible that the infusoria under the microscope do the same. No one gave a thought to the older worlds of space as sources of human danger, or thought of them only to dismiss the idea of life upon them as impossible or improbable. It is curious to recall some of the mental habits of those departed days. At most terrestrial men fancied there might be other men upon Mars, perhaps inferior to themselves and ready to

welcome a missionary enterprise. Yet across the gulf of space, minds that are to our minds as ours are to those of the beasts that perish, intellects vast and cool and unsympathetic, regarded this earth with envious eyes, and slowly and surely drew their plans against us. And early in the twentieth century came the great disillusionment.[1]

The idea of being watched by a superior, hostile intelligence is chilling. H.G. Wells captures the vulnerability, weakness, and limitations of humanity, despite all our technology. This theme is further emphasized in that mankind survives the Martian attack, not because of anything we could do to repel the invaders, but only because we happen to live on a planet inhabited by humble bacteria.

THE FACE

H. G. Wells's story not only was told and retold throughout the Twentieth Century, but it helped to fuel a culture that speculated about the actual existence of intelligent life on Mars. In July of 1976, NASA's Viking probe acquired a rather intriguing photograph from the surface of Mars. As the probe flew over the surface of our neighboring planet, it took photographs to map the surface for future space expeditions. In the Northern hemisphere of Mars, over a region known as Cydonia, a photo was taken that captured what looked to be a haunting humanoid face, complete with eyes, nose, and a mouth, seemingly staring out into space (Figure 1-1).

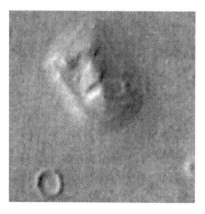

Figure 1-1. The Face on Mars.

This photograph of the "Face on Mars" sparked several years of eccentric speculation about an ancient civilization that had possibly lived on the planet Mars. This civilization supposedly had long ago carved out a face on the planet's surface, similar to the way ancient Egyptians had carved the Sphinx here on Earth. How else could a carving of a Face on Mars be explained? Through the Face on Mars, human beings were, in effect, indirectly detecting the existence of another intelligent life form, one that had since moved on or become extinct. For some, this photograph was not merely cause for speculation, but seen as proof that not only was there an ancient civilization that once existed on Mars; these intelligent beings had also visited Earth in the not-too-distant past. What was the evidence for this claim? Some claimed the Face on Mars shared an uncanny likeness with the Face of the Egyptian Sphinx.[2] Thus, a simple, fuzzy photograph of the surface of the planet Mars was cited as evidence that Egyptian artifacts were the products of space aliens!

Not every enthusiast took this photograph to such extremes, however. A few tried to remain objective and make a scientific case that a Face really did exist on Mars. The most obvious criticism of this Face-theory was our inherent tendency to see faces in everything. Anyone who has ever lain on the ground to stare at the clouds knows the human mind has a way of seeing faces that are not there. Not only can we see faces in the clouds, but if we look hard enough, we can see snakes, dragons, mountains, and just about anything else that can be conjured with the imagination.

To counter this claim, some people used computers to enhance this image[3] attempting to show that what merely resembled a face kept its face-like properties under higher resolution. Photograph enhancement appeared to reveal even more details that supported the Face hypothesis. For example, the mouth seemed to contain teeth. In addition, upon computer analyses, the Face appeared to remain under different viewing conditions and under different states of illumination.

It was further argued that the Face was surrounded by nearby polyhedral objects that appeared not only to be spatially aligned with it, but also did not appear to fit the overall geology of this part of Cydonia. The arrangement of these objects was suggested to be "out of place" if only natural causes were considered. Not only were they out-of-place, it was easy to envision these structures as being arranged and thus reflecting something that might be the ruins of an ancient city.

Such arguments worked to build a suggestive case around circumstantial evidence. Computer analyses of the Viking photograph indicated the Martian structure was indeed a face and the surrounding conditions provided a *context* in which the reality of a Face on Mars seemed more likely. Yet, a little more than twenty years after the Viking project, another photograph would be taken that would effectively discredit these arguments.

In 1998, the Mars Orbiter Camera on the Mars Global Surveyor captured a second image. Twenty years worth of improved technology meant this picture had a ten-fold higher resolution than the photo taken by Viking. This clearer picture allowed us to see once and for all that the Face on Mars is simply a Martian mountain (Figure 1-2). The eyes, nose, and mouth no longer were apparent. Instead, there are clearly seen ridges and cavities that could, with enough imagination, be roughly viewed as a face. The skeptical explanation that originally proposed that this face was simply a "trick of light and shadow" was verified. The Face on Mars was, in the end, an image in the clouds.

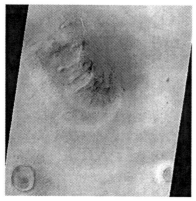

Figure 1-2. The Face on Mars Redux.

WHAT CAN WE LEARN FROM THE VANISHING FACE?

While the evidence has shown there is not an actual Face on Mars, the whole episode is worthy of consideration. True believers in the Face on Mars theory may ignore and downplay the Orbiter's pictures, and some may even suggest that NASA is engaged in a conspiracy to hide the "real evidence." Such people want the Face to exist, and have incorporated this "evidence" into their beliefs about alien civilizations and their ancient contact with humankind. More serious scholars might regard this as a case study in human psychology, where we create a reality based on our expectations. Most people, however, will simply forget the whole episode and move on. The Face on Mars theory was only one among many of the small and somewhat interesting disputes of the late Twentieth Century. Yet there is something more to be considered—the hypothesis of a Face on Mars could very well have turned out to be correct!

Imagine if the Orbiter's picture did in fact show a structure that looked very much like a humanoid face on the surface of the planet Mars. That is, under Orbiter's higher resolution and more advanced photography, the eyes, nose, and mouth not only remained, but looked even more like a chiseled eyes, nose, and mouth. Imagine further that space explorers actually then land on Mars twenty years from now and take close-up photos showing that the Face is every bit as detailed as the Egyptian Sphinx. If this were to happen, the Face on Mars would be a revolutionary discovery. Why? Reasonable people would acknowledge that some form of intelligent beings did indeed design and build this face. This would mean we are not alone. But why would this inference be made?

Zoologist Richard Dawkins explains how such an inference is made with reference to other sculptured faces found here on Earth:

> The sheer number of details in which the Mount Rushmore faces resemble the real things is too great to have come about by chance. The faces are clearly recognizable, moreover, when seen from different angles. . . . Its four heads are clearly designed. A sculptor conceived them, drew them out on paper, made meticulous measurements all over the cliff, and supervised teams of workmen who wielded pneumatic drills and dynamite to carve out the four faces, each sixty feet high. The weather could have done the same job as the artfully deployed dynamite. But of all the possible ways of weathering

a mountain, only a tiny minority would be speaking likenesses of four particular human beings. Even if we did not know the history of Mount Rushmore, we'd estimate the odds against its four heads being carved by accidental weathering as astronomically high—like tossing a coin forty times and getting heads every time.[4]

If the Mars Global Surveyor had shown the Face on Mars to be as detailed as the faces on Mount Rushmore, we would easily infer design because natural processes would be extremely unlikely to carve out such a structure. Of all the ways natural processes can erode a mountain, only an infinitesimal number could conceivably carve out such a face.

Since an actual discovery of a detailed Face on Mars would lead to an inference of design, let's think about non-human design and how we might detect it in nature. To infer design from a Face on Mars, two criteria would be inherently employed. The first criterion is that of familiarity. The Face appears humanoid. If a non-humanoid face was carved into the surface of Mars, it is unlikely we would recognize it and speculate about its origin. If the alien face had thirteen eyes, five noses, and three mouths arranged in an asymmetric fashion, the carving, as seen in a low resolution picture, would probably not catch our attention. Something could be designed but go un-noticed, meaning that our ability to detect design is limited to that which is familiar in some fashion.

Of course, familiarity is not enough by itself. After all, the mountains on Mars are also familiar, but nothing about this leads us to a design inference. The Face on Mars is familiar in two specific ways. First, it looks like a face. This familiarity allows us to recognize it, without which, we have no recognition, and without recognition we cannot hope to detect design. But the Face on Mars is also familiar in a deeper sense: as a carved face in the same category as the faces on Mount Rushmore. This deeper sense of familiarity allows us to employ reasoning by *analogy*. In other words, we would argue that since all known carved faces originate from design, this new carved face likewise originated from design. Such analogous reasoning is at the heart of all attempts to detect design.

This leads us to the second criterion of design inference—discontinuity. Not only does a carved face fit nicely into the category of faces that have been designed, it is "out-of-place" if we consider only the various rocky structures that have not been designed. That is, the familiarity is misplaced among the things that arise without design. In the Face on Mars example, people thought they saw a familiar humanoid face. But the Face was judged to be out-of-place because there were no other faces on the surface of Mars. From our knowledge of earth-based geology, detailed faces do not form naturally on planet surfaces. The Face would not fit with what we know about geological processes and the surface of Mars, but it *would* fit with what we know about designers and design.

As we have seen, there is not an actual Face on Mars. With better photographs, the Face on Mars looks much more like any old mountain. The mouth disappears, the features look less like facial features, and the whole structure looks far less symmetrical. The familiarity criterion still applies, only now the Face on Mars simply looks like a familiar mountain. Thus, it is no longer out-of-place and in fact fits nicely as just one more mountain on the surface of Mars.

In this hypothetical example, it is important to note what information we would *not* need to draw our conclusion. If an actual carving of a Face on Mars had been discovered in reality, we would have concluded the presence of design without having any knowledge of the designers. Likewise, we would not need to know exactly how the Face on Mars was made, nor would we need to know when it was made. These are all interesting questions that would be asked after we detected such a design, but the answers to these questions would not be required in order to *detect* the design. The Face itself would be enough. This is important because it is often asserted that we need to know a lot about the designer before we can detect design. After all, archaeology studies human design and previous knowledge about humans and their methods is important in detecting things like pots and arrowheads as the products of design. While such knowledge can be helpful, and sometimes essential, it is not always necessary. If we did, in fact, need previous knowledge about designers to detect designs, then we could never conclude that the discovery of a high-resolution Face on Mars, every bit as detailed as the faces on Mount Rushmore, was the product of design. Here, we are faced with a choice. We can either acknowledge that non-human design could be detected *vis-à-vis* the Face on Mars therefore rejecting the notion that independent knowledge about designers is absolutely and always required to detect designs. Or we could adhere to the view that independent knowledge about designers is necessary to detect designs and thus argue that the discovery of a Face on Mars could never be attributed to design without knowledge of the designers.

The Face on Mars episode teaches us that a design inference without knowledge of the designers could have worked. It just did not. It did not fail to work because we lacked information about the hypothetical designers. It failed because the patterns involved in forming this structure turned out to be better explained by natural processes than by intelligent forces. Something that appeared designed under low resolution was shown to be a natural phenomena under higher resolution.

THE FACE OF LIFE

Let's turn our attention from the sterile surface of Mars to the thriving surface of Earth. What sets Earth apart from all other known planets is that it teems with life. For centuries, humans have noticed that living things and their features look designed. Many great Western thinkers and philosophers have used these properties to point out that there is a purpose behind nature and that such apparent design indicates a Divine Designer. Perhaps the best known proponent of such reasoning was the Nineteenth Century Anglican clergyman, William Paley. He argued that if we were to find a watch and study it, we would conclude the watch was designed, based on all its intricate parts and the manner in which they all worked together to carry out a purpose. Paley employed the analogous reasoning that is at the heart of all design inferences. Like the watch, the eye is built of many intricate parts that all work together, in a very organized manner, to bring about sight. Paley postulated that since the eye is like the watch in terms of its various features, the eye is also like the watch in terms of its origins, namely, it was designed.

There are two ways to respond to Paley's argument. The first is to refer to Charles Darwin and his Theory of Evolution. We shall discuss Darwin and natural selection in more detail in later chapters of this book, but suffice it to say that Darwin proposed an evolutionary mechanism called *variation* and *natural selection* that could produce a biological feature like the eye without the need for an intelligent designer. We can ignore Darwin's thesis for the moment because Darwin never *refuted* Paley's argument. Darwin provided an alternative explanation for the origin of biological features that has become part of mainstream science, yet this only means there are now two different ways to explain the eye. So let us turn our attention to the second rebuttal to Paley's argument, as this one functions more as a refutation.

This second rebuttal is that the design Paley saw in nature is really like the Face on Mars. Yes, it may appear designed from a distance, but on closer inspection the eye looks much more like something that was not designed. Philosopher David Hume makes a similar case. Since the inference of design is ultimately an inference from analogy, Hume argues that living things are quite unlike man-made objects on a most basic level. For example, living things reproduce but man-made objects do not. Living things are built of chemicals suspended in water, not the nuts, bolts, and springs of man-made objects. We might even say that life, at the most basic level, much more resembles a soup than someone's watch.

The human eye may indeed look like a camera, but the camera is built upon various metal and plastic parts that interact in specific ways, whereas the eye is built upon cells. Cells are small membranous sacs, with the walls of the sac being composed of lipids and the contents of the sac loaded with molecules called proteins, carbohydrates, and nucleic acids. What takes place in the cell is nothing more than an amazingly complex set of interactions between molecules such that certain properties *emerge* endowing the cells with properties that in turn make up the eye. At this most basic level, the eye is structured and functions as it does simply because molecules assemble according to their chemical bonds and generate a structure that looks like it was designed. Like the Face on Mars, when life is viewed under higher resolution, it looks as though it was not designed. Or does it?

A Fly in the Soup

The Soup View of the cell long dominated biology. Scientists thought of the cell as little more than a membrane sac filled with soupy contents that randomly interacted with one another to produce all the processes characteristic of life. Bruce Alberts, a leading molecular biologist who was also the President of the National Academy of Sciences, wrote:

> We have always underestimated cells. Undoubtedly we still do today. But at least we are no longer as naïve as we were when I was a graduate student in the 1960s. Then, most of us viewed cells as containing a giant set of second order reactions: molecules A and B were thought to diffuse freely, randomly colliding with each other to produce molecule AB—and likewise for many other molecules that interact with each other inside a cell.[5]

Speaking of the simple bacteria, scientists Lucy Shapiro and Rich Losick also remarked:

> When the authors were graduate students in the late 1960s, the bacterial cell was generally viewed as an amorphous vessel housing a homogeneous solution of proteins.[6]

Donald Ingber, from the Departments of Pathology and Surgery at Harvard Medical School, likewise noted:

> At this time, the late 1970s, biologists generally viewed the cell as a viscous fluid or gel surrounded by a membrane, much like a balloon filled with molasses.[7]

Biologists John Scott and Tony Pawson note that in the early 80s, the contents of the cell were thought to exist in an "an unstructured milieu" and they echo the observations of Ingber:

> At that time, cells were viewed as balloonlike bags filled with a soupy cytoplasm containing floating proteins and organelles (membrane-bound compartments, such as the nucleus and mitochondria).[8]

In many ways, this perspective of a soupy cell was understandable. Science has learned about cells by breaking them open and studying all their parts and pieces suspended in a test tube. In essence, biochemists turn a population of cells into a soup. By analyzing this soup, we can learn about life because many of the pieces and parts still work in this artificial state. For example, enzymes (which are proteins that speed up chemical reactions) function just fine in the test tube soup and because of this we can describe and quantify their properties. From here, it is not hard to imagine that the soup in the test tube essentially reflects a soup encapsulated by the membrane. Many of the differences might stem from the fact that the soup in the test tube is more dilute than what you find in a cell, but a thin soup is not significantly different from a thick soup. To then understand the origin of this soup, we simply postulate the existence of a pre-biotic soup on the primitive earth where eventually small drops were captured by membranous sacs. The story could not be more straightforward.

While the Soup View of life made sense, and succeeded in generating much scientific knowledge, it would seem obvious something was missing. Yes, it is easy to break open cells and study their parts, but what about putting the parts back together to resurrect the cells? If the cell was truly a complex soup, and the test tube was filled with a complex soup, there should be no Humpty Dumpty problem. But there is. Imagine having a large beaker full of bacteria, the smallest and simplest known cells of life. You split the bacteria into two beakers and physically treat one to burst all the bacterial cells. This beaker would contain our bacterial soup. The chemical composition of the soup beaker and the beaker of cells would be essentially the same, as both would be filled with the same ingredients of life. Yet the soup beaker would not contain life. It would contain only the remnants of life. Further imagine that you try to resurrect life by introducing different forms of energy into the soup beaker. Zap it with electricity or heat it on the stove. All you will end up with is a warm, stinky soup. Clearly, energy plus all the ingredients of life fail to produce life. Why?

What makes the bacterial soup different from the bacteria is organization. Life is not pieces and parts suspended in a soup. Life is pieces and parts organized in a rather specific spatial and temporal manner. In his book, *The Way of the Cell*, biochemist Franklin Harold explains:

> Even the simplest uni-cellular creatures display levels of regularity and complexity that exceed by orders of magnitude anything found in the mineral realm. A bacterial cell consists of more than three hundred million molecules (not counting water), several thousand different kinds of molecules, and requires some 2,000 genes for its specification. There is nothing random about this assemblage, which reproduces itself with constant composition and form generation after generation.[9]

Many other scientists have commented on the orderly state of the cell at the smallest levels. For example:

> Cells are highly ordered structures. . . . At all levels of analysis from the light microscope to the molecular they are high information content (low thermodynamic probability) entities. So far as their internal dynamics is concerned, this means that most physicochemical processes are channeled or "directed" rather than random and suggests that little occurs in the cell on the basis of chance or as a simple consequence of the law of mass action.[10]

When the cells are burst open to form a soup, the organizational information needed to impart life is lost and cannot be replaced by throwing things back together with the haphazard introduction of energy. A soup is complex and in this sense it does reflect life. However, life is more than complexity. Life is *organized complexity*. As Harold notes, organization "sums up the essence of biological order."

Hume's objection to Paley's argument could have been seriously strengthened by scientific discovery. The perception of the cell as "an amorphous vessel housing a homogeneous solution of proteins" could have been verified. The perception of the cell as "a viscous fluid or gel surrounded by a membrane, much like a balloon filled with molasses" could have been confirmed.

Amorphous vessels and balloons filled with molasses would not arouse suspicions of design. But this is not what science has discovered. Modern science teaches us that "the cell is understood to be highly organized, with specialized areas for different functions and molecular motors shuttling components around."[11] Hume's objection to Paley's argument certainly has not been strengthened by scientific discovery.

The High-Resolution Face of Life

Earlier we saw that the design inference behind the Face on Mars failed because, under high-resolution, the structure no longer looked like a face or appeared designed. However, if such high-resolution photographs had turned up an actual carving of a face, it is safe to say that today many scientists would be seriously considering that Mars was once inhabited by intelligent beings. Similarly, life, under low resolution, appears designed. We see hearts that work as pumps, eyes that work as cameras, joints that work as fulcrums, and so on, all having the appearance of design. But what if we look at life itself at a higher resolution—the level of the cell?

Cells also have the appearance of design. Within the cell are smaller particles and membranous sacs and tubes called organelles. These organelles impose spatial organization inside the cell and this organization is coupled to function. For example, the mitochondria function as a factory that regenerates ATP molecules, the energy currency of the cell. The lysosome functions as a degradation chamber to remove the unneeded and defective material inside the cell. Organelles called Golgi bodies function to sort the various proteins so that they reach their proper destination. The nucleus is thought of as the control center of the cell. Some scientists even argue that one organelle may function as the cell's eyes![12] The cell indeed has its own organs, they are just very small.

But what if we look at an even higher resolution, the level of the molecules contained within the cell? Here we find proteins organized into large complexes that are thought of as molecular machines because they actually look and work like machines. Other proteins form tracks to connect and shuttle the molecular machines via motor proteins. The proteins in the membranes work as selective gates, pumps, and sensors. This entire intricate organization of gadgets is due in large part to the encoded information stored by the molecule of DNA. As Harold notes, "The unique mark of a living organism, shared by no other known entity, is its possession of a genetic program that specifies that organism's chemical makeup."[13] Thus, at the molecular-level, the contents of a cell look like a factory full of miniature robotic machines that are following encoded instructions to interact with one another to breakdown and synthesize material. At even higher resolution inside the cell, at the molecular-level, the appearance of design remains.

Unlike the Face on Mars, the biotic face of design remains at the highest relevant resolution. When we look inside the cell, the appearance is reminiscent of the inner workings of a watch. Organization does not simply emerge. Organization is encoded. It exists because of instructions. And where there are instructions, there may also be intelligence.

References

1. Wells, H.G., 1986. *The War of the Worlds*. Penguin Books, New York, p. 1.
2. "The Mars Egypt Connection." http://www.earthchangestv.com/face-mars/overlay.htm; last accessed 06/01/05.
3. Carlotto, M.J. "The Martian Enigmas: The Face, Pyramids and Other Unusual Objects on Mars." http://www.newfrontiersinscience.com/martianenigmas/; last accessed 06/01/05.
4. Dawkins, R., 1996. *Climbing Mount Improbable*. W.W. Norton & Company, New York, p. 6.
5. Alberts, B., 1998. "The Cell as a Collection of Protein Machines: Preparing the Next Generation of Molecular Biologists." *Cell*, 92:291-294.
6. Losick, R. and Shapiro, L., 1999. "Changing Views on the Nature of the Bacterial Cell: From Biochemistry to Cytology." *Journal of Bacteriology*, 181:4143-4145.

7. Ingber, D.E., 1998. "The Architecture of Life." *Scientific American*, 278:48-57.
8. Scott, J.D. and Pawson, T., 2000. "Cell Communication: The Inside Story." *Scientific American*, 282:7279.
9. Harold, F.M., 2001. *The Way of the Cell: Molecules, Organisms and the Order of Life*. Oxford University Press, Oxford, pp. 10-11.
10. Agutter, P.S., Malone, P.C. and Wheatley, D.N., 2000. "Diffusion Theory in Biology: A Relic of Mechanistic Materialism." *Journal of the History of Biology*, 33:71-111.
11. Galatzer-Levy,J.,2006. "Movement of Chromosome in Nucleus Visualized." http://www.eurekalert.org/pub_releases/2006-04/uoia-moc041206.php; last accessed 04/18/06.
12. Albrecht-Buehler, G., 1998. "Cell Intelligence." http://www.basic.northwestern.edu/g-buehler/cellint0.htm; last accessed 06/20/05.
13. Harold, F.M., 2001. *The Way of the Cell: Molecules, Organisms and the Order of Life*. Oxford University Press, Oxford, p. 44.

CHAPTER 2

THE EXPLANATORY CONTINUUM

Imagine walking into a room where there are two groups of scholars having a rather heated debate. One group argues that living things are the products of Mind. These scholars discuss things like the human eye, arguing the optimal arrangement of parts seen in these structures point to a designer as their cause. This group also highlights the harmony and beauty that is all around us, insisting that a form of wisdom lies behind the natural world. The second group of scholars claims the harmony and optimal arrangements found in nature could well have arisen by chance. According to this group, natural forces working over huge spans of time stabilized these arrangements and ordered configurations, removing the need to invoke any type of designer.

Striving to maintain objectivity as you follow these two groups of scholars, you might notice they are looking at the same world, yet perceiving a "big picture" that is very different. The first group looks at the world and sees some kind of purpose behind it. They are called the teleologists. The second group looks at the same world but sees no purpose behind it. We will call this group the non-teleologists.

You might be thinking that I have been talking about a group of creationists and evolutionary scientists arguing in the auditorium of a local college. You would be wrong. These two groups of scholars once argued in the halls of Ancient Greece. The teleologists were represented by men such as Socrates, Plato, Diogenes, and Aristotle. The non-teleologists were represented by such men as Democritus, Leucippus of Elea, and Epicurus of Samos. These great and scholarly thinkers debated their opposing views over a period of about two hundred years. Their works would later influence European scientists and philosophers, including Robert Boyle, William Paley, and David Hume.

It is not uncommon for people to approach the topic of design from a myopic perspective, thinking that "Intelligent Design" is an American idea invented back in the 1990s by sneaky creationists with a socio-political agenda. Those with a somewhat broader historical perspective may go back to 1925 and the infamous Scopes Trial, where the teaching of evolution was put on trial. Others may go all the way back to 1802 and William Paley's *Natural Theology; or, Evidences of the Existence and Attributes of the Deity, Collected from the Appearances of Nature.*

The perspective of a world that was designed did not start with Paley, nor did it begin with naïve religious believers. It began with some of Western civilization's greatest philosophers. In their book, *The Anthropic Cosmological Principle,* astronomer John Barrow and mathematician Frank Tipler document this fact.[1] For example, Socrates once extolled the human eye as a proof of the wisdom of the gods:

> Is not that providence, Aristodemus, in a most eminent manner conspicuous, which because the eye of man is delicate in its contexture, hath therefore prepared eyelids like doors, whereby to screen it, which extend themselves whenever it is needful, and again close when sleep approaches? . . . And cans't thou still doubt Aristodemus, whether a disposition of parts like this should be the work of chance, or of wisdom and contrivance?

Aristotle and his followers would take the teleological perspective much further. As Barrow and Tipler point out:

> Aristotelian science was based upon presupposition of an intelligent natural world that functions according to some deliberate design. Its supporters were therefore very critical of all those pre-Socratic thinkers who regarded the world structure as simply the inevitable residue of chance or necessity.

But what of the non-teleologists? Barrow and Tipler write:

> The Epicureans were, of course, anxious to scotch any notions of supernatural causation or the appeal to any entity who controls or or-

dains events. Interestingly, no useful scientific structure was erected upon this materialistic foundation because Epicurus had a very low view of mundane scientific investigation.

And then there was the Roman poet Lucretius Carus (99-55 BC):

> Lucretius believed life to have originated at some definite moment in the past by natural processes but that created beings included 'a host of monsters, grotesque in build and aspect' who were subsequently eliminated by their sterility.

These ideas bear resemblance to those of Charles Darwin. In fact, Lucretius even wrote:

> In those days, again, many species must have died out altogether and failed to reproduce their kind. Every species that you now see drawing the breath of the world survived either by cunning or by prowess or by speed. In addition, there are many that survive under human protection because their usefulness has commended them to our care.

This is not the only argument that is familiar. Consider the following:

> When we see some example of a mechanism, such as a globe or clock or some such device, do we doubt that it is the creation of a conscious intelligence? So when we see the movement of the heavenly bodies. . . how can we doubt that these too are not only the works of reason but of a reason which is perfect and divine?

No, this was not written by William Paley, but instead by the Roman lawyer and orator, Marcus Cicero (106-43 BC). Cicero would also write something else that sounds equally familiar:

> Can I but wonder here that anyone can persuade himself that certain solid and individual bodies should be moved by their natural forces and gravitation in such a manner that a world so beautiful adorned should be made by fortuitous concourse. He who believes this pos-

sible may as well believe, that if a great quantity of the one and twenty letters, composed of gold or any other matter, were thrown upon the ground, they would fall into such order as legibly to form the 'Annals of Ennius'. I doubt whether fortune could make a single verse of them.

The debate between teleology and non-teleology is at least 2500 years old and has involved some of history's greatest thinkers. The notion that current arguments about design are nothing more than a fundamentalist reaction to the painful truth of Darwinism is a notion divorced from historical context. If history stretches back no further than one hundred years or so, it is easy to get the impression that the non-teleological perspective has been vindicated and teleology has been refuted. But if history spans 2500 years or more, consider the possibility that the non-teleological view has just recently gained the upper hand with more sophisticated versions of the same arguments from old. Teleologists have the potential of evening the playing field somewhat by also reviving their arguments in more sophisticated versions. Is the 2500 year-old debate really over? Of course not.

Then what of Charles Darwin? Today it would seem that since his Theory of Evolution was formulated, the non-teleological view has surfaced as the clear victor. Evolution has been scientifically established. Evidence from various fields strongly support a historical, genetic relationship between species. It is a scientific fact that random mutations generate variability and natural selection culls this pool of variability to produce the fittest state. Yet while it is clear that evolution has occurred, and mutations and natural selection have been significantly involved in evolution, there still remains the distinct possibility that there is more to the story than accidental changes captured and propagated by natural selection. A teleologist has no reason to exclude an important role for natural selection in the evolution of life, but a role is not a cause. For example, an actor may play an important role, such that his absence will bring a halt to the play, but the actor's role is not the cause of the play.

The concept of Intelligent Design need not contradict anything science has discovered about evolution. If design at the hands of an intelligent agency intersects with our biological reality, this does not mean that mutation and natural selection would not exist. On the contrary, an intelligent agent that sought to design an entity and deposit it on this planet might very well exploit processes such as natural selection to play a role in biotic history. This interpretation comes from the realization that a human-like designer would be likely to recruit evolution to serve design objectives. For example, what if a scientist today was put in charge of designing a microbial life form capable of surviving on its own? He would not design it such that it could not adapt in response to environmental challenges. To do so would be to design an organism that was prone to extinction. Not only would he lack good design reasons for prohibiting evolution, I'm not even sure it could be done.

Over time, any design is going to decay. If one wants a design to persist over time, there are only two options: a) continually intervene to deposit replacement designs or, b) design them such that they self-perpetuate. The self-perpetuation of a design is called replication or reproduction. There are good design reasons for using this strategy. Daniel Koshland, a scientist from the University of California, Berkeley, explains the importance of re-production:

> This is not the only way the living system regenerates. The constant resynthesis of its proteins and body constituents is not quite perfect, so the small loss for each regeneration in the short run becomes a larger loss overall for all the processes in the long run, adding up to what we call aging. So living systems, at least the ones we know, use a clever trick to perfect the regeneration process—that is, *they start over.* Starting over can be a cell dividing, in the case of *Escherichia coli,* or the birth of an infant for *Homo sapiens.* By beginning a new generation, the infant starts from scratch, and all the chemical in-gredients, programs, and other constituents go back to the begin-ning to correct the inevitable decline of a continuously functioning metabolizing system.[2] (emphasis added)

Reproduction is the means to forward a design into the future. Yet be-cause of the inevitability of mutation, and its effects, replication over large spans of time will lead to evolution. It would thus seem that a good designer would take this "problem" and turn it into something to be exploited or used. This is just one example to illustrate that Intelligent Design and evolution may complement, rather than contradict each other. Life itself could have been designed and evolution, by natural selection, would have subsequently followed. What's more, life might even have been designed in such a way that Darwinian evolution was recruited to carry out distinct design objectives meaning that evolution could have been "rigged by design." Or perhaps evolutionary mechanisms themselves may have been designed. How could we ever hope to address such fascinating possibilities?

The Traditional Template

Due to the ancient nature of this debate, both sides have developed a consensus on the proper way to approach the question of design in nature. This consensus has in turn shaped all present and future debate on this topic. I shall call this consensus the Traditional Template. The template looks like this: proponents of design look for some feature that cannot possibly be explained by natural causes. Then, once such a feature has been proposed, it is argued that only a designer can account for the existence of this feature. Such an approach to detecting design is actually quite ambitious, and if successful, would indeed revolutionize the way we view the living world. There is nothing inherently wrong with imposing this template on our inquiry, but we should recognize how it sets up the overall debate.

The Traditional Template assigns the non-teleological explanation the default status. This perspective basically presumes that non-teleological mechanisms are to be assumed unless it can be demonstrated, with great certainty, they do not apply. Since the theory of Darwinian evolution is the most well developed non-teleological mechanism, it becomes the default explanation. As a result, the arguments for design end up becoming arguments about the inadequacies of Darwinian evolution. Design proponents tend to argue that Darwinian evolution cannot possibly explain the origin of some biological features and therefore design must be invoked to account for their existence.

This template can be seen in Charles Darwin's *The Origin of Species*. In Chapter Six of his book, Darwin anticipates his skeptics objecting that gradual changes in species would be deemed impossible, and thus responds by arguing for their mere possibility. For example:

> Secondly, is it *possible* that an animal having, for instance, the structure and habits of a bat, could have been formed by the modification of some animal with wholly different habits? . . . Nor can I see any insuperable difficulty in further believing it *possible* that the membrane-connected fingers and fore-arm of the Galeopithecus might be greatly lengthened by natural selection. . . we must own that we are far too ignorant to argue that no transition of any kind is *possible*. . . If it could be demonstrated that any complex organ existed, which could not *possibly* have been formed by numerous, successive, slight modifications, my theory would absolutely break down. . . . In the cases in which we know of no intermediate or transitional states, we should be very cautious in concluding that none could have existed, for the homologies of many organs and their intermediate states show that wonderful metamorphoses in function are at least *possible*. (emphasis added)

Note that not only does Darwin argue for the mere possibility of transitions, he even challenges his critics to come up with something that could not possibly be explained by gradual transformation. This context has since become the fulcrum of this debate, where Darwinian explanations are to be preferred unless one can demonstrate they are impossible.

Once we begin to appreciate the central role that possibility plays in this debate, further insights follow. For example, because this template pushes the design proponent into the position of opposing Darwinian evolution, the design proponent ends up trying to prove a negative. Proving a negative is notoriously difficult to do *for any topic*. Consider how our legal system is set up. If Jones is accused of murdering Smith, the burden of proof is not on Jones to prove he did not murder Smith. It is too difficult to prove that you did not do something. Instead, the burden is on the State to prove Jones *did* murder Smith. Jones is innocent until proven guilty. In philosophy, this is recognized as the burden of proof, where such burden rests on the shoulders of the person making the proposition.

This dynamic is both important and inherent in the template. Darwin's theory, by itself, does not refute a teleological explanation for biological complexity. Instead, Darwin's theory offers us an *alternative* explanation. The success of Darwin's theory has nothing to do with proving design is impossible. The success stems from the manner in which Darwin's theory has been successfully used to guide research and generate insights into biology. Such research and insights have, in turn, generated much circumstantial evidence that supports the Darwinian thesis.

What if Darwin had formulated his argument differently? Imagine that instead of looking for facts that support the possibility of gradual transitions, Darwin had attempted to argue that design was impossible. Imagine further that he took this approach as a defensive posture in response to someone's challenge that if it could be proven impossible that life's features were designed, we would have to abandon the conclusion of design. Darwin would have been in the position of attempting to prove that a claim is not true, rather than trying to explain what was true. His attempts to prove that design was impossible may have become significant in the realm of philosophy, but I doubt they would have formed a scientific hypothesis that developed into a larger explanatory theory. If Darwin had taken this position, which is the negative approach he challenges his opponents to take, I think it is safe to conclude that Darwin's own thesis would have never been developed and he would not have become a significant figure in the history of science.

There is yet another aspect to this Traditional Template that is perhaps even more important. When design proponents raise examples of things that "could not have evolved," while scientists speculate how these things "could have evolved," we often lose sight of the important fact that this is a debate about history. Let us not forget the central issue surrounding design in nature is whether something was, in fact, designed. Darwin's explanation was likewise intended as an explanation of natural history, an attempt to account for the present by things that actually happened in the past.

By focusing on what is and what is not possible, debates concerning design versus the Darwinian perspective tend to take on a philosophical, rather than historical, essence. The argument itself evolves into competing claims, where one side says X could have evolved while the other side insists that X could not have evolved. Yet there is no symmetry in the opposing positions. While it is true, from the design perspective, that if X could not have evolved, then it did not evolve, it is not true that because X could have evolved that it did evolve. The possible does not always translate into the actual. History is full of things that could have happened, but never did happen. In fact, in the set of all possible events, the things that could have happened vastly outnumber the things that actually did happen. Nevertheless, because of the philosophical nature of the debate, and the impetus it creates, a strange spin-off argument often emerges. This argument, although rarely stated in such explicit terms, tends to conform to the following pattern: if a biological feature could have evolved through a Darwinian process, then the design inference fails, and since the design inference fails, the biological feature did evolve through a Darwinian process. The realm of the possible then becomes transformed into the actual.

The final way in which the Traditional Template shapes the design debate is with the very familiar evolution versus design paradigm where it is assumed that the two explanations somehow contradict each other and are mutually exclusive. In fact, in the debate between evolutionary scientists and creationists, the only place there ever seems to be agreement is with the claim that evolution is incompatible with design. Those who have followed this debate in any sense know it is common for creationists to argue that evolution implies there is no design and no God. What many people may not know is that this creationist assertion is also made by many mainstream evolutionary biologists and scholars. For example, in his book *Science on Trial*, evolutionary biologist Douglas Futuyma writes:

> Some shrink from the conclusion that the human species was not designed, has no purpose, and is the product of mere mechanical mechanisms—but this seems to be the message of evolution.[3]

Dr. William Provine, Professor of History and Biology from Cornell University, is even more radical. In 1998, Provine was invited by a group of biologists at The University of Tennessee, Knoxville to give the keynote address for their Darwin Day celebration (an educational outreach program

designed to highlight the importance of evolution in a biological education).
In his address to the UT community, Provine asserted:

> Naturalistic evolution has clear consequences that Charles Darwin
> understood perfectly. 1) No gods worth having exist; 2) no life after
> death exists; 3) no ultimate foundation for ethics exists; 4) no ulti-
> mate meaning in life exists; and 5) human free will is nonexistent.[4]

Provine adds confusion to the ambiguity as there is nothing about evolution
that implies there are no "gods worth having."

The problem with creationists and scholars asserting that the existence
of evolution means there is no design or purpose behind nature is that, while
creationism obviously equates with teleology (where a Mind acts as the Cre-
ator), it is not true that evolution equates with non-teleology. Again, it is
important to emphasize that evolution is not inherently opposed to design.
This can be clearly shown by a quick consideration of the way evolution is
defined in the scientific community. First, it is often defined as a change
in gene frequencies in a population over time. This definition is not anti-
design. We know from artificial selection that such evolution can be and is
guided by design, where human intelligence intervenes to manipulate mat-
ings, as well as the environmental conditions of the resulting offspring. For
example, the gene frequencies of the world's dog population differ from that
which existed in the ancestral population of wild dogs and those which were
first domesticated. But this change in gene frequency does not mean there
was no design behind the process or behind the changes in gene frequencies
of the current population of dogs today.

Another definition of evolution entails the twin concepts of "descent
with modification" and a "common ancestor." This definition proposes that
organisms, along with their historical lineage, are biologically connected
and that organisms have changed in appearance and function over time due
to genetic and environmental changes. But once again, artificial selection
shows that this definition of evolution does not preclude the involvement of
intelligent intervention. After all, the domestication of an original population of wild dogs involved both intelligence and descent with modification.

It is very important to keep in mind that evolution can indeed incorporate intelligently prescribed interventions and is not the opposite of design. Evolution, is a process that heavily involves historical contingencies, and as such, allows plenty of room for intelligent interventions. A view that truly opposed evolution would contend that gene frequencies do not change in populations over time or that organisms are not related through common descent.

In summary, it is helpful to understand the way the Traditional Template shapes the debate about design in nature. Design proponents have found themselves in the position of proving a negative, which is extremely difficult to accomplish for any topic of dispute. The historical aspect of the dispute is often overlooked or downplayed at the expense of arguments about what could and could not possibly happen. Evolution itself is needlessly set against design as if we could not exist in a reality where both are true. There is nothing inherently wrong with this approach and from the perspective of a design proponent, it offers the potential of a huge payoff. However, there are differing ways of approaching the question of design in nature.

INDUCTIVE GRADUALISM

To consider other ways of addressing the issue of design in nature, we need only adjust our approach. Instead of arguing whether something *could* happen, we can place more emphasis on whether something *did* happen. This adjustment helps, for the purposes of clarity, to eliminate the arguments about what is and is not possible. Instead of focusing on abstractions and posing challenges to the imagination, we can take a forensic approach and seek out the best explanation that accounts for a historical event. Instead of downplaying history to focus on abstractions, history is emphasized. The topic of origins is approached from the point of view of an investigator who gathers clues and examines evidence. An analysis of data patterns may lead us more clearly to one explanation rather than another. And throughout this process, we will bear in mind that an evolutionary explanation is not necessarily in conflict with a teleological explanation.

The Traditional Template has design proponents making very strong claims as they try to prove something is impossible. This creates a need to uncover extraordinary evidence and develop arguments that are completely immune from any counter argument. The forensic approach, on the other hand, proceeds as an investigation. Investigations are built around clues and hunches, taking on a hugely different dynamic.

Most of us are familiar with crime stories and how detectives go about trying to recreate the scene of a crime in order to bring the suspect to justice. The analysis of a crime scene is really an analysis of a small piece of history that has recently occurred. If we return to our previous example of Smith being accused of murdering Jones, imagine that all the prosecution had to prove was that it was merely possible that Smith was guilty. The defense is then put in the untenable position of trying to prove that Smith could not have murdered Jones. It is safe to say that defense lawyers everywhere would have an extremely hard time proving their clients could not have possibly committed the crime. In such a situation, any hunches or clues will always work in the prosecution's favor. It is clear that a mere hunch or clue is not sufficient to show it was impossible for Smith to have murdered Jones. On the contrary, a mere hunch or clue works in favor of establishing the possible.

The investigative approach that I will apply to the question of design in nature is something I will call Inductive Gradualism. While the Traditional Template offers only two explanations (X could evolve and X could not evolve), Inductive Gradualism provides a continuum of explanations. The continuum can be envisioned as it relates to a question about the evolution of some biological feature, X (Figure 2-1).

This Explanatory Continuum captures the simple fact that many beliefs involve different degrees of conviction. As we proceed from the top to the bottom, our sense of conviction about X's evolution increases. It is important to lay this continuum out so we can understand the difference between the Traditional Template and the forensic-historical approach. The Traditional Template focuses only on the first step in the continuum. Tremendous energy and thought is put into this step, as a demonstration that X could not possibly evolve renders the remaining steps unnecessary. However, if it is concluded that X's evolution is possible, we are still a long way from resolving issues in a forensic-historical sense. Many questions remain to be addressed.

THE EXPLANATORY CONTINUUM

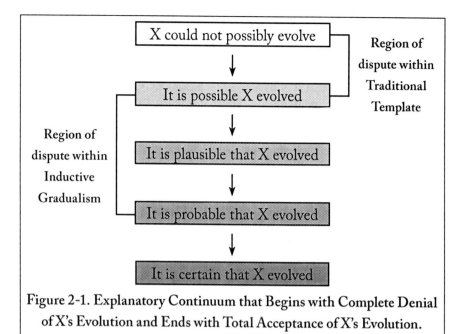

Figure 2-1. Explanatory Continuum that Begins with Complete Denial of X's Evolution and Ends with Total Acceptance of X's Evolution.

This is where Inductive Gradualism comes into play. Here we try to gather more clues and play out our hunches as we attempt to proceed through the continuum. We begin by granting the possibility of X, and since certainty is not truly achievable when debating ancient history, the goal is only to reach the probable stage of the continuum. We attempt to move beyond the possible into the realm of the plausible, and from there, into the realm of the probable. Note, however, that Inductive Gradualism does not truly contradict the Traditional Template. It allows that debate to play out separately and simply grants the possibility for the sake of the investigation. If, while the investigation is ongoing, it is determined that the explanation about X is impossible, we can pull the plug on the investigation. The investigation might even uncover clues and arguments that could end up feeding back into the Traditional Template. Thus, in a rather oblique manner, the Traditional Template and Inductive Gradualism can complement each other.

Inductive Gradualism permits three levels of explanation: *the possible, the plausible,* and *the probable*. To clarify the differences in these three explanatory forms, consider again the case of Smith and Jones. Since Smith is Jones's neighbor, it is entirely possible that Smith murdered Jones. Even if Smith was out of town at the time of the murder, it is possible that Smith could have paid someone to murder Jones. The possibility that Smith could have murdered Jones is of little importance since the same claim could be made for anyone else living on the same street. Possibilities do not really carry much weight when trying to account for something that actually happened.

To improve the explanation, we must move from the realm of possibility to plausibility. A plausible claim is a possibility that is supported by some circumstantial evidence. For example, if it were true that Smith was a violent man who intensely disliked Jones and had threatened to kill him, then the claim becomes plausible. However, it remains equally plausible that Smith did not kill Jones, as many people make threats without actually acting on them. Plausible explanations function to arouse or heighten suspicion but are in need of more evidential support. Plausible explanations are further differentiated by degrees of strength. For example, the plausibility of the explanation might increase if it were true that Smith acted strangely when questioned by the police. Even though there may be an alternative explanation as to why this was the case, it coincides nicely with our original explanation and thus improves its plausibility. Nevertheless, an explanation that remains only plausible can be legitimately denied.

Plausible explanations take another leap when they become probable. A probable claim is a plausible claim supported by a vast amount of data that all converge and best make sense in light of the explanation. The probable explanation emerges when it becomes clear to unbiased observers that the explanation is the best way to account for all the relevant data. In this case, witnesses and physical evidence (such as fingerprints and ballistics) could be added to the case such that it becomes very probable that Smith murdered Jones.

To summarize, a possible explanation can be easily denied, a plausible explanation can reasonably denied, and a probable explanation is difficult to deny. Of course, the border between the possible, plausible, and probable can be indistinct and it is therefore up to those who dispute a claim to arrive at some form of consensus about such matters. In this scenario, both sides would have to agree, for example, that suspicious behavior is justification for a plausible explanation and evidence such as fingerprinting analysis and witness testimony would justify a probable claim.

The success of Inductive Gradualism depends on an investigator's ability to proceed through the Explanatory Continuum. There are certain traits any good investigator should possess. He should be able to approach the object in dispute with an open mind. If he comes to the dispute with a bias, he is likely to consider only the data that support his bias and ignore those that appear to contradict it. Second, the investigator must have a certain level of sensitivity to detect the existence of clues, coupled with a tolerance for ambiguity. These characteristics are even more important if the clues are subtle. If someone approaches the investigation with the mind-set of demanding various proofs, they might very well miss a subtle clue that could turn the tide of the entire investigation. Third, when the investigator develops a hypothesis, it must be held to tentatively. Until the hypothesis reaches a state of high probability, the investigator must be psychologically prepared to abandon the hypothesis if the evidence mandates it. The investigator must also be careful to use the hypothesis only as a *working hypothesis*, recognizing that alternative explanations might well explain the same data. Fourth, the investigator must show patience. Sometimes, important data only come to light with careful research. Sometimes, it is just plain luck. Without patience, an investigator might abandon a valid hypothesis prematurely. Finally, the investigator should try to see the big picture amid all the data as well as having the ability to see how one clue is relevant to the others.

All investigations must begin with a hunch or suspicion. These are generated by an observation that leads one to draw up the hypothesis. The hunch or suspicion plays a crucial role in the investigation. Not only does it spark the investigation, it provides the intellectual guidance throughout the search for evidence to strengthen or remove the suspicion. It provides an impetus for a follow-up analysis and further aids in recognizing where the hard facts fit into the big picture. Are there more facts that support the suspicion? Or are there facts that undercut and weaken the suspicion?

The type of data that can spark a hunch is not the same as the type of data that might be needed to convince a skeptic. Someone looking for evidence to support their hunch may be satisfied with a quantity of evidence that a skeptic would find totally inadequate. If we again return to our example of where Smith is accused of murdering Jones, a detective might find Smith's behavior suspicious enough to embrace the hypothesis that Smith murdered Jones. When pursuing this hunch, the detective might uncover a witness who claims to have seen Smith run out of Jones's house the night of the murder. This might be viewed as further supporting evidence, strengthening the plausibility of the hypothesis. Of course, Smith's lawyer, who is paid to be extremely skeptical of Smith's guilt, could easily argue that Smith ran out of the house after stumbling upon the dead body. The lawyer might even question the reliability of the witnesses' account.

STUMPING DARWIN

Inductive Gradualism probably sounds like common sense to many people. So why make a fuss about it? The problem is that the Traditional Template, which permeates all design debates, works from a very different approach, with the issue revolving around possibilities. The Traditional Template is not fertile ground for an investigation. If we return to the debate between teleologists and non-teleologists, data that might cause one to suspect teleology behind life is completely insufficient to convince a non-teleologist. Thus, a teleologist trying to convince a non-teleologist will find data to be of little or no use if they only generate suspicions. A non-teleologist, expecting to be shown that evolution is impossible, is unlikely to recognize any data that only cause suspicions of "evidence for design." Neither teleologists nor non-teleologists will recognize true clues as such, since both sides are looking for a proof rather than a mundane clue. Yet what investigation advances without clues?

Sometime around 1860, Asa Gray, a professor of botany from Harvard, apparently asked Darwin what it would take to convince him of design. Darwin replied:

> Your question what would convince me of design is a poser. If I saw an angel come down to teach us good, and I was convinced from others seeing him that I was not mad, I should believe in design. If I could be convinced thoroughly that life and mind was in an

unknown way a function of other imponderable force, I should be convinced. If man was made of brass or iron and no way connected with any other organism which had ever lived, I should perhaps be convinced. But this is childish writing.[5]

Darwin is effectively stumped by the question and offers answers that he concedes as "childish." Darwin states clearly that he needs to see an angel to be convinced of design. Apparently, this would prove the existence of the supernatural and Darwin can only view design as a supernatural phenomenon. Darwin further admits that he needs to be convinced that life or mind was the product of some force that we cannot even ponder. This statement is in the same category as saying that life or mind could not possibly have been produced by natural forces. Finally, Darwin says a brass or iron man, not connected to other life forms, would convince him of design. Yet we could also put this statement in the category of something that could not have been produced by evolution. In the end, clearly what Darwin needed was a supernatural sign or a demonstration that natural explanations are impossible in order to be convinced of design.

Note that Darwin's answers are useless from an investigative perspective. Investigative analyses do not gradually converge on things like angelic appearances or imponderable forces. These are things we stumble upon and are thus detected fortuitously. As for brass men, we already know from the start that humans are not made of brass or iron. No one is going to investigate for iron men. The data that Darwin admits would convince him of design, fail as data that would merely arouse suspicions. If man was made of brass or iron and was in no way connected with any other organism which had ever lived, this finding would go far beyond justifying a mere suspicion. It would, after all, work to convince Darwin, himself a skeptic of design. This type of data would allow us to leap, in a single step, from the possible to the almost certain along the Explanatory Continuum. Miraculous signs and proofs of the impossible are shortcuts through the Explanatory Continuum, but as investigators, we must be willing to take the long road. To do this, we must have a starting place from which we can roll up our sleeves and begin sifting through the data in a search for more clues. We need to know what kind of things would even suggest design before we can proceed. In the next three chapters, I will cite some of the data that cause *me* to suspect design behind life's origin. We can then further consider whether there are ways to strengthen those suspicions to continue on through the Explanatory Continuum.

REFERENCES

1. For the following quotes, see Chapter 2 in Barrow, J.D. and Tipler, F.J., 1988. *The Anthropic Cosmological Principle*. Oxford University Press, Oxford.
2. Koshland, D.E., 2002. "The Seven Pillars of Life." *Science*, 295:2215-2216.
3. Futuyma, D.J., 1983. *Science on Trial: The Case for Evolution*. Pantheon Books, New York, p. 13.
4. Abstract of Will Provine's 1998 Darwin Day Keynote Address. http://web.archive.org/web/19990219210609/fp.bio.utk.edu/darwin/1998/provine_abstract.html; last accessed 05/05/03.
5. Charles Darwin to Asa Gray. Down, September 17 [1861?]. http://web.archive.org/web/20040224220254/http://pages.britishlibrary.net/charles.darwin/texts/letters/letters2_03.html; last accessed 10/20/06.

PART II — THE CLUES

CHAPTER 3

ECHOES OF TECHNOLOGY

I n a well-known science fiction television series, *Star Trek: The Next Generation*, one of the most popular characters is Data, an android who, like Pinocchio, wants to be human. This tension between the character's desire to be human and the reality that he is an artificial life form allowed the writers of the TV show to explore many concepts that define what it is to be human, often in a humorous way, while keeping the underlying premise that humans remain different from androids. Humans are biological creatures born as products of nature. They are made of cells and organs and body fluids. Androids, on the other hand, are artificial life forms, products of applied technology, composed of circuits, metals, and synthetic fluids. While the writers of *Star Trek* call into question the validity of these differences with regard to behavior, perhaps the real significance of these differences lies elsewhere.

Distinctions between artificial and natural life forms are beginning to look less significant as the field of molecular biology develops, where biological organisms appear much more similar to technological products than anyone could ever have predicted. The fictional android, Data, is a technological product built around silicon, silver, and copper atoms. In a similar fashion, living organisms, built around carbon, nitrogen, and hydrogen atoms, can also be viewed as products of technology.

An understanding of human technology and the logic behind it is often used to clarify how our own bodies work. The concept of homeostasis will help us visualize this. Homeostasis is a process by which all living things interact and respond to their changing environment to maintain a constant internal environment. A basic example of homeostasis is the temperature maintenance system in the human body. Your body maintains an average internal temperature of 98.6 degrees Fahrenheit. When you are in a cold environment, without layers of clothing, your body quickly begins to lose heat and your core body temperature begins to decrease. Thermal sensors are activated to signal your brain that your body temperature is decreasing. In response, your brain attempts to compensate by signaling your muscles to begin short bursts of contractions which cause you to shiver. As you shiver, the muscle contractions work to generate heat, which in turn warms the blood that travels through them, increasing the body's core temperature. In essence, it's as if your body is activating a program to solve a problem posed by the environment.

Biologists do not teach homeostasis to students by drawing from the fundamentals of chemistry and physics. Instead biology textbooks often introduce the concept of homeostasis by using a furnace and thermostat as an analogy for how such constant internal states can be maintained.[1] Homeostasis could be described in terms of chemistry and physics, just as the interaction of a thermostat and furnace could be described in terms of chemistry and physics. However, the biology lesson is not found in such a discussion, rather it is found in the similarity between the body and the design of a thermostat and furnace. The body echoes the design principles of our own technology.

This technological echo is even louder when we look inside the cell. Enter into the world of molecular biology and you will find a place described in ways that would make an engineer or computer programmer feel quite at home. Common concepts and labels that can be found in the indexes and glossaries of most standard college molecular biology textbooks include such terms as: carriers, channels, chaperones, checkpoints, circuits, cycles, coding regions, codons, cooperativity, couplers, domains, enhancers, expression, feedback, induction, initiators, integration, messengers, modules, motifs, motors, organizing centers, operators, primers, promoters, pumps, reading frames, receptors, sequences, signals, silencers, suppressors, templates, terminators, transcriptions, translations, uncouplers, and vectors. As scientist C. R. Lowe explains:

> The molecular machinery of nature out performs anything that mankind currently knows how to construct with conventional man-

ufacturing technology by many orders of magnitude . . . . Almost without exception, there exist biomolecular analogues of conventional functional devices, including structural components, wires, motors, drive shafts, pipes, pumps, production lines and programmable control systems.[2]

In fact, the technological echo inside the cell is so strong that we can think of life as carbon-based nanotechnology, where cells are endowed with a myriad of machinery built around carbon atoms. K. Eric Drexler, a pioneer in the field of nanotechnology, defines nanotechnology as technology that is based on the manipulation of individual atoms and molecules in order to build structures that conform to complex, atomic specifications.[3] Nanotechnology involves microscopic machines that function at a microscopic level. This is an excellent description of what happens in any living cell. It was, after all, life itself that led many scientists to believe the futuristic science fiction of nanotechnology would become an eventual scientific reality and today billions of dollars are being spent developing this new field of engineering. As scientist D. S. Goodsell noted, "Biological molecules are proven examples of the feasibility, and utility, of nanotechnology."[4] Concerning the humble bacterium that lives in your large intestines, *E. coli*, Howard Berg, a professor of molecular and cell biology from Harvard, writes:

> Thus, in addition to rotary engines and propellers, *E. coli*'s standard accessories include particle counters, rate meters, and gear boxes. This microorganism is a nanotechnologist's dream.[5]

The scientific literature is rife with similar descriptions, where molecular structures inside the cell are treated as if they are products of advanced technology. Consider just a few of these examples.

- The bacterial flagellum, used to propel bacteria, is a complex that consists of roughly forty proteins. Scientists Robert Macnab and John Parkinson, in explaining how to understand the working processes of the bacterial flagellum, note, "We need to think almost in engineering terms about transmission shafts, mounting plates and bushings."[6] David DeRosier, another researcher who studies the flagellum, writes "the flagellum resembles a machine designed by humans."[7]

• The F1-ATP synthase is a protein complex found in bacteria and mitochondria that works to synthesize ATP. Paul Boyer, an expert on this topic, reviewed the research and entitled his review, "The ATP Synthase—A Splendid Molecular Machine."[8] The mechanism by which this complex synthesizes ATP was confirmed by a group of Japanese scientists. *Science News*[9] helped publicize these findings as follows: "With parts that resemble pistons and a drive shaft, the enzyme F1-ATPase looks suspiciously like a tiny engine. Indeed, a study demonstrates that's exactly what it is." In fact, when Stephen Block reviewed these same findings for the journal *Nature*, his article began, "Some enzyme complexes function literally as machines, and come equipped with springs, levers, and even rotary joints."[10]

• Eukaryotic cells all have an organelle called the nucleus which houses the cell's genetic material. For a long time, the nucleus was viewed as a "largely disordered, membranous-bound bag of DNA and other molecules."[11] In a review of research on the nucleus, scientists Angus Lamond and William Earnshaw note, "The currently available data lend support to the view that a nucleus is far from a randomly arranged bag of molecules, but rather functions as an integrated and highly ordered machine, albeit one with a high degree of structural flexibility."[11]

• Eukaryotes contain a microscopic network of protein strands called the cytoskeleton. These strands are composed of the proteins actin and tubulin. Another protein, kinesin, can attach to tubulin strands and use them as tracks to shuttle material to its proper destination. Ronald Vale and Robert Fletterick reviewed this protein and entitled their review "The Design Plan of Kinesin Motors."[12] Referring to this same motor, Sharyn Endow and Robert Fletterick wrote, "Microtubule motors are among the most fascinating machines in

Nature's vast repertoire of biological devices. These minuscule engines carry out many essential transport functions in the cell."[13]

- This list is nearly endless. Proteins known as cyclin-dependent kinases have been likened to "engines, clocks, and microprocessors."[14] Actin and myosin complexes are called "elegant machines" that reflect "the typical design in cell motility."[15] The structure of green fluorescent protein has been described as "so perfectly suited for its function it looks as if it were manufactured in a machine shop."[16] A DNA region that regulates the expression of genes has been described as containing an "analog computational device" and "logic device."[17]

It is important to remember the scientists quoted above are not proposing that life is indeed designed technology. But that is exactly what makes these descriptions of life all the more interesting. Why would a community of scientists, who draw heavily from a non-teleological perspective, continually treat the molecules they study as if they were technological products? Maybe is it so easy to treat life as carbon-based nanotechnology because it *is* carbon-based nanotechnology. Could scientists very well be studying a genuine form of nanotechnology, where biological molecules are truly machines functioning as molecular clocks, motors, information transducers, proofreaders, pumps, selective gates, springs, microprocessors, chaperones, sensors, and circuits? Or would it be an obvious mistake to take these concepts and terminology too literally?

Misleading Metaphors?

If I told my three-year-old daughter that she was the apple of my eye, she would giggle while telling me there was no apple in my eye. Her laughter would come from misunderstanding the use of metaphor. Merriam-Webster defines a metaphor as "a figure of speech in which a word or phrase literally denoting one kind of object or idea is used in place of another to suggest a likeness or analogy between them." Metaphors are just communication shortcuts that are not meant to be taken literally.

It is important to be careful when discussing metaphors. For example, a chemist might talk of oily molecules as those that do not "like" water, with the more technical term for such molecules being "hydrophobic" (literally meaning "water-fearing"). Surely molecules do not have the ability to actually dislike or fear water. Another metaphor would involve discussion of the energetic "cost" of the hydrophobic molecules in relation to a watery phase. But we do not mean that molecules really calculate energetic costs before performing a function. The human mind has a well-known tendency to project teleological metaphors onto the world. Yet nature does not really "abhor" a vacuum, the earth does not actually "groan," skies are not really "angry," and the weather is not truly "furious." Might biologists simply be using their metaphors similarly, as convenient ways to clarify and communicate difficult concepts? If so, it would be a serious mistake to read too much into these metaphors. After all, would anyone think we have evidence that oily molecules have feelings because chemists talk about them as if they have a phobia?

While we cannot rule out the possibility that the use of design language and concepts in biology is simply an elaborate maze of metaphors, there are four reasons for thinking there is a core, literal truth to such descriptions: 1) the metaphors used by biologists are unlike the metaphors I have cited above: 2) the metaphors used by biologists do not break down if taken literally; 3) the metaphors used by biologists are unlike the metaphors used in other areas of science and; 4) these metaphors are too useful. Let us consider each point in more detail.

The language of molecular biology is not in the same class as anthropomorphic metaphors, but rather, it is in the same class as the design terminology employed by engineers. Metaphors such as fear, cost, abhor and angry, commonly share the projection of consciousness onto the world, as if the outer world was, in fact, behaving like our inner world. Metaphors such as these represent the human tendency to view the world through anthropomorphic glasses. However, the metaphors employed by molecular biologists are not of this type. Properly understood, metaphors in the language of molecular biology do not project conscious awareness or emotion onto molecules. When molecular biologists interpret a protein as a "sensor," no one envisions the protein as a conscious entity that is sensing things and responding to what it sees or hears. Instead, when molecular biologists speak of protein sensors, they use this term in *the same way an engineer uses it* when he builds or describes a mechanical device. This is a point of major relevance to our investigation. It does not matter if biological molecules are not conscious. What matters is whether or not the biological molecules can be placed into the same class as mechanical components designed by humans.

Metaphors typically break down when we begin to take them literally. Any investigator who tried to use the literal interpretation of a metaphor as a research guide would quickly find themselves with a rather useless guide. For example, if the sky really is angry, this implies the sky contains some type of nervous system given that emotions, from a scientific viewpoint, are attached to nervous systems. However, since the sky has no brain, the understanding of meteorology is not at all advanced by seeking brains and neurotransmitters among the clouds. Neither will we find brains and neurotransmitters among the molecules that are hydrophobic. But all this changes when we turn to the use of metaphors in molecular biology.

The design terminology that is used in the language of molecular biology does not break down when interpreted literally. Consider the process of protein synthesis as an example. To make a protein, a specific sequence of twenty different building blocks, known as amino acids, must be linked together. Yet how does the cell know what sequence to put them in? That information comes from the DNA molecule, where a specific sequence of building blocks, known as nucleotides, encodes the amino acid sequence. The cell employs machinery that translates the nucleotide sequence of the DNA into the amino acid sequence of the protein.[18] We can thus legitimately think of the DNA as literally encoding the amino acid sequence, just as it is valid to think of the process of protein synthesis as an event that literally translates the DNA code-script into an amino acid sequence. While the sky does not actually possess emotions, the cell does actually encode and translate things.

The metaphors used by molecular biologists are also different from those used in other areas of science. While the metaphors of chemistry and physics may be used in biology, design terminology is rarely used outside of the biological sciences. For example, in talking about sodium and chloride ions interacting to form sodium chloride (common table salt), chemists do not speak of this reaction as the result of a "chemical program." Nor do they speak of the sodium-chloride circuit that is employed to shuttle sodium to chloride. And neither is the periodic table viewed as a conventional code. If we turn to physics, no one speaks about the oceans sensing the moon and regulating their motion in response in order to generate tides. When a ball is dropped from a tower, it is not shuttled to the ground as cargo. While these terms are foreign to the study of chemistry and physics, they are at the heart of the language of molecular biology.

Biology, and only biology, needs these types of design concepts and terms in order to make sense of what is being studied. Biologist Arnold De Loof defines life as "simply communication activity exerted by a communicating compartment (system)."[19] De Loof elaborates as follows:

> Communication is transfer of information. This transfer requires a communication system. Such a system typically consists of a sender-encoder, which emits a coded message, a transmission channel (air, blood, etc.), through which the message is transported along a gradient; and a receiver-decoder-amplifier-responder, in which energy must be stockpiled in order to allow an energy-consuming response. Very often, there is feedback. What constitutes "information"? A message of whatever nature contains information when, upon being decoded by the receiver, it can cause the mobilization of part of the stockpiled energy to do some sort of work sooner or later. What is the purpose of communication? To make the receiver work for the sender. Is information material or immaterial? Information in itself is immaterial, but it can need material support in order to be transported.

De Loof's description of life will make more sense to an engineer trying to build something than to a physicist trying to describe the earth orbiting the sun or a chemist trying to explain the role of oxygen in making fire. Yet even if his discussion of information and communication is merely a reliance on metaphorical language, such metaphors are rarely used outside of the engineering and biological sciences.

In his book, *The Fifth Miracle*, physicist Paul Davies surveys life in an attempt to outline the scientific case for abiogenesis (life arising from non-life). Although not a biologist, he nevertheless discovers that life is quite different from the non-living world in a manner that is so basic he wonders if new laws of physics will be needed. Davies then begins to sense the way in which biology is different from the physical sciences:

> Viewed in the light of the theory of computation, the problem of biogenesis appears just as perplexing as it does through the eyes of the physicist or chemist. And the difficulties are not purely technical. Thorny philosophical problems loom too. Concepts like information and software do not come from the natural sciences at all, but from communication theory, and involve qualifiers like context and mode of description—notions that are quite alien to the physicist's description of the world. Yet most scientists accept that information concepts do legitimately apply to biological systems, and they cheerfully treat semantic information as if it were a natural quantity like energy. Unfortunately, "meaning" sounds perilously close to purpose, an utterly taboo subject in biology. So we are left with the contradiction that we need to apply concepts derived from purposeful human activities (communication, meaning, context, semantics) to biological processes that certainly appear purposeful, but are in fact not (or are not supposed to be).[20]

It becomes clear that while the biologist views life as "communication activity exerted by a communicating compartment," the physicist notes that such notions are "alien to the physicist's description of the world."

To further evaluate whether the metaphors used by biologists are unlike the metaphors used in other areas of science, I searched three scientific databases for design terms in February of 2003. The first database is called Biological Abstracts, which includes 5500 biology and medical journals. The second database is called GeoRef, which includes 3500 geoscience journals. GeoRef was chosen because most scientists believe that life was spawned from geological processes. Finally, I searched the database, INSPEC, which provides access to the literature in physics, electrical engineering, electronics, communications, control engineering, computers and computing, and information technology. The results are shown in Table 3-I.

TABLE 3-I. Search of Scientific Journal Databases for Design Terminology			
Search Term(s)	**INSPEC**	**BIOABS**	**GEOREF**
Amplify	2096	6494	74
Adjust	9554	4768	193
Checkpoint	728	2665	0
Circuit	376401	11821	268
Circuitry	20258	3505	24
Communicate	12210	1799	123
Compensate	14576	8281	243
Control	860394	857841	27180
Correct	67072	35567	1823
Decode	1738	196	6
Dampen	259	301	16
Editing	10966	1978	263
Encode	3859	17855	4
Error	210492	35317	3996
Express	14789	53368	516
Fidelity	6577	4219	156
Message	31682	6897	137
Monitor	43528	27959	1820
Node	32337	43096	271
Proofreading	135	589	0
Quality control	27919	8405	1615
Regulate	3960	44413	127
Short circuit	15179	2863	15
Suppress	13797	23160	160
Translate	4325	1971	101

The first thing to notice from Table 3-I is that in every case, these design terms and concepts were far more common in the biological literature than the geological literature. Rather than clustering with geosciences, the number of hits from the biological database are more similar to the hits picked up from searching engineering and information science databases. In fact, almost 1.8 million hits were obtained from the engineering database with an average of 69,216 hits per search phrase. This is roughly the same picture the biological database presents, with a little more than 1.2 million hits and an average of 46,499 hits per search phrase. In stark contrast, the geological database returned only a total of a little over 39,000 hits and an average of only 1511 hits per search phrase. To ensure that these hits were not simply reflecting the size of the databases, the term "energy," was also searched, as this concept would be expected to be universally important in all sciences. In this instance, the engineering database returned 1,076,830 hits and the biological and geological databases were quite similar, with 230,280 and 199,059 hits respectively. While the biological database stored non-teleological terms such as "energy" only 1.16 times more often than the geological database, it stored the teleological terms over thirty times more often. Clearly, the biological research is using terms and concepts that look more like something from the engineering research literature than from the geological literature.

There is a final piece of evidence that suggests there is a basic and literal truth to the use of design terminology in molecular biology—these technological concepts are just *too* useful. Metaphors are certainly useful when explaining concepts to other human beings, yet the design terminology often goes beyond pedagogy—it provides true insight into the molecular and cellular processes. An understanding of our own designed artifacts, along with the principles required to make them, can guide the practice of molecular biology. As our own designs become more complex and sophisticated, they become better and better models for understanding life at the molecular level. For example, one genetics textbook notes that it is useful "to draw an analogy between polypeptide synthesis and the production of sound by a standard tape recorder."[21] Another genetics textbook talks about how mistakes during DNA synthesis are corrected such that this "process resembles that of a backspace delete key on a computer keyboard which is used to erase the incorrect character."[22] And a cell biology textbook describes the events in a cell as follows: "The cell-cycle control system operates much like the control system of an automatic washing machine. . . . These essential processes of the wash cycle are analogous to the essential processes of the cell cycle."[23]

Computers are a superior example. Biologists depend on them to store and manipulate data, but computers are also useful to molecular biologists *as crude models of the cell*. An understanding of how computers work serves as a model to better understand how cells work. Physicist Paul Davies notes that life is an information-processing system under software control.[20] Or consider how one Japanese biotechnology company, Yokoyama CytoLogic, described the cell on its 1999 web page :

> During the early stages of cell evolution a very clever system of information manipulation evolved: DNA became a repository of genetic information; messenger RNA served as an active copy of this information; and transfer RNAs together with various enzymes acted as adaptors/translators, producing functional products, i.e. proteins. This was a decoding process, which became fundamental logic of all future organisms. Interestingly, this process can also be viewed as a type of "computer." In the language of mathematics the DNA is the domain (or code table), the transfer RNA and associated enzymes a function, and the protein products the range. By changing the content of the domain or the structure of the function it is possible to produce a range comprising many products. Since there are many thousands of copies of the RNAs and enzymes involved in this process in a cell, this "computer system" can be thought of as being massively parallel, far beyond anything that can now be constructed using solid state computer hardware. The gradual understanding of this molecular logic, which has been preserved throughout evolution, has not only been a great success of basic science, but has also opened up the possibility of much new and interesting technology involving information and data processing. By employing the basic strategy of nature it is now possible to conceive of rationally modifying the DNA and/or the transfer RNAs and their associated enzymes in order to produce a wide variety of products.[24]

James Shapiro, a microbiologist from the University of Chicago, also likens a cell to a set of computer programs:

> . . . the actual result of molecular studies of heredity, cell biology and multi-cellular development has been to reveal a realm of sensitivity, communication, computation and indescribable complexity. This year's Nobel Prize in Medicine illustrates this point: the recipients

were recognized for identifying components of the molecular computational network that regulates the eukaryotic cell cycle. Special mention was made of the concept of checkpoints, the inherently computational idea that cells monitor their own internal processes and make decisions about whether to proceed with the various steps in cell division based on the information detected by surveillance networks. . . . Applying the computer storage system metaphor, the ideas summarized in Tables 2 and 3 can be restated by saying that the genome is formatted for interaction with cellular complexes that operate to replicate, transmit, read, package and reorganize DNA sequence information. Genome formatting is similar to the formatting of computer programs in that a variety of generic signals are assigned to identify files independently of their unique data content. We know that different computer systems employ different signals and architectures to retrieve data and execute programs. In an analogous fashion, diverse taxonomic groups often employ characteristic DNA sequences and chromosomal structures to organize coding information and to format their genomes for expression and transmission.[25]

Even more explicitly, he notes that the best metaphor for the genome (the complete set of genes found in a cell) is a computer:

The best current metaphor for how the genome operates is to compare it to the hard drive in an electronic information system and think of DNA as a data storage medium. The metaphor is not exact, in part because genomes replicate and are transmitted to progeny cells in ways that have no precise electronic parallel. Nonetheless, the information-processing metaphor allows us to view the role of the genome in a realistic context. DNA by itself is inert. Information stored in genomic sequences can only achieve functional expression through interaction of DNA with other cellular information systems.[25]

Ion Petre, a scientist from the Turku Centre for Computer Science in Finland, echoes this same theme and further provides an example of an interesting convergence between cells and computers:

Viewed as information processing systems, biological organisms possess amazing capabilities to perform information-handling tasks such as: control, pattern recognition, adaptability, information-storage, etc. Thus, the functioning of biological organisms as information-processing systems is of great interest to computer scientists, and we are witnessing now a fast growing research in this field. This research is genuinely interdisciplinary in nature, involving both computer scientists and molecular scientists (biologists, biochemists, biophysicists, crystallographers. . .). One of the leading paradigms of this research is *"cell as a computer."* A beautiful example of this paradigm is a single cell organism called *ciliate*—the gene assembly process in ciliates has turned out to be a very elegant computational process which even *uses one of the basic data structures of computer science: the linked lists!* This process of gene assembly (assembling genes of macronucleus from their micronuclear form) is *the most involved DNA processing known in living organisms.*[26]

That cellular processes are likened to computer processes clearly indicates that our understanding and design of computers has illuminated cellular processes. Is it simply a strange coincidence that an understanding of things we design helps us to understand how life works?

When we talk about tape recorders, washing machines and computers, we are not employing anthropomorphic metaphors. We are actually using the knowledge about our own designed artifacts to shed light on biology and how it works. Imagine if there were no computers, tape recorders, and washing machines. Take away human technology, and suddenly, there are no good metaphors left to describe life. How could research gain accurate insight into the cell that works like an advanced computer without knowing about computers?

If life was designed, it is reasonable to assume that such design would be advanced beyond our current capabilities, given it is not yet possible to design life from scratch. In terms of the history of science, this means that *our ability to recognize life as designed would be dependent upon our own technological development.* It is not simply a question of developing the technology needed to process the information necessary to understand life. It is not simply needing computers and programmers to process the biological information. It is the weird way in which our technology parallels, and thus illuminates, life processes—we can learn about the latter by appreciating the former. The computers and programmers *themselves* provide very good models for understanding cells.

The natural world provides plenty of metaphors that are not dependent on human design. Biological processes could be likened to meteorological, astronomical, or geological processes. To understand the cell, instead of talking about circuits, codes, machines, and programs, we could be talking about storms, eruptions, tides, sedimentation, clouds, tornadoes, eclipses, orbits, and wind. Yet while such metaphors may have some albeit limited descriptive power, they could never really replace these types of technological concepts.

All of this, of course, makes sense if life really is carbon-based nanotechnology. To understand an alien technology, we would have to use our own technology as a model, and the more similar the technologies, the more easily we could characterize and understand this alien technology. As our designed artifacts have become more advanced, complicated, and sophisticated they provide better and better models for thinking about biology. This would lead me to the following prediction: as our technology improves, as we design things that are smaller, more complex, and more sophisticated, I would expect our understanding of how life works to improve accordingly.

None of the points discussed above amount to a *proof* of teleology in biology. We are only concerned, at this point, about things that might cause the suspicion of design behind life. Those who share in this suspicion might want to explore the world as if biological metaphors have a literal meaning that is, at least, partly true. Crude technology gives us at least partial insight into much more advanced biotechnology. Is there any reason why we would be wrong to do this? Is there any evidence that strongly demonstrates that a literal interpretation of such metaphors is indeed in error? For example, what argument can be raised against viewing a protein as like a sensor versus viewing a protein *as* a sensor? Why is protein synthesis not an example of translation? To follow up on this suspicion of design, let us take an even closer look at some of the similarities between biology and engineering.

A Convergence Between Biology and Engineering

In a scientific essay about molecular machines, Bruce Alberts offered a most interesting acknowledgment at the end of his article.[27] Alberts stated that he was indebted "to Jonathan Alberts for his explanation of how engineers analyze machines." A biologist is seeking engineering explanations to better understand biology? Following Alberts's lead, let us consult David Ullman's text, *The Mechanical Design Process*, which is part of Schaum's Outline Series in Mechanical Engineering.[28]

A biologist reading this text would feel quite at home as Ullman explains how mechanical engineers go about designing machines. In his discussion of machines, Ullman speaks of a system that is "considered a conglomeration of objects that perform a specific function." This is exactly how biologists view biological systems. Ullman explores the process of component assembly, which again is something quite familiar to the molecular biologist. Ullman further addresses the form-function relationship inherent in components, something that is central to our understanding of proteins and other cell components. In mechanical engineering, devices are often named after the function they impart. Consider the screwdriver. It is named as such because it works to drive screws into a surface. A stapler staples paper. A copy machine copies and a washing machine washes. Mechanical engineers mentally index the mechanical world by function. Biologists follow exactly this same process. Proteins likewise are often named according to their function. For example, DNA polymerase is a complex of proteins that functions to form polymers of nucleotides. The activation domain of a transcription factor is part of a protein that functions to activate the process of transcription. ATP synthase works to synthesize ATP. The degradosome degrades RNA. Signal transduction complexes convey signals. The list is long.

Ullman also notes that knowing what something does in the mechanical world does not tell us how it goes about its task. He writes, "To answer *how* we must have some information on the *form* of the device. The term 'form' is used to relate any aspect of physical shape, geometry, construction, material, or size." Once again, what is true for mechanical engineering is true for biology, where form is used to understand function. For example, in molecular biology, x-ray crystallography is a sophisticated technique used to determine the actual form of proteins. When these forms are determined, biologists are often able to rationally interpret how it is that the functions associated with the protein are performed. Such information is also essential in designing experiments to better characterize the mechanisms by which a protein carries out its function.

The specific similarities that mechanical engineering and molecular biology share can be further appreciated by a survey of the detailed functions employed by both disciplines. Consider Table 3-II, which reproduces a series of functions provided by Ullman (p. 145). He describes these as "typical mechanical design functions" which are verbs used by engineers to actualize and analyze the design of a machine. Note that most of the verbs/functions work to impose order. They all function as specifications. All of these verbs not only have a place in mechanical design, but they have also long been employed by molecular biologists to describe the processes of life.

Table 3-II. Typical Mechanical Design Functions		
CHANGE	VERIFY	CONVERT
INCREASE/DECREASE	DRIVE	TRANSFORM
COUPLE/INTERRUPT	POSITION	TRANSLATE
JOIN/SEPARATE	RELEASE	ROTATE
ASSEMBLE/DISASSEMBLE	DISSIPATE	START/STOP
CHANNEL/GUIDE	ORIENT	LIFT
RECTIFY	LOCATE	HOLD
CONDUCT	COLLECT	CLEAR
ABSORB	SECURE	SUPPORT
STORE	MOVE	SUPPLY

The similarity between "mechanical design functions" and biological functions is easily illustrated with a brief synopsis of some of the major events that take place inside a cell. I have employed most of the design verbs used by mechanical engineers (in italics) in a description that one might expect to find when studying basic molecular biology.

The cell nucleus is a large organelle that *stores* the genetic information, DNA. This DNA is replicated by a protein complex known as DNA polymerase, an enzyme which has a proof-reading component that *rectifies* mis-incorporated nucleotides. DNA polymerase also *verifies* that the correct base has been added to the growing strand of nucleotides before proceeding. The process of DNA replication is typically *coupled* to the process of cell division. But DNA polymerase is not the only complex that interacts with DNA, as other proteins known as transcription factors *assemble* on certain DNA regions to form a complex that *guides* another complex, known as RNA polymerase, to the DNA. The transcription complex also works to properly *position* and *orient* the RNA polymerase along the DNA. RNA polymerase will then bind and *move* along the DNA strand, synthesizing a complementary strand of RNA while some of these transcription factors are *released* from the complex after RNA polymerase begins to *move* away. Once the RNA is synthesized, other proteins and RNA molecules may *join* together to form a complex that splices different RNA pieces together. This RNA molecule is then removed from the nucleus and serves as the instructions for protein synthesis. During this process, certain proteins and other RNA molecules *join* together to *translate* the RNA sequence into an amino acid sequence. The processes of transcription and translation both *start* and *stop*. Protein expression levels may also be *increased* or *decreased* depending on events that take place during transcription and translation. Certain proteins work to *guide* these newly synthesized proteins to their proper destination. Once the proteins arrive, they function essentially by changing their conformations in response to specific interactions. Some proteins function as channels in the membrane to *conduct* ions across the membrane in a regulated fashion. In some cases, proteins work to *absorb* excess ions. Waste products can also be *dissipated* from the cell, as they are *channeled* to the outside through openings in membrane proteins. Some proteins interact with the membrane in such a way as to properly *orient* certain domains involved in protein-protein interactions.

Many proteins function to *convert/transform* chemical energy into work. Some proteins function as motor proteins that *drive* along protein strands as they *move* their cargo from one place to the next. Other proteins have specific sequences that serve to *locate* them to the correct organelle. Some proteins *secure* and *hold* various proteins and macromolecules at their correct address. And the components of some protein complexes, such as the bacterial flagellum and the ATP synthase, actually *rotate* around an axis.

What is most significant about the above paragraph is not merely how easy it was for me to transfer mechanical engineering concepts to a coherent synopsis about molecular biology, but how important these functional verbs are to our understanding of molecular biology. Without these mechanical design functions, molecular biologists would have tremendous difficulty understanding what is happening inside the cell, planning experiments and interpreting the meaning of the results of their experiments. In fact, I am not even sure it would be possible to understand and describe what happens inside a cell without referring to these mechanical design functions.

It is also worth re-emphasizing how foreign these concepts are in chemistry and physics. While molecular biologists easily apply these mechanical design concepts to research studies, and find them to be essential when interpreting and describing experimental results, the chemist or physicist would have great trouble employing even a fraction of these verbs. Returning to the Biological Abstracts, GeoRef, and INSPEC, a further search of these databases using Ullman's design functions was conducted in May of 2003 (Table 3-III). It again becomes clear that biology converges with technology rather than geology. In this case, the average number of hits found by using Biological Abstracts and INSPEC are almost identical, at 23,163 for INSPEC and 24,619 for Biological Abstracts. In contrast, GeoRef returned an average of only 1,985 hits, which represents only 8% of the average number of hits that occurred from both the biological and engineering literature. Much of this 8% probably traces to the tools used to analyze geological phenomena. For example, a paper describing a new way of storing data about earthquakes is likely to be picked up with the search phrase "store."

The similarity between engineering and biology is uncanny if all biology can be reduced to nothing more than the laws of chemistry and physics. In mechanical engineering, the devices that are designed do not violate these laws, but the same devices do not seem entirely reducible to just those

Table 3-III. Search of Databases for Mechanical Design Functions			
Search Term(s)	INSPEC	BIOABS	GEOREF
Absorb	4237	2958	130
Assemble	2838	3902	89
Conduct	8417	5915	590
Convert	12246	7516	333
Couple	12932	5868	996
Dissipate	1473	583	66
Guide	33877	12054	11705
Join	5695	1770	729
Locate	12141	39441	1303
Move	31115	11099	1176
Orient	1740	1545	282
Position	179989	119505	13316
Rectify	803	266	22
Release	34533	200054	4941
Secure	14803	2352	138
Start	32831	38723	1139
Stop	13719	14180	1451
Store	22747	12395	461
Translate	4414	2040	105
Verify	32715	10222	736

laws. The mechanical design functions are more plausibly attributed to the intentions and planning of the designer who imposes spatial, temporal, and geometric constraints on materials that channel the forces of chemistry and physics to a predetermined end. To properly describe the origin of the device, the design must be considered in tandem with the laws of chemistry and physics. The design itself is not obviously reducible to these, as no law dictates the shape of a carburetor or where it is attached to the engine. One could attach a carburetor to the roof of a car. It just would not work. But the shape of the carburetor, its parts, and its positioning must be accounted for to fully understand an engine. And such understanding must entail some notion of intelligent intervention.

While Tables 3-I and 3-III provide a snapshot of the usage of teleological concepts and language, how has this usage fared over time? Consider the term checkpoint used in the quote by Shapiro earlier in the chapter. In May 2003, this term was used to search PubMed, a database from the National Library of Medicine. This database stores over 12 million citations since the mid-60s, mostly related to biology and medicine. From 1965-1975, the search phrase "checkpoint" returned no hits. From 1976-1990, it returned six hits. From 1991-2003, it returned 2413 hits. Of these, almost half (1108) are from 2001-2003. Thus, here is a new teleological concept that surfaced when biologists began to think of the cell as being filled with machinery and the incidence of use of this term is growing rapidly.

Or what if we surveyed the concept of design itself? Searching the PubMed database with the term "design" returns the results shown in Figure 3-1. Note again that from the 1990s onward, the use of the term "design" skyrockets. Of course, this could simply be attributed to the growing number of scientific journals in the database. That is why the term "energy," was also searched. This term is a basic, centuries-old concept in science. Note the use of the term "energy" does not skyrocket similarly since the 1990s, but instead maintains a constant and gradual increase. Another possible explanation is that since the 1990s, computers have become more widely used in science. The term "design" might simply be picking up scientists' design of new computer programs and models. While there is an increase in the use of the term "computer" since 1990, it still lags far behind the use of the term "design." Thus, it appears that this term became more popular since it became clear that the "entire cell can be viewed as a factory that contains an elaborate network of interlocking assembly lines, each of which is composed of a set of large protein machines."[27] At the very least, the term "design" refuses to be exorcised from biology.

If living processes are the products of design, it comes as no surprise that so much of biology is more akin to the study of engineering than to chemistry or physics. Furthermore, it would make sense that as our understanding of the cell advances, that teleological concepts, including the very concept of design, would proliferate in the biological literature. Much of this design terminology stems from the fact that biologists have discovered that cells are filled with miniature machines and that coded information is stored and

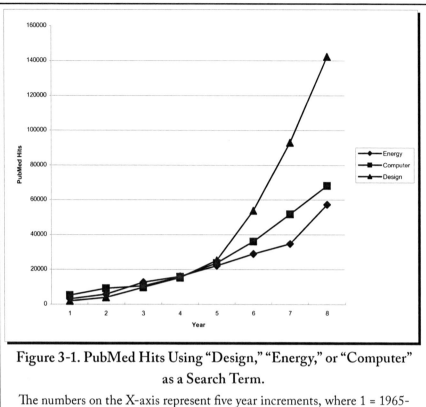

Figure 3-1. PubMed Hits Using "Design," "Energy," or "Computer" as a Search Term.

The numbers on the X-axis represent five year increments, where 1 = 1965-1970, 5 = 1986-1990, 6 = 1991-1995, 7 = 1996-2000, and 8 = 2001-2005.

employed for the synthesis of these machines. We will therefore look more closely at the code and the machines in the next two chapters.

In conclusion, none of the above arguments are intended as proofs of design. None of these arguments work to establish design in a probable sense. We are merely trying to traverse the Explanatory Continuum from the realm of the possible to the plausible. Furthermore, the discussion in this chapter has not considered whether much of the teleological language inherent in biology can be attributed to natural selection, something we will consider in Chapter 6. We are simply looking for clues; causes for suspicion; reasons to consider that design may indeed be behind life. If we return to our earlier example of the murder investigation involving Jones and Smith, the convergence of biological and engineering concepts does not amount to Jones being caught in the act of murdering Smith. It simply amounts to

ECHOES OF TECHNOLOGY

Jones behaving suspiciously. Biology, and the language of biology, is not behaving in a manner similar to the related sciences of chemistry, physics, geology, meteorology, etc. In comparison, that biology, and the language of biology, is out of sync with other natural sciences catches our attention and leads to the development of a hunch. If life was designed, these are exactly the patterns we would expect. These patterns are positive evidence that render design behind life a plausible explanation.

REFERENCES

1. For just two examples among many, see Salidin, K.S., 1998. *Anatomy & Physiology: The Unity of Form and Function.* WCB McGraw-Hill, Boston, Massachusetts, p. 21 and Knapp, L., 1998. *Perspectives in Human Biology.* Wadsworth Publishing Company, Belmont, California, pp. 76-77.

2. Lowe, C.R., 2000. "Nanobiotechnology: The Fabrication and Applications of Chemical and Biological Nanostructures." *Current Opinion Structural Biology*, 10:428-434.

3. Drexler, K.E., 1986. *Engines of Creation: The Coming Age of Nanotechnology.* Anchor Press, New York.

4. Goodsell, D.S., 2000. "Biomolecules and Nanotechnology." *American Scientist*, 88:230-237.

5. Berg, H.C., 1999. "Motile Behavior of Bacteria." http://www.aip.org/pt/jan00/berg.htm; last accessed 11/10/04.

6. Macnab, R.M. and Parkinson J.S., 1991. "Genetic Analysis of the Bacterial Flagellum." *Trends in Genetics,* 7:196-200.

7. DeRosier, D.J., 1998. "The Turn of the Screw: The Bacterial Flagellar Motor." *Cell,* 93:1.

8. Boyer, P.D., 1997. "The ATP Synthase—A Splendid Molecular Machine." *Annual Review of Biochemistry,* 66:717-749.

9. Wu, C., 1997. "Molecular Motor Spins Out Energy for Cells." *Science News,* 151:173.

10. Block, S.M., 1997. "Real Engines of Creation." *Nature,* 386:217-219.

11. Lamond, A.I. and Earnshaw, W.C., 1998. "Structure and Function in the Nucleus." *Science,* 280:547-553.

12. Vale, R.D. and Fletterick, R.J., 1997. "The Design Plan of Kinesin Motors." *Annual Review of Cell and Developmental Biology,* 13:745-777.

13. Endow, S.A. and Fletterick, R.J., 1998. "Reversing a 'Backwards' Motor." *BioEssays,* 20:108-112.

14. Morgan, D.O., 1997. "Cyclin-Dependent Kinases: Engines, Clocks, and Microprocessors." *Annual Review of Cell and Developmental Biology,* 13:261-291.

15. Goldman, Y.E., 1998. "Wag the Tail: Structural Dynamics of Actomyosin." *Cell,* 93:1-4.

16. Boxer, S.G., 1996. "Another Green Revolution." *Nature,* 383:484-485.

17. Yuh, C.H., Bolouri, H. and Davidson, E.H., 1998. "Genomic Cis-Regulatory Logic: Functional Analysis and Computational Model of a Sea Urchin Gene Control System." *Science,* 279:1896-1902.

18. This description omits the fact that DNA is first copied into an RNA format and it is the RNA that guides the process of protein synthesis.

19. De Loof, A., 1999. "Life as Communication." *HMS Beagle. The BioMedNet Magazine,* 68, p. 5. http://www.biomednet.com/hmsbeagle/68/viewpts/op_ed; last accessed 04/12/01.

20. Davies, P., 1999. *The Fifth Miracle: The Search for the Origin and Meaning of Life.* Simon & Schuster, New York, pp. 121-122.

21. Fristrom, J.W. and Clegg, M.T., 1988. *Principles of Genetics.* Chiron Press, New York, p. 381.

22. Russell, P.J., 1998. *Genetics,* 5th ed. Benjamin/Cummings, Menlo Park, California, p. 357.

23. Alberts, B., Bray, D., Johnson, A., Lewis, J., Raff, M., Roberts, K. and Walter, P., 1998. *Essential Cell Biology.* Garland Publishing, New York, p. 572.

24. Yokoyama Cytologic. http://web.archive.org/web/19990915232616/http://www2.jst.go.jp/erato/project/yjb_P/yjb_P.html; last accessed 01/27/01.

25. Shapiro, J., 2002. "Genome Organization and Reorganization in Evolution: Formatting for Computation and Function" *Annals of the New York Academy of Sciences,* 981:111-134.

26. Petre, I., 2005. "Computational Processes in Living Cells." http://www. abo.fi/~ipetre/compproc/; last accessed 06/24/05.

27. Alberts, B., 1998. "The Cell as a Collection of Protein Machines: Preparing the Next Generation of Molecular Biologists." *Cell*, 92:291-294.

28. Ullman, D.G., 1992. *The Mechanical Design Process*. McGraw-Hill, New York.

Chapter 4

Error Correction Runs Deep

As a boy, I learned there were four basic food groups—meat, dairy, bread, and fruits and vegetables. Every day, you were supposed to eat a certain amount from these four groups, but when you are a boy, there are more important things to worry about. Like football. It was Mom's job to worry about the four food groups. But when it's finally time to go off to college, you have to start fending for yourself. How in the world is a young college student supposed to balance their diet when there are more important things to worry about? Like parties. The answer became obvious—pizza.

What is food? If you return from the grocery store, take your frozen pizza out of its plastic wrapper, and cook it, why is it that you are able to eat the pizza and not the pizza wrapper? Surely, the pizza tastes much better, but what if you were starving? There is a very simple reason: the pizza wrapper is not made up of the right types of molecules that your body can absorb, use, and incorporate. Yes, the pizza wrapper—like plastic cups and batteries—are all made up of molecules; but they are not of the type your body can process. In contrast, food is composed of the same type of molecules as your body and so are the right sort to provide nutrients.

When you study biology in college, you no longer learn about the four basic food groups. Now it's time to learn the four basic biological molecules: lipids, carbohydrates, proteins, and nucleic acids. These are the molecules that life is very good at making and the rest of the world has a much harder time making. All of these molecules play various roles in life, but each class of molecule plays a primary role. Lipids are important because they are used to make the membrane of a cell, the basic unit of life, which in turn makes it possible to compartmentalize the chemical reactions essential to life. Carbohydrates typically serve as the energy source, or fuel, of a cell. Proteins are the workhorses of a cell. Not only do they provide much of the basic structural material for making a cell, but most of the enzymes are proteins, playing an essential role in speeding up the myriad of chemical reactions that make life possible. Nucleic acids come in two forms: RNA (ribonucleic acid) and DNA (deoxyribonucleic acid). DNA is the information storage molecule of the cell. RNA is a transient copy of certain parts of the DNA used to make proteins, and carries out many other specialized roles in the cell as well.

Throughout the rest of this book, we shall discuss two of these important biological molecules, namely, proteins and nucleic acids. Because much of the information in later chapters will depend on some basic knowledge of these molecules, I will begin this chapter by briefly surveying them. If you are already familiar with this material, just skip ahead to the section entitled "The Code."

Proteins and Nucleic Acids

What is life? Biology textbooks never truly define it, they merely describe it. Life is described as a process with certain features, including growth, metabolism, the ability to reproduce, and the ability to react to the environment. Furthermore, all known life exists either as a single cell or a larger complex of many cells.[1] A cell can be simply viewed, at least for the moment, as a membranous sac that houses a large and complex network of chemical reactions. These reactions carry out many variations on two basic themes: (a) complex molecules are either broken into simpler molecules, often with the release of energy that can be captured, stored, and used and/or; (b) simpler molecules are built into more complex molecules to control and harness the events within the cell. Within each cell thousands of chemical reactions occur, all of which make it possible for you to move your arms, yawn, think, and get up from your chair.

Proteins are major ingredients of the cell. A protein is a large molecule consisting of a chain of subunits called amino acids. Some amino acids are large, others are small. Some have no charge associated with them, others are positively charged, while still others are negatively charged. Some readily associate with water molecules (called hydrophilics), while others more readily associate with oil (called hydrophobics). Life uses a set of twenty different amino acids. When these various amino acids are linked in a chain, their individual physical and chemical properties interact with each other and the water that surrounds them.[2] For example, positives attract negatives, but repel other positives. Since proteins are surrounded by water, hydrophobic amino acids seek refuge from the water. This results in a chain with hydrophobic amino acids crowded together to form the core, and hydrophilic amino acids forming the surface. Any chain with a particular sequence of amino acids has a preferred shape (or a fairly small set of preferred shapes), because the folded shape represents a compromise between the chemical properties of all the different subunits, resulting in a three-dimensional arrangement that tends to be quite stable

Proteins play many important roles in the cell. They not only function as enzymes that speed up the thousands of chemical reactions inside a cell, they also organize the environment inside and outside the cell. As biologist Thomas Lee notes, "What distinguishes the chemistry of life from that of non-living systems is, in a word, organization."[3] Proteins bind to other proteins to form complex architectures, similar to the way a child can form all kinds of things by linking Lego blocks. Proteins link up with each other largely because of complementary surfaces (for example, a specifically placed and unique protrusion on one protein might fit into a particular crevice on another protein). Like Lego blocks, proteins come in many different shapes, allowing for very specific and complex linkages to occur. The structures formed by the linking of proteins together not only organize the contents of the cell, but also serve as railways for the transport of material inside a cell.

Whether it is speeding up a chemical reaction or building an essential structure inside the cell, these protein functions are dependent on the protein's shape. The amino acid sequence determines the protein's shape but what determines the amino acid sequence? To answer this question, we now turn to the nucleic acids.

Nucleic acids come in two forms, known as DNA and RNA. Both of these nucleic acids are similar to proteins in that they consist of a chain of subunits. The subunits of the DNA and RNA are called nucleotides. Each nucleotide consists of three parts: a phosphate group, a sugar, and a nitrogenous base. A nucleotide is constructed with a phosphate group attached to one specific part of the sugar molecule while the nitrogenous base is attached to another specific region. A chain of nucleotides is then linked in such a way that two sugars share a common phosphate group.

While proteins use twenty different subunits, RNA and DNA use only four different subunits. The nitrogenous base attached to the sugar molecule is what differentiates one nucleotide from another. DNA uses four different nitrogenous bases called adenine (A), guanine (G), cytosine (C), and thymine (T). RNA uses A, C, and G, but uses a nitrogenous base called uracil (U) instead of thymine. Because nucleic acids are a string of nucleotides, scientists can represent them as a string of letters. For example, if a nucleotide containing thymine is attached to one with adenine which is in turn attached to one with guanine, we can represent this arrangement as "TAG." In fact, in the 1990s, a science fiction movie that explored the potential negative outcomes of genetic engineering on human society used the four bases as its title. The movie was called *GATTACA*.

DNA and RNA differ in significant ways. In addition to using a different nitrogenous base, their sugar molecules are slightly different. In RNA, a chemical group known as a hydroxyl group is present at a specific location on the sugar, but is missing from the same location on DNA molecules. This chemical group allows RNA to act as a catalyst, however, this also makes RNA more unstable and likely to degrade. Typically, the nitrogenous bases in a single strand of nucleotides can form chemical bonds (known as hydrogen bonds) with each other, where U binds to A and G binds to C. These interactions allow the RNA to fold into a three-dimensional structure, which is another feature that enables it to act as a catalyst. In contrast, DNA exists as two distinct chains of nucleotides wrapped around each other (like a spiral staircase) and held together by complementary sequences of nitrogenous bases (A's bind to T's and G's bind to C's), called the double helix. Because of the way nitrogenous bases in DNA interact, if the sequence of one strand is known, the sequence of the other strand can easily be inferred. For example, if one strand has the sequence GATTACA, the other strand that is bound to it has the complementary sequence CTAATGT.

Encoding Life

Why is DNA so important to life? Put simply, the sequence of nucleotides in a DNA molecule literally encodes the sequence of amino acids in a protein. Since the amino acid sequence is responsible for the protein's shape, and the shape is responsible for the function, the DNA encodes three-dimensional shapes and their functions in one-dimensional terms.

Every amino acid is encoded in the DNA as a set of three nucleotides in sequence called a codon. Since a sequence of nucleotides can represent an amino acid, a *genetic code* relates amino acids to DNA. For example, there is an amino acid called phenylalanine. It is a bulky, oily amino acid and in DNA language, it is represented by two codons: AAA and AAG. For a protein with 100 amino acids arranged in a particular fashion, this sequence is encoded in the DNA as a sequence of 300 nucleotides. If the last amino acid in that protein is phenylalanine, the last three nucleotides in the DNA encoding that protein will be AAA or AAG. This span of the 300 nucleotides is called a gene, meaning that genes can be thought of as encoded proteins.

So how do cells take the nucleotide sequence in a gene and use it to make the coded protein? Imagine a cell in your pancreas. Pancreatic cells secrete various digestive enzymes that break down the carbohydrates, proteins, and fats found in your pizza. One such digestive enzyme is trypsin, which cleaves proteins into smaller pieces. So let us consider how this trypsin is made.[4] We will start with a protein machine known as RNA polymerase, which binds to a region just in front of the gene for trypsin (the nucleotide sequence which represents the amino acid sequence of trypsin). This protein machine will unwind the double helix of DNA and travel down one of the strands in a manner similar to a train on its track. As the RNA polymerase begins to travel through the trypsin gene, it reads the nucleotide sequence and makes an RNA copy. When it progresses to the last portion of the gene, RNA polymerase is typically dislodged from the DNA such that the finished product is an RNA molecule containing the complete set of codons representing trypsin's amino acid sequence. The synthesis of this RNA molecule is called *transcription*, as the DNA nucleotide sequence is being transcribed into an RNA format. It is like making a copy of an essay on your computer's hard drive and saving it on a compact disc. The RNA formed is called messenger RNA (mRNA).

Transcription takes place in a specialized compartment of the cell known as the nucleus. When the RNA is made, it is picked up by carrier proteins that shuttle it out of the nucleus where it is then handed off to another protein machine known as the ribosome. The ribosome is considered the protein synthesis factory of the cell. It is composed of dozens of different proteins itself, along with special RNA molecules known as ribosomal RNA (rRNA). The ribosome works with another set of RNA molecules known as transfer RNA (tRNA). This is the key to decoding the nucleotide sequence into an amino acid sequence. Transfer RNA are special molecules in that not only are specific amino acids attached to them (by other enzymes), but they also recognize specific codons on the mRNA. Protein synthesis works simply by threading the mRNA into the ribosome such that codons enter special cavities that can interact with the proper tRNAs. When specific tRNAs line up under the instructions of the codons on the mRNA, then the specific amino acids they carry can be detached from the tRNA and linked together by the ribosome. Thus, the ribosome uses the mRNA to sequentially line up appropriate tRNAs that happen to carry specified amino acids so that these amino acids can be linked together. One college genetics text book describes this whole process as follows:

> It is useful at this point to draw an analogy between polypeptide synthesis and the production of sound by a standard tape recorder. . . . The recorder is the machine that converts the electromagnetic data stored on recording tape into meaningful sounds. The nature of the information stored on the tape determines the nature of the sounds produced, whether an opera by Wagner or a rock concert. As the tape moves across the head, or reader, electrical impulses are instantaneously produced that subsequently result in a sequence of sounds. Polypeptide synthesis is analogous. The mRNA (tape) moves across the ribosome (tape reader) and a polypeptide (music) is produced as a linear sequence of amino acids connected by peptide bonds. In the tape recorder, it is the electronic components of the

recorder that translate the information encoded on the tape into music. If the analogy holds, comparable components will translate the nucleotide sequence of the mRNA into the amino acid sequence of a polypeptide.[5]

The analogy holds. Molecular biologists thus refer to this process of protein synthesis as *translation*.

It is clear why DNA is so important to life. Its primary role is to encode the information necessary for the life processes of the cell. It is quite astonishing to realize that coded information is at the heart of all life. This realization allows us to think of the cell as a very small and self-supporting supercomputer, a concept which we have explored previously in Chapter 3.

THE CODE

When I first learned about the genetic code I was totally struck by the fact that biologists behaved as if they had discovered something ordinary. In philosophy and other areas of science, people would comment on the uncanny implications of the Big Bang or quantum physics. But that life is encoded raised no one's eyebrows.

Most biologists did not originally expect life to be built around coded information. Before understanding the true nature of DNA, biologists expected proteins to be the genetic material of the cell. Because biologists believed that proteins were more complex than DNA, they thought that proteins were the biological substance that ultimately accounted for the complex form and function of organisms which was passed on from generation to generation. Biologists knew that DNA was part of the cell's nucleus and was also passed on from generation to generation, but DNA, being rather inert and constructed with only four building blocks, was thought to be too simple to account for the complexity of biological organisms.

In the 1940s and 50s, engineers and physicists, using the newly developed fields of cybernetics and information theory, began to speculate about a code inherent to life. Simple components could generate great complexity if those simple components reflect the way we *communicate*—coding material. For example, something as simple as the twenty-six letters of the alphabet has generated the great body of Western literature. Such teleological speculations spilled over into biology and eventually led to the successful cracking of life's code. Nevertheless, as Brian Hayes, writing in *American Scientist*, commented:

> Imagine that in 1957 a clairvoyant biologist offered as a hypothesis the exact genetic code and mechanism of protein synthesis understood today. How would the proposal have been received? My guess is that *Nature* would have rejected the paper. "This notion of the ribosome ratcheting along the messenger RNA three bases at a time—it sounds like a computer reading a data tape. Biological systems do not work that way. In biochemistry we have templates, where all the reactants come together simultaneously, not assembly lines where machines are built step by step."[6]

If communication is a key to understanding how life works, it would help to consider a very basic fact about the way humans encode their world—human language is completely conventional. We see a round, red fruit and attach a sequence of letters to it such that it is now an "apple." There is no law of nature determining that we attach this sequence of letters to the red, round fruit; each language has its own sequence, and even different alphabetical characters.

The genetic code is likewise conventional. For example, there is no law of nature which determines that the codon UCU must represent the amino acid serine, because other codons can also represent this amino acid, for example, AGC. There is no chemical reason why the codon could not have been UUU. The genetic code is also conventional in that the organelles inside the cell known as mitochondria have their own DNA and use slightly different codes in various organisms. In their book, *The New Biology*, philosopher Robert Augros and physicist George Stanciu make this same point:

> The genetic code itself is not a product of physical or chemical necessity either. Unlike the periodic table of elements which is determined by the necessities of atomic structure, the genetic code is conventional. There is no natural or necessary connection between

the proteins manufactured by the cell and their equivalents in the DNA code.[7]

Because of its conventional essence, when biologists introduce the genetic code and describe how DNA encodes proteins, they often draw from human codes. Biologists do not teach and explain the basic elements of the genetic code by drawing from the fundamentals of chemistry. Rather, they often introduce this concept with analogies to the products of purposeful activity, such as Morse code.

Morse code is an entirely appropriate analogy because it is strikingly similar to the genetic code. Biologist Mary Anne Clark outlines this relationship as follows:

> Morse code uses combinations of two elements, the dot and the dash, to specify letters of the alphabet and punctuation marks. In genetic code, combinations of the four subunits A, T, C, and G are used to specify the twenty amino acids of the protein alphabet.

> Morse code uses coding combinations of various lengths, from a single dot (a short pulse) or dash (a longer pulse) to four dots/dashes for the 26 letters of the English alphabet. Genetic code always uses combinations of the same size—three units. The DNA codons, e.g. AAA, CGA, CAT, specify the 20 amino acids, the alphabet of protein structure. Transmitted Morse code uses a brief period of silence to mark the boundaries between codons (e.g. to distinguish the letter combination "et" from the letter "a" in the message "beta globin"). Genetic code is read continuously, parsing the DNA data string into triplets, and depends on the translating ribosomes to get the reading frame right.

> Morse code begins with the first character of the message and uses a stop codon (.-.-.-) to specify the end of the message. Genetic code also begins with the first character of the message and ends with one of three stop codons: TAG, TAA, or TGA. In both codes, the codons are laid out in the same sequence as the letters of the message.[8]

ERROR CORRECTION RUNS DEEP

Teleologists have noted that the genetic code is so similar to Morse code the "so-called Shannon information laws apply equally" to both codes (that is, mathematically, the two codes are essentially the same). These scientists write, "DNA information is not just analogous to a message such as Morse code, it *is* such a message sequence."[9]

The fact that DNA contains encoded information in the form of a one-dimensional linear string of symbols is very suggestive *positive* evidence for Intelligent Design behind the fabric of life. If we set aside life for the moment, then every other example of a sequence of characters representing convention is because of Intelligent Design. If a sequence of dots and dashes, or zeroes and ones, or scribbles, encode something, we rationally infer an intelligent cause ultimately behind the existence of that sequence. In fact, this is often perceived as a working assumption behind SETI, the Search for Extra-terrestrial Intelligence. To detect intelligence, SETI might eventually find a sequence of signals that appears to encode something. In striking contrast, geologists do not look for a sequence of characters that encode the formation of mountains or cause volcanoes to erupt. Nor do meteorologists look for a sequence of characters that encode the formation of rain or hurricanes. Nor do chemists look for a sequence of characters that encode the formation of crystals or gases. If every other example of encoded information points to Intelligent Design, and encoded information in science is specific to life, it is reasonable to follow this lead and make the same tentative inference for the ultimate origin of genetic information and life itself.

The genetic code as evidence of Intelligent Design, represents a very real pattern not easily credited to natural law. Initially, it would seem that natural law cannot account for such a pattern, for then the pattern would exist because of necessity and therefore not be conventional. So what is the source of this pattern? Many biologists have long attributed the source to mere chance, where the genetic code has been referred to as a "frozen accident." This view is clearly derived from the non-teleological approach, where by chance, the code just happened to fall into place and since living things quickly came to depend on it, the code was immediately frozen into place. This is a common way to interpret a product of design from a non-teleological perspective. However, before we further consider this view, it is important to keep in mind that it is entirely reasonable to merely suspect Intelligent Design behind life based on nothing more than the existence of this code itself. It makes perfect rational sense to argue, "Because of the existence of a code, I suspect an intelligent cause behind the origin of life," whereas it is rather odd reasoning to argue, "Because of the existence of a code, I suspect a non-intelligent cause behind the origin of life." Codes suggest intelligent, rather than non-intelligent origins.

An Optimized Code

As noted previously, the genetic code shares many likenesses with Morse code. Nevertheless, they differ in an important way. In Morse code, every letter of the alphabet is represented by only one codon of dots and dashes. In the genetic code, the same amino acid is typically represented by more than one codon. For example, in Morse code, the letter V is represented strictly by "dot-dot-dot-dash." The letter O is represented by "dash-dash-dash." But in the genetic code, the amino acid proline is represented not only by CCU, but also by CCC, CCA, and CCG. Because amino acids are encoded by multiple codons, the genetic code is said to be degenerate. Yet this very degeneracy is helpful to the cell because it protects the cell against the harmful effects of mutations. For example, if a mutation occurs such that the codon CCC is changed to CCA, the correct amino acid proline is still encoded. Thus, an error in copying does not necessarily result in the wrong amino acid being used during protein synthesis.

The code protects against the deleterious effects of mutations much better than anyone anticipated. In the late 1990s, powerful computer analyses were used to compare the natural genetic code with a large assortment of randomly generated codes.[10] For example, instead of CCA and CCC coding for proline, what would happen if UUG and UGU coded for this amino acid? What would happen if all the codons were different? This analysis showed that the genetic code we observe in just about every cell is extremely resistant to deleterious errors, such that only one in a million randomly generated codes was more error-proof. This indicates that the genetic code is optimized to prevent destructive mutations or, as one science reporter puts it, the code "isn't simply the product of chance."[10] Then in 2000, a much more robust and sophisticated analysis was used to confirm these findings. These researchers concluded:

> If our definition of biosynthetic restrictions are a good approximation of the possible variation from which the canonical code emerged, then it appears at or very close to a global optimum for error minimization: the best of all possible codes.[11]

Chance alone would not be expected to produce a code that was better than any other million randomly generated codes when it comes to protecting against harmful mutations. If the code is too optimal to be attributed to chance and too conventional to be attributed to chemical law, then it was selected, meaning that its origin can only be explained either as design by natural selection or design by an intelligent agent. Since many biologists are constrained by a non-teleological outlook, they attribute these non-random aspects of the code to mutation and natural selection, where simpler and sloppier codes once existed and were then fine tuned over millions of years. However, there is another aspect of the code that works against this thesis—the universality of the genetic code.

Almost all organisms use the same genetic language or code called the *canonical* code. For example, the same code used in human cells is also employed in everything ranging from baker's yeast to roses to flies. There are, however, a very small number of organisms that use slightly altered codes. Yet the consensus among scientists is that these altered codes are secondarily derived from the canonical code. These slightly different codes all appear to be inferior with respect to the canonical code, as they do not protect against the effects of mutation as well.[11] Nevertheless, since the canonical code is found in the vast majority of organisms, and the alternative forms are nearly identical, it is the origin of the Universal Optimal Code that is in question.

The existence of a Universal Optimal Code presents a problem for Darwinian interpretations as a function of its universality. Since all organisms share the same code, there is a lack of evidence of any type of precursor state, or set of precursor states, to be arranged into a phylogenetic tree. One can always imagine precursor states and try to find circumstantial evidence to support such speculation, but the fact will always remain that such speculations involve a significant element of assumption. If there is no evidence of any precursor states, there are no solid reasons to believe, without reservation, that they once existed.

The universality of the code is in conflict with a view that imagines simpler and sloppier states which are gradually molded into the Universal Optimal Code. Recall that what makes the code optimal is that it protects against the existence of harmful mutations by decreasing their likelihood. It would seem that organisms could indeed exist with all kinds of different genetic codes, even if the codes were inferior. In fact, that is exactly what the Darwinian thesis proposes during the long period of evolution towards the establishment of the Universal Optimal Code. Because of both the complexity and the optimality of the code, one might reasonably expect this period of evolution to be long and to involve a large number of precursor states. Since evolution does not work as a linear sequence, but instead proliferates like the branches of a bush, the lineage leading to the Universal Optimal Code would represent only one among many of these thousands of lineages. This means there would have once existed many, many more different life forms with codes different from the canonical code. It is therefore not at all unreasonable to suppose there must have been thousands of different codes, slouching toward the canonical code over hundreds of millions of years. Although there should be, there is no evidence of the descendants of all these evolutionary experiments. It is startling to realize that there is not a trace of these pre-Universal Optimal Code organisms, or their codes, existing anywhere on this planet.

One might argue that organisms that evolved the Universal Optimal Code out-competed and replaced these earlier versions. But such a scenario seems *ad hoc*. Most people think of evolution as one species competing against another, but this is often not what occurs. Instead, different species tend to make peace with each other by developing lifestyles, called niches, that do not conflict. For example, a hyena and lion both may eat antelope meat. Yet just because lions are better predators does not mean they have driven hyenas into extinction. Most single-celled protozoa have an organelle called the mitochondria which is efficient at producing energy rich molecules. Some protozoa have lost their mitochondria, but these inefficient cells have not been driven to extinction through competition with protozoa who have retained their mitochondria. Many bacteria have lost their flagella, but they have not been competed out of existence by bacteria who have retained their flagella. It would seem that cells with inferior genetic codes need not always have competed with cells with less error-prone codes. So it is again surprising that at least some of these inferior cells did not find niches that would have allowed them to survive to this day. After all, organisms exist today with derivative codes that are less optimal than the Universal Optimal Code, making it an established fact that life forms with different codes can co-exist on the same planet. Furthermore, since mutations are the raw fuel of evolution, it is possible that a less error-proof code might have been advantageous somewhere when new evolutionary solutions were being developed. In some cases, it would thus seem reasonable to propose that more error-prone cells might have actually out-competed the less error-prone cells, as they would be more likely to stumble on mutations needed to adapt.

Both the universality and the optimality of the genetic code fit well with the hypothesis of Intelligent Design. The code is optimized to resist potentially deleterious mutations as a consequence of intelligent foresight. It is universal because this single, optimal solution was implemented by the designer. These are the type of data we would expect from Intelligent Design. After all, what if the code was thoroughly sub-optimal? Would this not be a popular argument against Intelligent Design (and rightly so)?

PROOFREADING

Biological processes often involve the flow of information. When cells divide, the program contained in the DNA (the nucleotide sequence) of any cell is replicated and passed on so the new cell will have a copy of this information. When genes are expressed, the nucleotide sequence of the DNA is transcribed to make an RNA molecule that has a complementary nucleotide sequence. When proteins are synthesized, the ribosome factories translate the nucleotide sequence of the RNA into an amino acid sequence. Since all these information transfers are very important in the cell, it would make good design sense to ensure these transfers occur with few errors. The process of correction used by cells is the same one I (and my computer) used to type this chapter to ensure there are no (or only a few) mistakes—the process of proofreading.

When I typed this chapter, the word processing program immediately underlined any mis-spelled words that occurred because intelligent programmers designed the program to proofread as I type. Cells use a similar, although more sophisticated, mechanism during every step of information transfer, where each step depends on machinery reading a sequential template of nucleotides accurately. DNA replication provides an excellent example of this process.

Recall that DNA consists of two chains of nucleotides intertwined in a helical fashion. These two strands are also complementary in sequence. When DNA is replicated, various proteins bind to and unzip the DNA molecule so that single strands are exposed. The exposed single strands then serve as the template to direct the replication machinery and determine which individual nucleotides get added to the newly synthesized strand. For example, if the template strand has the exposed sequence GGGGG, the replication machinery traveling along this strand, will read this sequence and compose a new strand of CCCCC which hydrogen bonds to the GGGGG to create a new double helix. This replication machinery is quite efficient, with the new strand being synthesized at a rate of about 300-500 nucleotides per second. In addition, this process is very accurate, with only one mistake made in every 100,000 nucleotides.

The replication machinery further increases its accuracy with components that perform an additional proofreading function for the new nucleotides added to a growing strand. This proofreading function increases the fidelity such that only one mistake in every 10 billion nucleotides then occurs.[12, 19-21] Proofreading occurs because the replication machinery has two cavities or active sites, one which forms chemical bonds between individual nucleotides (the polymerase) and another which breaks apart the chemical bonds between individual nucleotides (the nuclease). When the replication machinery reads an 'A' on the template strand, it must pick from a pool of G's, C's, T's, and A's. The correct choice would be T. If a T is then chosen and added to the newly forming strand by the polymerase cavity of the machine, the machinery chugs along to the next nucleotide on the template.

ERROR CORRECTION RUNS DEEP

However, when adding at a rate of 500 per second, mistakes can happen. If, for example, the machinery adds a G by mistake, this mistake is recognized and the improper base pair is shifted into the nuclease cavity where the G is then cut away. The template strand is returned to the polymerase cavity to select again.

What is most intriguing about this process of DNA replication and proofreading is its elegant sophistication when faced with a very difficult problem. This machinery must discriminate between four different nucleotides which are extremely similar. Remember that A forms hydrogen bonds with T and G binds to C. These are known as Watson-Crick base pairs (named after the scientists who first described the structure of DNA and proposed this base pairing relationship). Mismatching is clearly possible as hydrogen bonds can also form between C-A and T-G (through something biochemists call wobble-like interactions). The replication machinery discriminates between nucleotides through subtle conformational shifts that depend on the base pair conforming to the geometry of standard Watson-Crick base pairs (where non-Watson-Crick base pairs have only a modestly different geometry with respect to distances between one of the carbon atoms of the sugars and with respect to bond angles). To use an analogy, the replication machinery is not reading a template string of red, green, white, and black beads. It is reading four beads that are closely continuous shades of gray. Yet it discriminates between these shades of gray at a rate of 500 beads per second while making a mistake only once every 10 billion beads. The replication of DNA thus involves discrimination near the very threshold where the basis for discrimination begins to fade away. Yet it is exactly here that we find information processing events essential to life. This is quite an amazing feat of nanotechnology.

Molecular proofreading underscores our intuitive suspicion of Intelligent Design. The process of proofreading is well-known in teleological endeavors, but quite out of place in non-teleological realties, much like a stone Face on Mars. Computer programs and term papers are proofread, while mountain and rain formation are not. Proofreading also constitutes *prima facie* evidence of specificity, since proofreading material is not necessary unless specific information is required.

Remember also that every step of information transfer is proofread: when DNA is replicated; when tRNA molecules interact with the codons on the mRNA molecules during protein synthesis[13]; and when amino acids are attached to their proper tRNA molecules.[14]

This latter example of proofreading is intriguing. The enzyme that attaches amino acids to their proper tRNAs has two active sites, a synthetic domain and an editing domain, separated by significant distance. Basically, it appears that the acceptor stem of the tRNA (the region where amino acids are bound) can adopt two conformations, such that mismatched amino acids end up in the editing domain where they can be cut away and properly matched amino acids remain in the synthetic domain. What is interesting is not just that the proofreading takes place, but that the general mechanism of proofreading is analogous to that which is used by the DNA polymerase when it synthesizes DNA. It appears that the process of replicating DNA molecules and attaching amino acids to tRNA molecules employs a similar mechanism not due to common descent. We see an abstract engineering-like principle at work here, where the same basic *logical* strategy (a dynamic competition between synthetic and editing functions) is being employed in different proteins carrying out different processes. It is difficult to resist the subtle implications of design, where not only is proofreading itself an echo of design, but the same basic logic of a proofreading mechanism, found in different contexts, amplifies this echo.

A Parity Code

Computers store, use, and transmit information in the form of bits. A bit, short for binary digit, comes in the form of zeros and ones. A single bit is thus capable of representing two different values—one or zero. Because errors may occur in a stream of bits, computers employ a strategy to recognize corrupted data known as a parity code. The idea behind the parity code is to attach one more bit to a data string that represents whether there is an even or an odd number of ones in a string. For example, the string 0001 0011 would contain an odd numbers of ones, so another 1 is attached to the string which represents "odd." The data string thus becomes 0001 0011 1. If one bit changes such that the data becomes corrupted, the number of ones would be even, the parity code would be incorrect and the computer would detect an error.

Dónall A. Mac Dónaill, a chemist from Trinity College in Dublin, has applied such error-coding theory to the DNA molecule, noting that many have neglected this informatics perspective:

> Investigations into nucleotide alphabet composition have tended to focus on physicochemical and related issues. Yet nucleotide replication is at heart an information transmission phenomenon, and it seems reasonable to postulate that the evolutionary pressures shaping the nucleotide alphabet might not have been confined to physicochemical issues alone, and that considerations relating to informatics might have had a constraining evolutionary role, acting concurrently but independently of the physics and chemistry.[15]

Since nucleotides pair through hydrogen bonds, where one chemical group known as a donor pairs to another group from the opposite nucleotide known as an acceptor, Mac Dónaill realized it was easy to represent such interactions as a bit, where the donor is assigned a one and the acceptor is represented with a zero. Thus the nucleotide G can be represented as 011, as it has one acceptor and two donors, and the complementary nucleotide C is represented with 100. Mac Dónaill also noted the nucleotides come in two forms, pyrimidines and purines, and the two forms can represent a bit, where we assign a zero to a purine and a one to a pyrimidine. Now the nucleotides can be represented as four-bit numbers, where G is 011, 0 and C is 100, 1.

There are sixteen possible four-bit numbers, but DNA (or RNA) uses only four of them. What is striking is that all four have an even number of ones. From an informatics perspective, nucleotides can be viewed as code-words and it becomes quite significant that they all have an even number of ones:

> Given the centrality of parity in data transmission, the observation of a parity structure with the nucleotide alphabet is clearly of potential significance. . . if it is agreed that even-parity codewords will be employed, the arrival of an odd-parity codeword at the receiver clearly indicates an error.[16]

Mac Dónaill thus argues that the pyrimidine/purine nature of a nucleotide is related to its pattern of hydrogen bond donors and acceptors as a parity bit. The parity bit does not have to be attached to the coding material of life; the parity code is built into the fabric of the DNA! Mac Dónaill concludes, "The natural alphabet appears to be structured like a parity code, and it would appear that the error-coding theory proposed by Hamming in 1950 was actually anticipated by nature."[15]

This is an excellent explanation of why life uses A, G, C, and T but not other nucleotides. Previous studies have shown that artificial nucleotides (those other than A, G, C, T, and U) can be reliably used and replicated by polymerases. So why did nature not use any other nucleotides? Origin of life researcher, Leslie Orgel, suggested that "nature had simply failed to discover them."[15] Yet Mac Dónaill seems to have a meatier explanation: the use of other nucleotides would have made DNA more prone to error. It is also interesting to note a parallel with the genetic code. Originally explained as a "frozen accident," it became clear the code was a design used to lessen errors. Whether it is the choice of codons or the choice of nucleotides, the theme of minimizing errors repeats itself in a fractal pattern. This is a theme that may expose a vulnerable place in the non-teleological point of view, where frozen accident after frozen accident gives way to a deeper logic behind life.

But what about the origin of the parity code? Mac Dónaill writes, "The critical question is whether the parity code structure is accidental, or shaped by selection through evolutionary advantage." We can agree that the code was selected, but was it selected by an intelligent designer or by natural selection? Is there even a way to distinguish between the two? Perhaps in the end, all that we will have are two alternative ways to look at the same data. However, one consideration seems to be indicative of design.

Phillip Ball reviewed Mac Dónaill's work in *Nature* and explained the reasoning behind the evolution of a parity code:

The consequences of wrongly read or copied information can be disastrous. Malfunctioning genes can cause diseases and defects. Errors can occasionally have beneficial effects—they create the mutations that drive the evolutionary process—but they are usually detrimental. So cells have evolved molecular machinery for checking transcription and replication. This greatly reduces the chances of errors, but does not eliminate them. Mac Dónaill says that there is another mechanism for detecting errors—in the chemistry of DNA itself.[17]

It is understandable why mistakes in an incredibly complex entity such as a human being can be disastrous. But are we sure the same principle applies to simple, primitive quasi-life forms that originally evolved the use of DNA?

Viruses represent the simplest replicating entities, on the border between life and non-life. Because of their simplicity, viruses can exploit the highest mutation rates, often bordering on error-catastrophe. Low-information proteins, by definition, can tolerate the widest range of amino acid substitutions. It is these types of proteins that would likely have been spawned in the days of the quasi-life forms. Since mutation is the source of evolutionary variation, a simple, rather homogeneous population of low-information replicators would be well served by high mutation rates, creating massive variation to exploit great volumes of untapped niches and increasing the opportunities for adaptation. If we consider these altogether, it would seem that any original, simple quasi-life forms would be better served by preserving high error rates that appear to accompany simplicity and low-information states.

One way to distinguish between an intelligent designer and natural selection is that the former has foresight, while the latter is myopic, working only on immediate benefits. The error correction capabilities inherent in the DNA chemistry (and perhaps the genetic code) may reflect foresight, when such capabilities would become essential in the high-information state life forms that would exist hundreds of millions of years after the putative simple replicators. In contrast, natural selection is concerned only with immediate benefits, which might very well come from high error rates in such primitive life forms. Since evolution often boxes itself in, where a solution to an immediate problem becomes "locked in" and cannot be displaced in later evolution, it is not clear that quasi-life forms would have devised the type of fidelity that is needed by complex, modern-day organisms.

One thing is clear: very early on, life became obsessed with error correction. The chemistry of DNA, RNA, the genetic code, and the proofreading mechanisms behind information transfer are all biological universals. Apparently, one of the first objectives of evolution was to control evolution.

PROOFREADING IN THE LIGHT OF DESIGN

It is often said the whole concept of Intelligent Design is a scientific dead-end because it discourages research by proposing that "the designer did it" as the explanation behind the origin of some biological feature. It is further assumed that the thesis of design cannot guide investigative research because it merely uses gaps in our knowledge to assign a role for the designer and once something has been assigned to design, there is nothing left to say. Really?

Actually, the concept of design can be useful as a research guide. Several years ago, while reading some scientific articles describing the proofreading process of protein synthesis, it occurred to me that an important step of information flow appeared to lack proofreading. Already aware that the process of making DNA and protein synthesis was proofread, I wondered about transcription, the process of making RNA. I could not recall ever hearing anything about proofreading being associated with RNA polymerase activity (the protein complex that makes the RNA). It struck me that this was a great opportunity to use the hypothesis of design. Since the terminal step in information transfer (mRNA to protein) is proofread, could I use Intelligent Design to infer that the earlier step in information transfer (DNA to RNA) was likewise proofread? Yes. My thought processes proceeded in the following manner:

Imagine you need to translate a book from English into German and then German into Chinese. If it was important that this translation was as accurate as possible, you would employ proofreaders at both stages. It would not make much sense for an intelligent designer to employ proofreaders to ensure the German text was accurately translated into Chinese without also using proofreaders during the first step (the English to German translation). The purpose of carefully scrutinizing the second translation is defeated if your first translation is inaccurate. Proceeding from this logic base,

I predicted that proofreading should exist during transcription (if we also hypothesize that cells, much as they exist today, were originally designed by a rational agent). Confronted with some rather sophisticated and specified proofreading near the terminal stages of information flow, it seemed most logical to expect its existence at a preceding stage as well.

With this hypothesis in hand, I could go into a lab and design experiments to discover whether proofreading does indeed occur during transcription. If I had, in fact, performed these experiments, my prediction would have been borne out. A literature search I performed *after* coming up with this hypothesis[18] provided support that there is good evidence that RNA polymerase can proofread.[12] Thus, the suspicion of design was able to direct a line of thinking that not only could generate research, but could also uncover truths and further understanding of our biological world.

Note that it was not necessary for the researchers to draw on the concept of Intelligent Design in order to discover that proofreading occurred during transcription. The question of Intelligent Design's utility is different from its necessity. Something can be useful without being needed. That I have paper clips on my desk does not render my stapler useless.

It could further be argued that Darwin's Theory of Evolution would also predict the existence of proofreading during transcription, using *ad hoc* reasoning to suggest that proofreading transcription provided a selective advantage. While this could possibly be true, the fact remains that the researchers cited above did not use Darwinian evolution to predict the existence of such proofreading. When scientists originally believed RNA polymerase could not proofread, Darwinian logic was used to explain why this was the case.[18] Further, it is not clear that Darwinian evolution could be used to really make a prediction of proofreading being associated with RNA polymerase activity. I was able to make such a prediction because the assumption of *Intelligent* Design entails that the design displays rationality. Darwinian evolution does not entail the ability to make predictions based upon systems behaving in a rational manner. Evolution only requires that things work in *any way* that works to enhance reproductive output. The objective of Darwinian evolution is merely survival and reproduction. Any feature, no matter how clumsy or irrational, that serves these ends is adequate.

The Suspicion Deepens

In the last chapter, we saw the importance of teleological concepts and language and how they illuminated the workings of the cell. We also saw that the study of molecular biology shares many uncanny similarities with the study of human design (engineering). This provides a basis to suspect design behind life, since these are the type of dynamics we would expect to exist if life is indeed carbon-based nanotechnology. Unlike the Face on Mars, it does not seem that the suspicion of design disappears with a closer look.

Protein synthesis employs mechanisms and processes strikingly similar to Morse code. The genetic code has been shaped to minimize the effects of errors. The process of DNA/RNA synthesis appears to employ a parity code. Each phase of information transfer, DNA-to-DNA, DNA-to-RNA, and RNA-to-protein, is proofread. The echoes of technology continue to resonate under higher resolution, enhancing our suspicions of design. Yet since processes like protein synthesis and DNA replication are completely dependent on molecular machines, with a closer look, we would expect that they too will continue to suggest Intelligent Design.

References

1. I will ignore the question of whether or not viruses can be considered a life form for the sake of simplicity.
2. For the sake of simplicity, this description ignores the shared properties of amino acids that cause all proteins to adopt similar high-resolution shapes; structures known as alpha helices and beta sheets.
3. Lee, T.E., 1993. *Gene Future: The Promise and Perils of the New Biology*. Plenum Press, New York, p. 9.
4. This explanation ignores the complexities involved in the trypsin gene structure and in modifying the RNA.
5. Fristrom, J.W. and Clegg, M.T., 1988. *Genetics*, 2nd ed. Chiron Press, New York, p. 381.
6. Hayes, B., 1998. "The Invention of the Genetic Code." *American Scien-*

tist, 86:8-14.

7. Augros, R. and Stanciu, G., 1988. *The New Biology: Discovering the Wisdom in Nature.* New Science Library, Boston, p. 189.

8. Dunn J. and Clark M.A. "Life Music: The Sonification of Proteins." http://web.archive.org/web/20040221165714/mitpress2.mit.edu/e-journals/Leonardo/isast/articles/lifemusic.html; last accessed 02/27/04.

9. Thaxton, C.B., Bradley, W.L. and Olsen, R.L., 1984. *The Mystery of Life's Origin.* Philosophical Library, New York, pp.211-212.

10. Vogel, G., 1998. "Tracking the History of the Genetic Code." *Science,* 281:329-331.

11. Freeland, S.J., Knight, R.D., Landweber, L.F. and Hurst, L.D., 2000. "Early Fixation of an Optimal Genetic Code." *Molecular Biology and Evolution,* 17:511-518.

12. Jeon, C. and Agarwal, K., 1996. "Fidelity of RNA Polymerase II Transcription Controlled by Elongation Factor TFIIS." *Proceedings of the National Academy of Sciences of the United States of America,* 93:13677-13682.

13. Yoshizawa, S., Fourmy, D. and Puglisi, J.D., 1999. "Recognition of the Codon-Anticodon Helix by Ribosomal RNA." *Science,* 285:1722-1725.

14. Silivan, L.F., Wang, J. and Steitz, T. A., 1999. "Insights into Editing from an Ile-tRNA Synthethase Structure with tRNA and Murpirocin." *Science,* 285:1074-1077.

15. Mac Dónaill, D.A., 2002. "A Parity Code Interpretation of Nucleotide Alphabet Composition." *Chemical Communications,* 18:2062-2063.

16. Mac Dónaill, D.A., 2003. "Why Nature Chose A, C, G, and U/T: An Error-Coding Perspective of Nucleotide Alphabet Composition." *Origins of Life and Evolution of the Biosphere,* 33:433-455.

17. Ball, P., 2002. "DNA Codes Own Error Correction." *Nature.* http://www.nature.com/nsu/020916/020916-4.html; last accessed 05/23/03.

18. I document the widespread traditional view that transcription was not proofread at: http://www.idthink.net/biot/proof2/index.html.

19. Thomas M.J., Platas, A.A. and Hawley, D.K., 1998. "Transcriptional Fidelity and Proofreading by RNA Polymerase II." *Cell,* 15:93:627-637.

20. Wang, D. and Hawley, D.K., 1993. "Identification of a 3'-->5' Exonuclease Activity Associated with Human RNA Polymerase II." *Proceedings of the National Academy of Sciences of the United States of America,* 90:843.

21. Orlova, M., Newlands, J., Das, A., Goldfarb, A. and Borukhov, S., 1995. "Intrinsic Transcript Cleavage Activity of RNA Polymerase." *Proceedings of the National Academy of Sciences of the United States of America,* 92:4596-4600.

CHAPTER 5

WELCOME TO THE MACHINES

Waiting to meet her friend for dinner, Emily wanders aimlessly about the hotel lobby. Noticing a door to a conference room, she peeks in out of curiosity. She pauses to listen for a few moments as a speaker addresses the room full of people. "This sophisticated machinery is under the control of a tightly regulated feedback loop, causing it to express the correct information at the proper time, which then enables the simultaneous activation of multiple functions," says the man at the podium. Emily gently eases the door closed and smiles as she sees her friend Sarah approaching her across the lobby. Later that evening, as Emily and Sarah are finishing dinner, a small group of people are seated at the table next to them. Recognizing the speaker from the conference room, Emily introduces herself. "I saw a small part of your presentation a little while ago. You know, my brother is also a computer programmer." The speaker frowned briefly in confusion and then chuckled, realizing Emily's mistake. "I am not a computer programmer," the speaker replied, "I am a molecular biologist."

Given that biologists increasingly find themselves talking about programs and coded information, Emily's confusion is quite understandable. In his book, *Engines of Creation: The Coming Age of Nanotechnology*, K. Eric Drexler highlights one reason why molecular biologists talk so much about life's coded information:

> But by itself, DNA is a fairly worthless molecule. It is neither strong like Kevlar, nor colorful like a dye, nor active like an enzyme, yet it has something that industry is prepared to spend millions of dollars to use: the ability to direct molecular machines. . . .[1]

The information contained in the DNA molecule and expressed using the Universal Optimal Code serves as the instructions for synthesizing molecular machines inside the cell. Molecular machines are complexes of many different proteins (and sometimes RNA) that fit together like pieces of a three-dimensional puzzle. These well-matched pieces then interact with each other to elicit a specific function that is important for the life of the cell. The DNA information encodes the machines and the machines decode the DNA information. The code and the machines are partners in an elaborate dance we call Life.

Life, when viewed as carbon-based nanotechnology, not only employs an information processing system complete with software and error-checking mechanisms, but the cellular hardware consists largely of the very things physicist Paul Davies has noted—"tiny structures that might have come straight from an engineer's manual." Davies provides some examples:

> Miniscule tweezers, scissors, pumps, motors, levers, valves, pipes, chains, and even vehicles abound. But of course the cell is more than just a bag of gadgets. The various components fit together to form a smoothly functioning whole, like an elaborate factory production line. The miracle of life is not that it is made of nanotools, but that these tiny diverse parts are integrated in a highly organized way.[2]

There are hundreds of these "gadgets" that are responsible for a variety of cellular activities. These machines can be categorized according to their basic functions: 1) the DNA processing machines; 2) the RNA processing machines; 3) the protein processing machines; 4) membrane-associated machines; and 5) basic cell physiology machines.

The DNA processing machines make a copy of the DNA just prior to cell division, repair any damages to the DNA caused by chemicals, and reshuffle the genes in the DNA. One of the DNA processing machines, the replisome, is a complex of proteins involved in the replication and repair of DNA. The replisome is similar to a factory full of machines and includes the DNA polymerases, which are proteins that synthesize a new strand of DNA, and the helicases, which unwind and separate the strands of DNA's double helix.[3] The replisome also includes sliding clamps, which are circular proteins that form rings around the DNA to anchor the machinery, and "clamp loaders" that pry open the rings and attach them to the DNA.

Other machines also crucially interact with the DNA. For example, the topoisomerases do a remarkable job of untangling the DNA strands if they become knotted.[4] Proteins such as Rad50 and RecA are part of a diverse set of dynamic machines that sense DNA damage and repair it in a highly regulated fashion.[5]

The RNA processing machines use the information in the DNA to construct an RNA molecule. The transcriptosomes are massive protein complexes that recognize the genes in the DNA and make RNA copies of them.[6] Other machines modify the RNA. The spliceosome, which is currently considered to be the most complex molecular machine, is composed of over 140 proteins and five RNA molecules.[7] The function of the spliceosome is to cut the RNA into pieces, remove the sequences that are not part of the instructions for protein synthesis and splice the instruction pieces back together. The editosomes are protein machines with more than twenty parts which function to carefully select and precisely edit the protein synthesis instructions inherent in the RNA molecule.[8] Degradosomes and exosomes, comparable to molecular paper shredders, degrade the RNA molecules when there is a problem with the instructions or they are no longer needed.[9]

The protein processing machines use the information in the RNA to make all the cell's proteins. The ribosome is a machine composed of about fifty proteins and three different RNA molecules that interact to form a complex architecture complete with tunnels and grooves. It works as a "tape player" that synthesizes proteins by using the information stored in an RNA molecule, where RNA is threaded into the ribosome and a newly forming chain of amino acids correspondingly emerges from its exit tunnel.[10] Proteins, once made, are also processed by yet more machines. Chaperones are proteins that assist other proteins to fold into their proper three-dimensional shape.[11] They often associate with the newly formed proteins that are emerging from the exit tunnel of the ribosome. Many of the chaperones simply work to prevent these newly formed proteins from getting entangled prior to folding. A special class of protein folders, known as chaperonins, look like a cylinder with a lid.[12] Newly synthesized proteins are channeled to the chaperonin, stuffed into the cylinder and the lid is closed. This process allows the newly formed amino acid chain to fold in protective isolation from the rest of the cell's internal environment. When the folding process is completed, the lid pops open, and the freshly folded protein is released. Improperly folded or defective proteins are destroyed by another protein cylinder known as the proteasome, which has very similar dimensions to the chaperonin. Defective or outdated proteins are often tagged by yet another protein (known as ubiquitin) which causes the cell's machinery to select them for elimination. Once tagged, these proteins are sent to the proteasomes, unfolded, threaded into the cylinder's chamber, and cut into small pieces.[13]

The membrane-associated machines are embedded in or associated with the cell membrane, playing a vital role at the cell's interface with the environment. These machines are responsible for shuttling material into and out of the cell, where they function as secretion machines.[14] Other machines act as switches, converting signals outside the cell into signals inside the cell.[15] Nuclear pore complexes are machines composed of up to thirty proteins that regulate protein and RNA traffic across the membrane of the nucleus, the special compartment that houses the DNA.[16]

Basic cell physiology machines oversee protein and organelle movement and coordinate the overall cycle of events that take place within in the cell. Among the basic cell physiology machines are the motor proteins, which transport newly synthesized proteins and organelles to specific destinations in the cell. One scientific paper reviewing these motors describes them as follows:

> Life implies movement. Most forms of movement in the living world are powered by tiny protein machines known as molecular motors. Among the best known are motors that use sophisticated intramolecular amplification mechanisms to take nanometre steps along protein tracks in the cytoplasm. These motors transport a wide variety of cargo, power cell locomotion, drive cell division and, when combined in large ensembles, allow organisms to move. Motor defects can lead to severe diseases or may even be lethal.

Basic principles of motor design and mechanism have now been derived, and an understanding of their complex cellular roles is emerging.[17]

Also included in this class is the mitotic spindle, which coordinates the division of cells and their genetic material.[18] Living cells even have self-destruction machines known as apoptosomes, which allow the cell to destroy itself in a programmed and coordinated manner.[19]

It is clear that biologists commonly recognize these protein complexes *as machines.* If you search the biological literature for the string, "protein machine" or "molecular machine," you will find hundreds of research papers describing and analyzing various machines that carry out a myriad of roles in the cell. The results of a December 2005 PubMed search using the search string "molecular machine" are shown in Figure 5-1. Note that as with the teleological term "design," the number of hits again begins to skyrocket after 1990. For example, from 1986 to 1990, the search returned thirty-three hits. But from 2001 to 2005, 613 hits were returned. In fact, over 90% of the

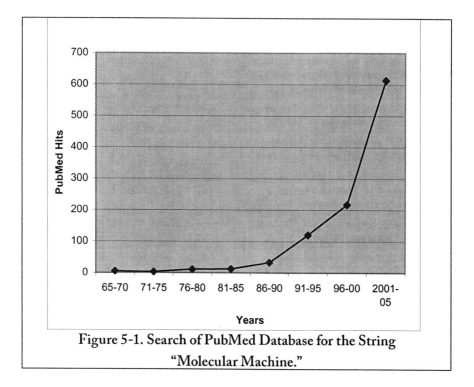

Figure 5-1. Search of PubMed Database for the String "Molecular Machine."

hits recovered come from the years 1991-2005. Because this increase might reflect a general increase in articles in the scientific literature, the number of hits was divided by the total number of articles during the specific time span and the ratio supported the pattern of data shown here. Similar patterns are also evident for any particular molecular machine searched within the scientific literature.

A simple scan of the titles of research articles in respected scientific journals demonstrates that biologists commonly recognize these protein complexes as machines (Table 5-I). Protein complexes (that sometimes include RNA) are treated as machines, described as machines, and like manmade machines, are often named after the primary function they carry out for the cell.

TABLE 5-I. Sample Journal Article Titles from the Scientific Literature	
Title of Journal Article	**Journal/Date**
The chaperonin folding **machine**.	Trends Biochem Sci 2002 Dec;27(12):627-32
Motors and switches: AAA+ **machines** within the replisome.	Nat Rev Mol Cell Biol 2002 Nov;3(11):826-35
Interactions between telomerase and primase physically link the telomere and chromosome **replication machinery**.	Mol Cell Biol 2002 Aug;22(16):5859-68
Bacterial secretome: the **assembly manual and operating instructions** (Review).	Mol Membr Biol 2002 Jul-Sep;19(3):159-69
The mRNA **assembly line**: transcription and processing **machines** in the same **factory**.	Curr Opin Cell Biol 2002 Jun;14(3):336-42
Cyclin-dependent kinases: **engines, clocks, and microprocessors**.	Ann Rev Cell Dev Biol 1997; 13:261-91
An extensive network of coupling among **gene expression machines**.	Nature 2002 Apr 4;416(6880):499-506
Ribosome as a **molecular machine**.	FEBS Lett 2002 Mar 6;514(1):2-10
Apoptosome: the seven-spoked **death machine**.	Dev Cell 2002 Mar;2(3):256-7
RNA polymerase as a **molecular machine**.	Mol Biol (Mosk) 2002 Mar-Apr;36(2):208-15
The 26S proteasome: a **molecular machine** designed for controlled proteolysis.	Ann Rev Biochem 1999;68:1015-68

Title of Journal Article	Journal/Date
Caught in the act: how ATP binding triggers cooperative conformational changes in a **molecular machine**.	Mol Cell 2002 Jan;9(1):3-5
Opening of the clamp: an intimate view of an ATP-driven **biological machine**.	Cell 2001 Sep 21;106(6):655-60
F1-ATPase: a highly efficient **rotary ATP machine**.	Essays Biochem 2000; 35:3-18
A moving DNA **replication factory** in Caulobacter crescentus.	EMBO J 2001 Sep 3;20(17):4952-63
The terminase enzyme from bacteriophage lambda: a **DNA-packaging machine**.	Cell Mol Life Sci 2000 Jan 20;57(1):128-48

WHAT'S IN A MACHINE?

While we all have an intuitive understanding of machines, it is helpful to precisely define what they are. K. Eric Drexler writes:

> One dictionary definition of a machine is "any system, usually of rigid bodies, formed and connected to alter, transmit, and direct applied forces in a predetermined manner to accomplish a specific objective, such as the performance of useful work." Molecular machines fit this definition quite well. . . . Biochemists already work with these machines, which are chiefly made of protein, the main engineering material of living cells. . . like all machines, they have different shapes and sizes that do useful work.[20]

Drexler identifies two important properties of all machines: they are built with differently sized and shaped parts and it is the interaction between these parts that allows useful work to be done.

Bruce Alberts offers a definition that expands on the properties of a machine:

> Why do we call the large protein assemblies that underlie cell function protein machines? Precisely because, like the machines invented by humans to deal efficiently with the macroscopic world, these protein assemblies contain highly coordinated moving parts.[21]

Like all machines, the parts of a biological machine not only move, but their movement is highly coordinated.

Nanotechnology researchers offer an even more detailed definition of a machine:

> A molecular-level machine can be defined as an assembly of a distinct number of molecular components that are designed to perform machinelike movements (output) as a result of an appropriate external stimulation (input). In common with their macroscopic counterparts, a molecular machine is characterized by 1) the kind of energy input supplied to make it work, 2) the nature of the movements of its component parts, 3) the way in which its operation can be monitored and controlled, 4) the ability to make it repeat its operation in a cyclic fashion, 5) the timescale needed to complete a full cycle of movements, and 6) the purpose of its operation.[22]

The dictionary definition Drexler used states that the machine is "predetermined to carry out a specific objective." Can a machine be defined without reference to such teleology? I think so. In fact, let me propose my own definition of a machine:

> *A machine is a modular assembly of discrete parts with particular shapes that interact through their complementary conformations and display coordinated movement that is sequentially channeled through the interlocking topology of the parts as a consequence of energy input at discrete entry points. This input of energy elicits the uni-directional coordinated movement of parts resulting in an output we call function such that the function depends on both the physical interaction and particular arrangement of the parts and their coordinated movement.*

Anything designed by humans that would match this definition would be known as a machine.

The molecular machines of life also fit this rigorous definition. Proteins typically function as the discrete parts, whereas Alberts notes, "every major process in a cell is carried out by assemblies of ten or more protein molecules."

They come in specific shapes and it is these interacting, complementary shapes that allow these "ten or more proteins" to form specific complexes. The organization or positioning of these parts is crucial. The input of energy occurs when ATP (adenosine triphosphate) is bound by one of the "ten or more" proteins in the complex and eventually broken down into smaller ADP (adenosine diphosphate) and Pi (inorganic phosphate) molecules, triggering a cascade of shape changes among the other parts of the protein complex. It is the coordinated shape changes among the parts that ultimately enable the protein complex to carry out its function—the output. Molecular machines also display uni-directional movement, where the shape changes and repositioning of parts occur sequentially in one direction.

Consider how one scientist described one particular molecular machine, the ATP synthase:

> $F_o F_1$-ATPase is now frequently described as a molecular *machine* and the problem of its reversibility seems to be of great importance. If, according to several language dictionaries, a general definition of a machine is an "assemblage of parts that transit forces, motions and energy from one to another in a predetermined manner" is to be accepted, the question arises: do *reversible machines* exist? In my opinion the molecular machines created by Nature as well as those created by mankind are made exclusively for unidirectional energy transduction. Thus, a special mechanism(s) that can be switched on or off by the applied driving force, thus permitting unidirectional energy transmission, must be a component of any machine. If ATP synthase is a small electromechanical engine, its performance should be described as a mechanical device and not as thermal engine.[23]

This definition also implies that if the "interlocking topology of the parts" was disrupted (for example, by removing one of the parts), the flow of energy and cascade of shape changes would likewise be disrupted, resulting in the loss of function. Geneticists have shown this to be true of molecular machines. Mutations are introduced into a gene that codes for a particular part of a machine and if the mutation eliminates one of the parts, the entire machine ceases to function. Slight changes can also be introduced into one of the machine's parts to better characterize how the machine works and such changes often result in the slowing down or complete breakdown of the machine. As muscle physiologist Peter Hochachka notes:

> It is biological machinery we are talking about, but machinery, nevertheless. As in any man-made counterpart, fine-tuning (of isoform content and composition) is of course possible and may be desirable, but large-scale change in any one component of the overall system may well be expected to reverberate throughout the whole system. That is why the effects of any one of the host of modest mutations (causing single but large magnitude change in any one component of the system) are, in machinery analogy, like a spanner in the works. Misplaced spanners are intolerable in man-made and muscle machines.[24]

Machines Point to Intelligent Design

It is quite significant that life is machine-dependent. Nearly every major process taking place inside a cell (even the simplest one) is mediated by these molecular machines. Since our experience links the existence of machines with intelligence, that life is machine-dependent further supports the suspicion of Intelligent Design. One of Isaac Newton's rules of reasoning applies here: "Natural effects of the same kind must be assigned to the same causes, whenever possible."[25] If astronauts were to land on Mars and discover an odd object that, upon closer analysis, would best be described as "some type of machine," most people would infer that the machine was built and designed by an intelligent agent.

We do not normally infer non-teleological causes when confronted with machinery. Simply survey any textbook on evolution or biology to see if you can find one which cites a machine *as* evidence of a non-teleological cause. Can you find figures and descriptions of something like the bacterial flagellum followed by, "that this is a machine clearly shows non-intelligent forces were behind its origin?" Of course not. The existence of a machine is not something we expect, or predict, from non-teleological causes. A non-teleological perspective that is confronted with the reality of molecular machines *reacts* by insisting non-teleological causes could possibly explain their origin. But this is not the way the inferential winds are blowing.

The connection between machines and intelligent origins is widely recognized. In an article that is critical of Intelligent Design, philosopher and biologist Niall Shanks and Karl Joplin acknowledge, "If organisms are artifacts, it is natural to. . . assume they were designed."[26] Although Shanks and Joplin do not think organisms are artifacts, their statement implies that it would be reasonable to infer design if organisms were indeed shown to be artifacts. Thus, the stronger the case that X is an artifact, the more reason there is to think that X was designed.

Chemist Michael Polanyi writes, "If all men were exterminated, this would not affect the laws of inanimate nature. But the production of machines would stop, and not until men arose again could machines be formed once more."[27] Polanyi further illustrates why it is that machines stem from Intelligent Design rather than the non-teleological forces of nature. He writes:

> The structure of machines and the working of their structure are thus shaped by man, even while their material and the forces that operate them obey the laws of inanimate nature. In constructing a machine and supplying it with power, we harness the laws of nature at work in its material and its driving force and make them serve our purpose. This harness is not unbreakable; the structure of the machine, and thus its working, can break down. But this will not affect the forces of inanimate nature on which the operation of the machine relied; it merely releases them from the restriction the machine imposed on them before it broke down. So the machine as a whole works under the control of two distinct principles. The higher one is the principle of the machine's design, and this harnesses the lower one, which consists in the physical-chemical processes on which the machine relies.[27]

Polanyi defines this higher principle as a boundary condition. It is the structure and organization of the machine that imposes boundaries on the laws of nature. For example, because of the way the parts of a car are arranged, they impose boundaries on these laws such that the car functions effectively to provide transportation. These same laws will eventually turn a disassembled car into rust and dust. Polanyi also argues that these boundary conditions are factors to consider in addition to the laws of nature:

> A boundary condition is always extraneous to the process which it delimits. In Galileo's experiments on balls rolling down a slope, the angle of the slope was not derived from the laws of mechanics, but was chosen by Galileo. And as this choice of slopes was extraneous to the laws of mechanics, so is the shape and manufacture of test tubes extraneous to the laws of chemistry. The same thing holds for machine-like boundaries; their structure cannot be defined in terms of the laws which they harness. . . . The principles of mechanical engineering and of communication of information, and the equivalent biological principles, are all additional to the laws of physics and chemistry.[27]

The machine-like boundaries are imposed by a free and rational mind. Machines can thus be viewed as the physical actualization of the mind's conceptual world.

Polanyi also outlines the differences in the higher and lower principles at work in any machine by discussing language (which, in many ways, is analogous). He writes:

> Yet the strictly logical difference between the two consecutive levels remains. You can look at a text in a language you do not understand and see the letters that form it without being aware of their meaning, but you cannot read a text without seeing the letters that convey its meaning. This shows us two different and mutually exclusive ways of being aware of the text. When we look at the words without understanding them we are focusing our attention on them, whereas, when we read the words our attention is directed to their meaning as part of a language. We are aware then of the words only subsidiarily, as we attend to their meaning. So in the first case we are looking at the words, while in the second we are looking *from* them

at their meaning: the reader of a text has a *from-at* knowledge of the word's meaning, while he has only a *from* awareness of the words he is reading. Should he be able to shift his attention fully toward the words, these would lose their linguistic meaning for him.[27]

When we consider any machine, whether it be a washing machine or the bacterial flagellum, the same analysis applies. The parts can be considered in isolation and described in terms of their shape and their composition. But any attempt to account for the machine would be incomplete at this level, as it would not be clear why the parts have the shape and composition that they do. To understand this, Polanyi's *from-at* perspective is needed, where it is the function of the machine that assigns meaning to the shape and arrangement of the parts. This understanding will turn out to be quite helpful when we begin to explore how teleological explanations can guide us in our attempt to understand the living world.

Haven't We Heard This All Before?

For centuries, living processes have been compared to machines. The human body itself has been called a machine. Our hearts are likened to pumps, our eyes are likened to cameras and our nervous systems are said to contain wiring. Comparing the human body to a machine would appear to seriously undermine the suspicion of design inferred from the existence of molecular machines. Biologists do not require teleological causes for the origin of humans, eyes, hearts, and nervous systems because they have good working evolutionary explanations. If evolution has made the camera-like eye, why not explain the origin of molecular machines with the same mechanisms?

Intelligent Design can be inferred from molecular machines because they are real machines. But when dealing with organisms, organ systems, or organs, there is good reason for thinking the machine-descriptor is, in fact, a true metaphor. In their book, *The New Biology*, Robert Augros and George Stanciu consult the biological literature and easily find many features inherent to organisms and organs not found in man-made machines. They write:

All the properties of the organism we have discussed so far—its astonishing unity, its capacity to build its own parts, its increasing differentiation through time, its power of self-repair and self-regeneration, its ability to transform other materials into itself, its natural action from within, and its incessant activity—all these not only distinguish the living being from the machine but also demonstrate its uniqueness amid the whole of nature.[28]

Every feature that distinguishes a living organism from a machine fails to distinguish a molecular machine from other machines. Molecular machines do not build their own parts, do not truly "differentiate" simply as a function of time, do not undergo self-repair and self-generation, and do not transform raw material into themselves. It is clear that molecular machines do not behave as organisms; they fit in the same category as man-made machines.

Three other differences discussed at length by Augros and Stanciu are also relevant. First, living organisms and organs grow from a much simpler state, whereas both molecular and man-made machines are *assembled*. For example, the human heart has four valves, muscular walls, and four chambers with various attached blood vessels, yet these "parts" are not first synthesized as independent and complete valves, vessels, and chambers which are later pieced together. All the parts of the heart "grow" in unison during embryological development and never exist apart from the whole. In contrast, the parts of a molecular machine originally exist separately from the whole, where various individual protein components are independently synthesized and subsequently pieced together to form the machine. Molecular machines and man-made machines only differ in that the former represent an example of automated assembly while the latter require the use of human hands (although automated factories which use machines to build other machines are becoming more common).

Second, the parts of a machine can be completely separated from one another and then reassembled to restore the function of the machine. This cannot be done with organisms and organs. If a mouse was broken up into pieces, and its organs were laid out on a table, the organs could not be reassembled to form a mouse that would scurry off the table. But with molecular machines, biochemists routinely break them down into their respective parts inside a test tube and are able to reconstitute them to restore function.

Third, organisms can not be turned off indefinitely without damage. The only way to truly turn off an organism is to kill it and then it can not be turned back on again. But like all machines, if the power source of a molecular machine is removed, the parts stop moving and it ceases to function. But the machine is not damaged as a consequence of being turned off. It can be turned back on simply by restoring power.

It is not clear that the evolutionary explanations for the origin of organisms and organs smoothly extrapolate to the origin of molecular machines since they are so fundamentally different. Human beings are not machines, but are merely one example of living things which are unique expressions of encoded nanomachines. It is these nanomachines that spark the suspicion of Intelligent Design.

The Nanotechnologists

Despite the fact that the molecular machines conform to a rigorous definition of a machine and cannot be classified with organisms and organs, some may still insist that the concept of a "machine" is too subjective and may simply be another metaphor. After all, someone could describe a tornado as a "wind machine." Would we therefore infer an intelligent cause for every tornado that materializes? In Chapter 3, we considered the generic use of technological and teleological concepts in biology and whether such concepts were only metaphors or whether there was something more than metaphor at work. In this chapter, we are focused on one concept—the machine. Are these protein complexes really machines? A growing number of scientists not directly involved in this debate about design and evolution do not view these biological machines as metaphors. These scientists are convinced that biological protein complexes are indeed machines.

As we saw in Chapter 3, nanotechnology is a newer area of study which seeks to design things on a very small scale. Essentially, it is a field that is premised on the belief that human beings will be able to construct microscopic machines with the ability to create (and deconstruct) other material one atom at a time. Many scientists, engineers, and computer scientists who believe that nanotechnology is not only feasible, but inevitable, are hard at work developing this technology.

Every proposed advance in technology is met with skepticism. Skeptics once claimed that nanotechnology was doomed to failure because such small machines are unworkable. The problem, they often cited, was quantum physics. In quantum physics, Heisenberg's Uncertainty Principle states that particles cannot be located in any exact position for any length of time. Essentially, matter becomes too fuzzy at such small scales and machines can only function efficiently without fuzz. The nanotechnologists responded that the skeptics' interpretation of the Uncertainty Principle was mistaken. More importantly, the nanotechnologists pointed to the existence of machines already at work inside the cell. They pointed out that since machines already exist inside the cell, the skeptic's argument is plainly refuted.

For example, scientist David Goodsell notes that biological molecules "are proven examples of the feasibility, and utility, of nanotechnology."[29] K. Eric Drexler wrote, "One needn't study quantum mechanics to trust these conclusions, because molecular machines in the cell demonstrate that molecular machines work."[30] Ralph Merkle, who is the Principal Fellow at Zyvex, the first molecular nanotechnology company, writes:

> Peter Byrne recently claimed that quantum mechanics implies that molecular machines can't work. Oops. The most generally accessible argument that molecular machines are feasible is to observe that biological molecular machines exist. Enzymes can copy DNA with remarkable fidelity. Bacteria are propelled forward by flagellar motors (enter "flagellar motor" into your favorite search engine for more information on this fascinating subject). Ribosomes are programmable molecular machines that make proteins using instructions read from mRNA.[31]

Writing for the online journal *Hotwired*, Chris Peterson observed:

> Tearing their hair out, early nanotechnologists explained, for the thousandth time, why the Uncertainty Principle doesn't prevent nanotechnology. And pointed out, for good measure, that the molecu-

lar machines in nature are an existence proof that such machines can, indeed, exist without violating known physical law.[32]

The visionaries of nanotechnology did not view a "biological molecular machine" as merely a metaphor, but instead as a concrete reality that can be modeled, used, and learned from. In their eyes, nanotechnology already existed, a carbon-based nanotechnology we call life. As Ronald Bailey, *Reason's* science correspondent, writes: "Conceptually, nanotechnology and biotechnology are not all that distinct. In the words of Rita Colwell, the director of the National Science Foundation, 'Life is nanotechnology that works.'"[33]

The goal of today's nanotechnologist is to learn from life's nanotechnology and mimic it. Christopher Lowe, from the Institute of Biotechnology at the University of Cambridge, beautifully reflects these views in a scientific article on nanobiotechnology:

> The molecular machinery of nature outperforms anything that mankind currently knows how to construct with conventional manufacturing technology by many orders of magnitude. Almost without exception, there exist biomolecular analogues of conventional functional devices, including structural components, wires, motors, drive shafts, pipes, pumps, production lines and programmable control systems. Consequently, there is a growing realization that the new discipline of nanotechnology will provide the means to construct novel molecular architectures with greater precision and flexibility, and at a lower cost, than traditional manufacturing processes.[34]

Chemist George Whitesides argued that "biology outmatches futurists' most elaborate fantasies for molecular robots" and "considering the many constraints on the construction and operation of nanomachines, it seems that new systems for building them might ultimately look much like the ancient systems of biology."[35]

"Much of what we call biology is really nanotechnology," says Michael J. Heller, a professor of bioengineering. He adds, "We can learn a lot from molecular biological systems because, in a sense, they do a lot of things we want to do with nanotechnology."[36] Other scientists writing in the scientific journal *Biosystems* make the same point: "Biotechnology is biologically inspired nanotechnology. Biological systems excel at atom-by-atom manipulation, are capable of universal computation and self-reproduction and represent the only truly functional nanotechnology."[37]

The nanotechnologist's perception of biological machines as literal machines is driven home by an emerging distinction between the nanomachines humans are trying to build and the machines life depends on. Biological machines are considered "natural" and the man-made machines are "artificial."[22] What makes these machines different in the minds of researchers is not the essence of the structure or function, but the supposed origin of the machine. The man-made machines are known to be artificial, while the biological machines are believed to have been spawned by nature. Yet from the perspective of one gathering clues about origins, this distinction begs the very question.

Clearly, the consensus among the nanotechnologists is that nanotechnology can work because we already know it works inside our cells and we can learn from the cell's machines as we begin to design our own nanomachines. If biological molecules are machines only in a purely metaphorical, poetic sense, then the whole justification for the development of nanotechnology crumbles into dust. The "existence proof," the "proven examples," the demonstration, and the accessible argument would all boil down to pure metaphor. If our design inference is being misled by a metaphor, the nanotechnologists are likewise misled and are building on an illusion. The perspective that these molecular assemblies are only machines in a purely metaphorical sense is not only misguided in light of this developing and promising field, but if taken seriously, would eliminate the fundamental justification for pursuing this work.

So far we have seen that life is built around nucleic acids and proteins, which in turn represent encoded information and sophisticated machinery. To properly understand the cell, we not only need to think in terms of chemistry and natural law, but also in terms of design. As physicist Rob Phillips and engineer Steve Quake note, an understanding of the cell "will require merging two philosophical viewpoints. The first is that life is like a computer program: An infrastructure of machines carry out arbitrary instructions that are encoded into DNA software. The second viewpoint is purely physical: Life arises from a mixing together of chemicals that follow basic physical principles to self-assemble into an organism. . . . The two viewpoints are complementary, not incompatible."[38] All of this makes perfect sense if life is indeed carbon-based nanotechnology, as the mind is a known cause for the existence of encoded information and machinery elsewhere. It also explains why it is that teleological concepts and terminology shed so much light on the study of life. While none of these considerations may establish the reality of design behind life, and may in fact fail to persuade most skeptics of teleological explanations, it would seem to this author that a rather robust foundation has been laid down, upon which to base a healthy and serious hunch or suspicion. We have enough to start up the Explanatory Continuum and determine if further data add an increasing level of plausibility to our design suspicions. But in order to do this, we are going to have to come to terms with the reality of evolution and natural selection and the challenge they pose to any design inference.

References

1. Drexler, K.E., 1986. *Engines of Creation: The Coming Age of Nanotechnology.* Anchor Press, New York, p. 7.
2. Davies, P., 1999. *The Fifth Miracle: The Search for the Origin and Meaning of Life.* Simon & Schuster, New York, p. 20.
3. Jensen, R.B., Wang, S.C. and Shapiro, L., 2001. "A Moving DNA Replication Factory in *Caulobacter crescentus.*" *The EMBO Journal,* 20:4952-4963 and Baker, T.A. and Bell, S.P., 1998. "Polymerases and the Replisome: Machines within Machines." *Cell,* 92:295-305.
4. Wang, J.C., 1998. "Moving One DNA Double Helix Through Another By a Type II DNA Topoisomerase: The Story of a Simple Molecular Machine." *Quarterly Reviews of Biophysics,* 31:107-144.
5. Lukas, J. and Bartek, J., 2004. "Watching the DNA Repair Ensemble

Dance." *Cell*, 118:666-668 and Janicijevic, A., Ristic, D. and Wyman, C., 2003. "The Molecular Machines of DNA Repair: Scanning Force Microscopy Analysis of Their Architecture." *Journal of Microscopy*, 212:264-272.

6. Gall, J.G., Bellini, M., Wu, Z. and Murphy, C., 1999. "Assembly of the Nuclear Transcription and Processing Machinery: Cajal Bodies (Coiled Bodies) and Transcriptosomes." *Molecular Biology of the Cell*, 10:4385-4402.

7. Zhou, Z., Licklider, L.J., Gygi, S.P. and Reed R., 2002. "Comprehensive Proteomic Analysis of the Human Spliceosome." *Nature*, 419:182-185.

8. Stuart, K. and Panigrahi, A.K., 2002. "RNA Editing: Complexity and Complications." *Molecular Microbiology*, 45:591-596.

9. Raijmakers, R., Egberts, W.V., van Venrooij, W.J. and Pruijn, G.J., 2002. "Protein-Protein Interactions Between Human Exosome Components Support the Assembly of RNase PH-type Subunits into a Six-Membered PNPase-Like Ring." *Journal of Molecular Biology*, 323:653-663.

10. Spirin, A.S., 2002. "Ribosome as a Molecular Machine." *FEBS Letters*, 514:2-10.

11. Hartl, F.U. and Hayer-Hartl, M., 2002. "Molecular Chaperones in the Cytosol: From Nascent Chain to Folded Protein." *Science*, 295:1852-1858.

12. Saibil, H.R. and Ranson N.A., 2002. "The Chaperonin Folding Machine." *Trends in Biochemical Sciences*, 27:627-632.

13. Tanaka, K. and Chiba, T., 1998. "The Proteasome: A Protein-Destroying Machine." *Genes Cells*, 3:499-510.

14. Economou, A., 2002. "Bacterial Secretome: The Assembly Manual and Operating Instructions." *Molecular and Membrane Biology*, 19:159-169.

15. "G-Proteins: The Molecular Switches." http://www.idthink.net/biot/gprot/index.html.

16. Ryan, K.J. and Wente, S.R., 2000. "The Nuclear Pore Complex: A Protein Machine Bridging the Nucleus and Cytoplasm." *Current Opinion in Cell Biology*, 12:361-371.

17. Schliwa, M. and Woehlke, G., 2003. "Molecular Motors." *Nature*, 422:759-765.

18. Karsenti, E. and Vernos, I., 2001. "The Mitotic Spindle: A Self-Made Machine." *Science*, 294:543-547.

19. Salvesen, G.S. and Renatus, M., 2002. "Apoptosome: The Seven-Spoked Death Machine." *Developmental Cell*, 2:256-257.

20. Drexler, K.E., 1986. *Engines of Creation: The Coming Age of Nanotechnology*. Anchor Press, New York, pp. 5-6.

21. Alberts, B., 1998. "The Cell as a Collection of Protein Machines: Preparing the Next Generation of Molecular Biologists." *Cell*, 92: 291-294.

22. Balzani, V.V., Credi, A., Raymo, F.M. and Stoddart, J.F., 2000. "Artificial Molecular Machines." *Angewandte Chemie International Edition in English*, 39:3348-3391.

23. Vinogradov, A.D., 1999. "Mitochondrial ATP Synthase: Fifteen Years Later." *Biochemistry (Mosc)*, 64:1219-1229.

24. Hochachka, P.W., 1994. *Muscles as Molecular and Metabolic Machines*. CRC Press, New York, p. 136.

25. Quoted by William James Sidis. http://www.sidis.net/Unconscious%20 Intelligence.htm; last accessed 06/01/05.

26. Shanks, N. and Joplin, K. "Behe, Biochemistry, and the Invisible Hand," *Philo*, 4:1. http://www.philoonline.org/library/shanks_4_1.htm; last accessed 06/02/05.

27. Polanyi, M., 1968. "Life's Irreducible Structure." *Science*, 160:1308-1312.

28. Augros, R. and Stanciu, G., 1988. *The New Biology: Discovering the Wisdom in Nature*. New Science Library, Boston, pp. 20-33.

29. Goodsell, D.S., 2000. "Biomolecules and Nanotechnology." *American Scientist*, 88:230-237.

30. Drexler, K.E., 1986. *Engines of Creation: The Coming Age of Nanotechnology*. Anchor Press, New York, p. 15.

31. Merkle, R. C. "San Francisco Weekly Confused on Small Wonders." Foresight Nanotech Institute. http://www.foresight.org/hotnews/1999SFWkly.html; last accessed 06/12/03.

32. Peterson, C. "Nanotechnology: From Concepts to R & D Goal." Foresight Nanotech Institute. http://www.foresight.org/Hotwired.all.files; last accessed 06/12/03.

33. Bailey, R., 2002. "Forever Young: The New Scientific Search for Immortality." *Reason Online Magazine*. http://reason.com/0208/fe.rb.forever.shtml; last accessed 06/12/03.

34. Lowe, C.R., 2000. "Nanobiotechnology: The Fabrication and Applications of Chemical and Biological Nanostructures." *Current Opinion in Structural Biology*, 10:428-434.

35. Whitsides, G., 2001. "The Once and Future Nanomachines." *Scientific American*, 285: 78-83.

36. Burns, Katie, 2001. "Nanotechnology, Biotechnology Come Together." *North County Times*, August 2001. http://www.nctimes.com/news/2001/20010819/71506.html; last accessed 08/19/01.

37. Sowerby, S.J., Holm, N.G. and Petersen, G.B., 2001. "Origins of Life: A Route to Nanotechnology." *BioSystems*, 61:69-78.

38. Phillips, R. and Quake, S., 2006. "The Biological Frontier of Physics." *Physics Today*, 59:38-43. http://www.physicstoday.org/vol-59/iss-5/p38.html; last accessed 06/02/06.

PART III — THE CHALLENGES

CHAPTER 6

DUCKS AND RABBITS

I t is difficult to imagine life without trees. Our distant ancestors once lived in the trees and today we use our highly evolved brains to bring the trees down to us. Trees provide us with the wood to build our houses, fences, and furniture. We can also convert wood into a cellulose pulp that, in turn, is used to make paper. My ability to communicate to you through this book is made possible by trees. Your ability to read my words in a comfortable surrounding is also made possible by trees.

Since trees are living things, the wood itself is made up of various biological molecules. Wood can be exploited by other living things that might use it as shelter or food. So what is to keep bacteria and fungi from using our wood as food? We again use our highly evolved brains to treat the wood with chemicals that we have designed. One such chemical is known as PCP (pentachlorophenol), a manufactured chemical that is quite toxic to cells, making it a powerful insecticide, fungicide, and overall pesticide. Since PCP, known commercially as "Fungifen" and "Woodtreat," is toxic to cells, it is also used as a wood preservative for such things as utility poles and railroad ties.

Organisms that attempt to use such PCP-treated wood as food simply die. However, not all organisms are killed by PCP. There is a species of bacteria, known as *Sphingomonas chlorophenolica*, that can degrade this toxin and use its byproducts as a food source.[1] PCP was not introduced into the environment until the 1930s and is not believed to be a natural product. Since PCP is recent and man-made, and most bacteria cannot use PCP as food, it seems rather clear the ability to degrade PCP has recently evolved in *S. chlorophenolica*.

The metabolic pathway for PCP degradation has been established to involve at least three different protein enzymes called PepB, PepC, and

PepA.[2] For the purposes of simplicity, we can call these *start, continue,* and *finish* because one begins the process of degradation, the other continues it, and the last one finishes it. To accomplish the process of PCP degradation, these three enzymes work like an assembly line to complete the whole chemical reaction. How did this evolve?

S. chlorophenolica did not have to invent these enzymes from scratch, rather two factors worked in favor of their development. First, while most proteins have a primary function within the cell, they can also be promiscuous, at times taking part in other functions. Recall that enzymes work to speed up specific chemical reactions. For example, Enzyme E may speed up the conversion of A to B. Yet Enzyme E may also have the ability to speed up another similar chemical reaction, perhaps the conversion of F to G. In this case, we can say that Enzyme E produces both products B and G, but it is more often the case where a particular enzyme is very good at producing B and not so good at producing G. With *S. chlorophenolica, start, continue,* and *finish* are descendants of enzymes that originally worked on some other chemicals similar to PCP and its breakdown products.

The second factor working in favor of development of this three enzyme pathway was mutation, which is commonly thought of as causing harm. While this is often true, it is not always the case. Whether a mutation is harmful can depend on the context in which the mutation occurs. The mutation that occurred in *S. chlorophenolica* allowed the enzyme, *continue,* to be expressed at all times. Normally, this enzyme is under tight regulatory control, as its primary function is to assist in the degradation of specific amino acids. Thus, bacteria typically save energy and express the enzyme only when such amino acid degradation becomes necessary. If a mutation occurred such that *continue* was expressed all the time, these bacteria would be wasting energy and materials building an enzyme when it was not needed. Thus it would be at a disadvantage compared to other bacteria that were more frugal. But with various environmental changes, context becomes extremely important. If the same mutation occurred in a soil environment where PCP existed, the mistaken expression of *continue* would allow *S. chlorophenolica* to patch together a jury-rigged pathway of *start, continue,* and *finish* (since *start* and *finish* are constantly expressed). Because the three enzymes are promiscuous enough to recognize and react with PCP and its degradative byproducts, and because the mutation brings this new three-member patchwork on line, the bacterium with the new mutation is immune to the PCP. The descendants of this mutant bacterium can now survive in an environment that is toxic to the normal population of bacteria. The patchwork does not have to be perfect. It only has to work *well enough* to allow the mutant bacteria to exploit *some* area that cannot be exploited by other members of the population. Further mutations can then refine this patchwork over time.

S. chlorophenolica illustrate that variation and natural selection (the foundational keys of Darwinian evolution) can mimic a designer. Imagine an intelligent designer faced with the problem of determining how bacteria survive in an environment with the presence of the toxin PCP. Our intelligent designer might be a good biochemist, and on surveying the toolkit of enzymes synthesized by *S. chlorophenolica*, might come upon the design solution of expressing *continue* concurrently with *start* and *finish*. This solution would effectively design a pathway that could degrade PCP. Then, utilizing some basic skills of genetic engineering, our designer might mutate the regulatory regions of the *continue* gene to cause it to be expressed all the time. Yet *S. chlorophenolica* demonstrates that this type of process can happen without an intelligent designer. Instead of relying on the biochemist's insight, we have a large population of bacteria that continuously mutate *all* their genes over time. Sooner or later, when one bacterium just happens to mutate *continue* such that it is expressed at all times, natural selection "captures" and spreads this mutation. We need only consider that the discovery of this PCP degradation pathway has actually been patented to appreciate just how much variation and selection can behave as a "designer-mimic."[3]

It is important to recognize the essence of Charles Darwin's contribution to the ongoing debate about origins. Darwin's ideas were so profound because they provided a coherent non-teleological theoretical scheme by which to explain the order and optimal arrangements seen in biological organisms. With these ideas it became possible to explain away purpose and design in life as mere illusions. Darwin accomplished this in a brilliantly simple manner. For centuries prior, non-teleologists had explained the origin of biological features and their arrangements by chance alone. But chance, by itself, was never a convincing explanation as William Paley highlighted with his famous watch analogy. If a watch could not be formed by chance alone, then how could something much more complex, such as the human eye, be the result of chance? Darwin retained a role for chance in the explanation of origins, as chance events giving rise to new variations remain the cornerstone of modern Darwinism. His novel contribution was in explaining a mechanism by which certain chance variants could be maintained and perpetuated throughout time. This mechanism was natural selection. Natural selection posits that those chance variations that enable organisms to better survive in a particular environment are likely to spread throughout a population because the variation imparts an advantage over those organisms that have not changed. The essence of the Darwinian mechanism is that while minimizing the need for chance, it maximally exploits its occurrence. Chance is the raw source of novelty and natural selection is the means to propagate these useful novelties. Natural selection does not act as a conscious agent, actively choosing the useful novelties. It acts more like a passive sieve, where only the useful novelties get passed on through time.

The result of Darwinian evolution is that organisms are gradually molded to fit their environment. This is called adaptation and looks quite a lot like design. Those organisms that inherit random changes that allow them to better adapt to the demands of their environment have an advantage over those that lack this change. The resulting outcome is that these organisms tend to predominate over time and replace those that are not as well adapted. In many ways, evolution by natural selection is similar to making an organism by trial and error. Changes that happen to work get passed on, while mistakes are left in the dustbin of history. This would mean that every living thing today is the descendent of a historical lineage with a history of success.

A classic example of natural selection taught to most students learning basic biology is the case of the peppered moth. For a long time, most peppered moths in England were light-colored. This was because most moths would rest on trees during the daytime that were covered by pale lichens. The moths' light coloring, acting as a form of camouflage, made it more difficult for birds to find them and turn them into tasty snacks. One might marvel at how these moths came up with such a simple, yet ingenious, strategy to keep from becoming a bird snack. It certainly appears as though the moth was designed to escape predation. But then something changed. Because of the rise in pollution, the formerly light tree trunks became darkened. The light-colored moths became easier for birds to find and their former camouflage became a neon light that spelled "Eat Me" in bird language. In this changing environment, any dark-colored moth now had the advantage and the light-colored moths were eventually replaced with dark-colored variants. It appeared as though the moth's wings were redesigned to better evade predators. Yet this was simply the outcome of variation that naturally arose and was then pruned by natural selection.

Zoologist Richard Dawkins has written several books clearly outlining the manner in which Darwinian evolution can mimic a designer, therefore seeming to behave as a designer-mimic. He explains the challenge that Darwin poses to anyone trying to infer design among biotic reality simply from the appearance of design:

> Natural selection is the blind watchmaker, blind because it does not see ahead, does not plan consequences, has no purpose in view. Yet the living results of natural selection overwhelmingly impress us with the appearance of design as if by a master watchmaker, impress us with the illusion of design and planning. The purpose of this book is to resolve this paradox to the satisfaction of the reader, and the purpose of this chapter is further to impress the reader with the power of the illusion of design.[4]

Dawkins builds on this in a later book by pointing out:

> I think that the distinction between accident and design is clear, in principle if not always in practice, but this chapter will introduce a third category of objects which is harder to distinguish. I shall call them designoid. . . . Designoid objects are living bodies and their products. Designoid objects look designed, so much so that some people—probably, alas, most people—think they are designed. These people are wrong. But they are right in their conviction that

designoid objects cannot be the result of chance. Designoid objects are not accidental. They have in fact been shaped by a magnificently non-random process which creates an almost perfect illusion of design.[5]

The non-random process that Dawkins is referring to is natural selection and the products of natural selection only *appear* designed, thus causing Dawkins to label such products as designoid. It now becomes clear why Darwin has always posed a more serious challenge to design inferences than philosopher David Hume, who argued that when we look closely enough, life really does not appear designed. But Dawkins disagrees, arguing that life does indeed look designed: "Biology is the study of complicated things that give the appearance of having been designed for a purpose." He argues that this appearance of design is merely an illusion, as the real "designer" is natural selection, working in tandem with mutation and variation.

WHY NOT BACKTRACK?

In previous chapters, I have outlined various clues that might lead one to suspect life was designed. Such facts about life alone would be very strong indicators of Intelligent Design if there was no designer-mimic that could also take credit for the appearance of design. The existence of the blind watchmaker as the designer-mimic prevents us from progressing from these early suspicions of design to a solid conclusion of design. But why does the existence of the designer-mimic not go further and simply erase those original causes for suspicion? While it is possible the designer-mimic may account for the origin of the code and the machines (although there is no solid evidence to think so), there is no reason to automatically credit the designer-mimic for all things that appear designed. Biological reality may be more complicated than this.

That designoid phenomena exist is not evidence that everything that appears designed is, in fact, designoid. Nothing in evolutionary theory mandates against the possibility that we live in a reality that is a mosaic of design and designoid. We know this to be a fact simply because both design and Darwinian evolution already do co-exist in the same reality. Genetically engineered organisms, including mice, chickens, goats, and pigs, have already been created with our primitive forms of biotechnology. For example, the genes for spider silk were inserted into goats such that they produce spider silk protein in their milk[6] and pass this gene on to their offspring, resulting in a genuine genetic change in certain members of the species. This is a novel genetic constitution that was created by human intelligence. Scientists are continuing to research the genetic engineering of pigs such that their organs can be used for transplants in human beings without being rejected. These examples, and hundreds like them, prove that design and evolution can and do co-exist. Nothing in the laws of nature or the process of evolution poses an obstacle to design. Thus, the mere existence of Darwinian evolution does not force us to step backwards and erase our suspicions of Intelligent Design.

EVOLVOID

If the blind watchmaker can make organisms appear as though they were designed by an intelligent agent, then consider the other side of the double-edged sword. Without a way to clearly distinguish between designed objects and designoid objects, a biological feature that is actually designed might very well appear designoid. But we can go further than this. Following in Dawkins's footsteps, I would like to introduce another term to the origins lexicon, one that I will call "evolvoid." This is a feature that appears evolved, but is not. These features are designed in such a way that one could look at them and reasonably conclude that they might have evolved.

At first glance, evolvoid phenomena would seem to question the motivations and integrity of the designer. Why would a designer create an organism to make it appear as though it evolved? Is this deceptive? Positing a misleading designer is really not necessary, however, if evolvoid features exist. First, there is no reason to think the designer, in fact, designed organisms with the intention of making it clear to human beings that such organisms must have either evolved or did not evolve. Second, and more importantly, *design itself often produces things that our minds can interpret from an evolutionary perspective.* This would mean only that evolvoid features are a function of the way we impose beliefs upon reality. Let us consider some examples of evolvoid features—things that are designed, yet appear evolved.

Imagine you are a scientist working alone on genetically modifying hemoglobin to improve its capacity to bind and deliver oxygen. You design some sequence modifications and introduce the gene into the genome of a mouse with fairly standard genetic engineering techniques. While working late in your lab one night a terrible storm hits. A tree crashes into your lab, killing you. Yet the damage also causes the cages to pop open and the genetically modified mice run for safety. A spark then sets the lab on fire and the whole place goes up in flames. No one knows of your work, but the mice work their way into the world. Because of their oxygen-delivery advantages, they slowly begin to spread. Many, many years pass and the artificial sequences you used to deliver the gene decay away leaving nothing but the improved gene preserved by selection. Then, some scientists happen upon these mice and eventually sequence their hemoglobin gene. They find some rather significant sequence changes and then publish evidence on how natural selection is at work improving the hemoglobin gene in mice! In this case, the hemoglobin gene would be evolvoid. It would clearly be interpreted as the result of mutation and natural selection, when in reality, the changes were designed.

Tim M. Berra's book, *Evolution and the Myth of Creationism*, provides another example. Employing an analogy to illustrate descent with modification, Berra illustrates how the successive generations of Corvettes have changed in appearance, yet have also inherited certain features from previous generations.

> Everything evolves in the sense of "descent with modification," whether it be government policy, religion, sports cars, or organisms. The revolutionary fiberglass Corvette evolved from more mundane automotive ancestors in 1953. Other high points in the Corvette's evolutionary refinement include the 1962 model, in which the original 102-inch wheelbase was shortened to 98 inches and the new closed-coupe stingray model was introduced; the 1968 model, the forerunner of today's Corvette morphology, which emerged with

removable roof panels; and the 1978 silver anniversary model with fastback styling. Today's version continues the stepwise refinements that have been accumulating since 1953. The point is that the Corvette evolved through a selection process acting on variations that resulted in a series of transitional forms and an endpoint rather distinct from the starting point. A similar process shapes the evolution of organisms.[7]

In this instance, we know the mechanism behind this whole process of "Corvette evolution" was entirely dependent on Intelligent Design and planning. This is an excellent example of how a series of events that owe their origin to Intelligent Design can "look evolved," therefore, even descent with modification can be evolvoid.

In his book, *Darwin's Black Box,* biochemist Michael Behe used the example of the mousetrap to illustrate his idea of Irreducible Complexity. Behe described the mousetrap as a device composed of five distinct parts, all needed to elicit the function of mouse-trapping. Since the mousetrap was dependent on all five parts for its function, Behe argued that irreducibly complex structures could not evolve.

Biologist John McDonald attempts to counter this concept on his web page in an article entitled "A reducibly complex mousetrap," whereby he argues that simpler and simpler functional mousetraps could possibly exist.[8] McDonald posits a clever continuum of devices that use less parts, yet could, in principle, function to catch mice. Furthermore, by beginning with the simplest "mousetrap," this continuum can be viewed in evolutionary terms, where simpler mousetraps are modified to become slightly more complex with each step. Clearly, an evolutionary perspective is able to propose a continuum that looks like an evolutionary explanation for the origin of the mousetrap.

Biologist Ken Miller employs the same perspective, as reported in an article from the *Chronicle of Higher Education*:

Drawing on Mr. Behe's favorite analogy, Mr. Miller says that the various parts of a mousetrap have uses even on their own. Three out of the five components form a handy tie clip. Two of the five can serve as a clipboard.[9]

But as with Berra's example of evolving Corvettes, we have factual knowledge that the mousetrap was indeed designed. The simpler precursor states imagined by McDonald and Miller are not part of the mousetrap's actual history. The "reduced" constructs are simply imagined by McDonald and the mousetrap did not once exist as a clipboard, then a handy tie clip, only to eventually become a mousetrap. Berra, McDonald, and Miller provide examples that demonstrate the ease of perceiving something as evolved when it was, in fact, designed.

The evolvoid tendency can express itself in different ways. If Intelligent Design is subtle, yet builds on much knowledge (as in the case of redesigning hemoglobin), it will be viewed as evolvoid. If Intelligent Design does not re-invent the wheel every time around, but instead builds on previous design (as with cars), it will be viewed as evolvoid. And if an Intelligent Design can be deconstructed into simpler parts or forms in a purely imaginary realm (as with the mousetrap), it will be viewed as evolvoid. Just because something "appears evolved" is not sufficient evidence that it actually evolved.

Of Ducks and Rabbits

If we live in a reality where it is possible for Intelligent Design and evolution to co-exist, where evolved things can look like they were designed, and designed things could look like they evolved, it becomes clear that a design versus evolution dichotomy can be very misleading. That evolution and design may blur into each other highlights the deeply ambiguous nature of the dispute between these two competing concepts of origins. Adding to this ambiguity is the fact that we are often dealing with unique events embedded in ancient history, meaning that any hope of resolution is going to rest on indirect, circumstantial evidence. Given such thorough ambiguity, an alternative to the traditional either/or perspective should be considered; the both/and perspective.

Consider the picture in Figure 6-1. What do you see? If you look at the picture from the left, the two "prongs" could be a beak. The dark spot would

Figure 6-1. Duck/Rabbit Perspective [Reference 10].

be the eye and the picture would be that of a duck. Yet the two "prongs" could also be ears, the same circle is still an eye, but now the picture has the appearance of a rabbit. This is a classic example of an ambiguous figure which nicely illustrates the both/and principle. It would make no sense to insist it is a picture of a duck and not a rabbit. Neither would it make sense to insist it is a rabbit, not a duck. The picture is drawn such that either animal can be seen and is inherently ambiguous.

Perhaps this duck/rabbit image can assist us in expanding our thinking about the concepts of both design and evolution. Evolution is supported by a vast amount of evidence. If it walks like a duck, quacks like a duck, looks like a duck, it is a duck. So let us view non-teleological evolution as the Duck. In contrast, Intelligent Design is rooted in a long tradition of thinking, but supported mainly by suggestive clues. Following the trail of Intelligent Design may be akin to chasing Alice's rabbit down the rabbit hole. Let us think of Intelligent Design as the Rabbit.

Of course, in the end, any particular biological feature either arose through non-teleological evolution or it was intelligently designed. Yet if the situation is ambiguous, where both the Duck and Rabbit can be seen, we have a choice. We can choose to follow the Rabbit at the urging of our suspicions. As we chase the Rabbit, let us not worry about killing the Duck or attempting to convince ourselves there never was a Duck. Instead, let us keep our eye on the Rabbit and see where it goes.

Do You See What I See?

If you fill a glass halfway with water, is it half-full or half-empty? This type of question is designed to tell us something about our personality. It is said the optimists see the glass as half-full, while the pessimists see it as half-empty. Both the pessimist and the optimist see the same thing, however, their brains just interpret what they see differently. What we see is not simply a function of what is actually there, but is also a function of what we ourselves bring to the process of seeing.

In many ways, it is perception that is at the heart of the whole debate between design and non-teleological evolution. Regardless of their point of view on the subject, many people discuss and argue about "the evidence" as if this is all that matters. But what is evidence? It is not something we encounter or detect objectively, it is data that we *interpret*. This act of interpretation transforms data into evidence. But of what? Evidence for a hypothesis or theory—both of which are mental constructs, used to convert the raw data into something we call "evidence." What we detect with our senses is not evidence, but raw data; it is what our minds recognize, while interpreting the data.

Of our five senses, most people consider vision the most important. The first sentence of Aristotle's *Metaphysic* reads, "Of all the senses, trust only the sense of sight." Plato likewise ranked sight most important (and ranked touch the least important). Today, when people are asked which sense they would least like to lose, most answer "sight." Most of us think of sight as our most informative sense. It is therefore not surprising that our language associates the sense of sight with understanding, even to the point where our thinking can be described as *ocular-centric*. Consider the various metaphors that are associated with thinking and reason: insight, enlighten, illustrate, illuminate, foresight, shed light, show, reflect, clarity, envision, survey, and so on. If we happen to think someone is arguing illogically, we use words like "unclear," "clouded," "dull," or "myopic." Regardless of the topic of our intellectual inquiries (e.g., philosophy, theology, science), we are simply attempting to make sense of all the facts about the outside world by painting internal mental pictures. The human brain assigns meaning to facts in order to connect them. It actively grasps for patterns. The facts are simply dots and our inquiries are attempts to connect the dots. It is when you connect the dots that the mental image appears.

Psychologists have long studied perception, noting that human beings are not passive recorders of events, but are active participants in recording the event. As such active participants, we often shape what we record. Consider Figure 6-2. Read the phrases that are found in the triangles and then come back to the text.

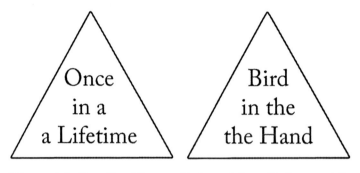

Figure 6-2. Familiar Phrases [Adapted from Reference 11].

What did you read? If you have not seen a similar example before, chances are that you did not notice anything unusual about the phrases. Did you read "Once in a lifetime?" Check again. There was an extra "a" in the first phrase and an extra "the" in the second phrase. Most people miss the duplicate words in these types of examples. Since such expressions are common, your brain draws on this experience and "cheats" for you when you read them. Your brain immediately recognizes such phrases as familiar and tells you what the phrase says before you actually read it. Writing for the Central Intelligence Agency, Richards J. Heuer used this same example to illustrate a basic fact about human perception: "We tend to perceive what we expect to perceive."[11]

This principle can be further illustrated with an experiment described by Daniel Chandler, a lecturer in Media and Communication Studies at the University of Wales, Aberystwyth.

In an experiment by Brewer and Treyens (1981), individual participants were asked to wait in an office. The experimenter said that this was his office and that they should wait there whilst he checked the laboratory to see if the previous participant had finished. After 35 seconds, he returned and took the participant to another room where they were asked to recall everything in the room in which they had been waiting. People showed a strong tendency to recall objects consistent with the typical "office schema." Nearly everyone remembered the desk and the chair next to it. Only eight out of the 30 recalled the skull (!), few recalled the wine bottle or the coffee pot, and only one recalled the picnic basket. Some recalled items that had not been there at all: 9 remembered books. This shows how people may introduce new items consistent with the schema.[12]

The experiment is intriguing in that most people failed to notice a skull sitting on the desk, while many others recalled seeing books that never existed. The "schema" that Chandler refers to is essentially the mind-set or context that we bring to the situation. Since the people knew they were in an office, they failed to notice objects that are not normally in an office. This is an excellent illustration of how perception is clearly shaped by people's experiences and expectations.

Perception is the "process of creating an internal representation of the outside world."[13] Two factors work together inside the brain to create this internal representation. First, *bottom-up processing* is where data are gathered from the world through the senses, providing the raw material upon which to create these internal representations. Second, *top-down processing* combines previous knowledge of the world with our expectations playing a significant role in how we then interpret these data. Such expectations help us assign meaning to data and designates some data to be interpreted as more significant than other data. Heuer explains this as follows:

Expectations have many diverse sources, including past experience, professional training, and cultural and organizational norms. All these influences predispose analysts to pay particular attention to certain kinds of information and to organize and interpret this information in certain ways. Perception is also influenced by the context in which it occurs. Different circumstances evoke different sets of expectations . . . . Patterns of expectations tell analysts, subconsciously, what to look for, what is important, and how to interpret what is seen. These patterns form a mind-set that predisposes analysts to think in certain ways. A mind-set is akin to a screen or lens through which one perceives the world.[11]

Ambiguous figures are one way to gauge the role of expectations in top-down processing. If you show the ambiguous rabbit/duck picture in Figure 6-1 to children on Easter Sunday, most will see the rabbit instead of the duck.[14] All the excitement about Easter bunnies creates a mind-set that favors the rabbit. A similar ambiguous figure can be viewed either as an old man or as a rat.[15] In one study, this ambiguous figure of the man/rat was shown to a group of experimental subjects.[16] Eighty-one percent of the subjects reported seeing a man. But when another group was first shown pictures of a rooster, a rabbit, a dog, and a cat, 100% reported seeing the rat. Heuer uses a series of drawings by Gerald Fisher that further highlights how context shapes perception.[17] Eight drawings are arranged in a continuum, with a man's face at one end, gradually transforming into an image of a sitting woman at the other end. Drawings in the middle of the spectrum are fairly ambiguous, where it is possible to view them either as a man's face or a sitting woman. Test subjects who were shown the detailed drawing of the man's face first, continued to see the face when subsequently shown increasingly ambiguous versions along the continuum. In contrast, subjects who were first shown the detailed picture of the woman continued to see the woman when shown the same ambiguous versions.[11] As Heuer explains, "Once an observer has formed an image—that is, once he or she has developed a mind-set or expectation concerning the phenomenon being observed—this conditions future perceptions of that phenomenon." These examples illustrate the powerful role expectations play in our perceptive processes. Previous experiences prime the mind such that it mainly sees what it expects to see. Our minds are drawn toward patterns, and once it appears that we are seeing a particular type of pattern, we assimilate the raw data and interpret it in a manner that is further consistent with that very same pattern.

The ancient origin of any biological structure is inherently ambiguous since we are dealing with events that are essentially unique and unobservable. When Charles Darwin proposed his Theory of Evolution by natural selection, he created a perceptual matrix with which to interpret the biological world around us. This non-teleogical matrix, the Duck, quickly replaced the previously more commonly held teleological matrix, the Rabbit since the Duck offered a novel perspective that allowed scientists to formulate a variety of testable hypotheses and models.

What is the true significance of this shift in perspective? Scientists have found the Duck to be a very insightful and productive guide to fit the pieces of data about the natural world into a coherent whole. The Duck became a useful template that not only made sense of the living world, but generated new data and understanding about life. Many would interpret this to mean that the Duck was the real image all along and the Rabbit disappeared when more data was added to clarify the ambiguous reality. Yet there is an alternative explanation. Darwin's template created an opportunity for top-down processing, where a certain conception of reality was being used to shape perception of all possible data. As Heuer noted, "New information is assimilated to existing images." For example, when it became clear the genetic code was not a product of chance, the Duck perspective led scientists to view this as evidence for natural selection. When molecular machines were discovered, this became evidence of the blind watchmaker's uncanny ability to mimic a designer. The Duck causes us to see more ducks. So have scientists embraced the Duck because that is the real image? Or might the Duck simply be priming our minds to convert all ambiguity into its image?

There are two factors that may help explain why the Rabbit has been neglected since the Duck appeared. First, the teleological perspective has long been intertwined with religion, metaphysics, and even mysticism. If nature is the product of a mind, it would stand to reason that most people would be more interested in the mind rather than the products of the mind. But the intellectual inertia that converts teleology into religion, for example, serves as a disability from an investigative perspective. Second, since Darwin's Duck was brought into view in 1859, it is not clear that analogies between human eyes and Nineteenth Century artifacts captured the true essence of life's design. Life as carbon-based nanotechnology would represent a highly advanced design, and our ability to catch a glimpse of this reality would depend on advances in our own designs and technology. Until our own technology reached a state that could fundamentally foreshadow that of life's technology, the true significance of the Rabbit could not be appreciated. Since it is our own advances in information technology and engineering that allow the suspicion of design to now resurface, the Duck may simply have had an investigative head start. If teleologists struggle with their Rabbit because many prefer to focus on the cause of the Rabbit, it is understandable that the Rabbit has been neglected. If teleologists do not quite know what to do with the Rabbit, simply because we do not have the experience and familiarity with the type of design that is embedded within life, it is likewise understandable that the Rabbit has been neglected. But perhaps we are nearing the point where the Rabbit can finally begin to hop and produce offspring of its own.

The Duck is not an illusion since the designer-mimic does have the ability to spawn things that appear designed. It is simply not possible to wave away the massive amount of evidence in support of Darwinian evolution with a consideration of the psychology of perspective. However, despite the popularity of the Duck, the Rabbit has never been erased and the discovery of life as carbon-based nanotechnology, complete with coded information and sophisticated machinery, has even caused the Rabbit to stir. In light of this, and the consideration of perspective and top-down reasoning, an interesting question arises: Why not follow the Rabbit and see where it leads?

BACK TO THE EVIDENCE

If we choose to focus on the perceptual matrix of the Rabbit, a serious problem emerges as a consequence of ambiguity, perspective, and top-down reasoning. When Heuer notes people tend to perceive what they expect to perceive, he adds:

> A corollary of this principle is that it takes more information, and more unambiguous information, to recognize an unexpected phenomenon than an expected one.

If one's perceptual view has long been the Duck, and only the Duck, and the Duck has also been a helpful guide, what would it take to see the Rabbit?

Astronomer Carl Sagan popularized the following rule: "Extraordinary claims require extraordinary evidence."[18] Surely, the notion that life was intelligently designed is an extraordinary claim. Such evidence as the genetic code, the existence of molecular machines, and a necessary reliance on teleological language and concepts in the biological sciences, do not constitute "extraordinary evidence." Sagan's maxim would then demand that the design hypothesis must be dismissed and abandoned. Yet Sagan's maxim does not fit within the Explanatory Continuum. It is something that better fits the Traditional Template, where Sagan, the skeptic, needs something compelling and unambiguous to cause a perspective shift in his mind before he could abandon the non-teleological perspective and embrace the teleological perspective, all in one step. The flaw in Sagan's maxim is that an extraordinary claim is simply a claim about an extraordinary event and the occurrence of an extraordinary event does not necessarily entail that it would come with extraordinary evidence. The fingerprints of an extraordinary event may produce only mundane or subtle clues. For example, when Darwin first proposed the theory of evolution by natural selection, it was perceived as an extraordinary claim, so much so that many scoffed at it. Yet Darwin's theory was subsequently popularized and accepted, not because he provided extraordinary evidence. On the contrary, Darwin simply presented some rather basic principles backed up by various observations that were weaved into the new perspective, which generated a track record of success when explaining the living world. It is this success that has caused it to be embraced.

In his book, *Finding Darwin's God*, biologist Ken Miller notes:

Fortunately, in scientific terms, if there is a God, He has left Himself plenty of material to work with. To pick just one example, the indeterminate nature of quantum events would allow a clever and subtle God to influence events in ways that are profound, but scientifically undetectable to us. Those events could include the appearance of mutations, the activation of individual neurons in the brain, and even the survival of individual cells and organisms affected by the chance processes of radioactive decay. Chaos theory emphasizes the fact that enormous changes in physical systems can be brought about by unimaginably small changes in initial conditions; and this, too, could serve as an undetectable amplifier of divine action.[19]

Miller's position is indeed reasonable and is echoed by many theologians and theistic evolutionists. If such a God were to subtly manipulate or design natural history in this manner, the evidence for such extraordinary events would certainly be nonexistent.

Sagan and Miller are good examples of opposing but extreme perspectives on the ability to detect design. From these differing perspectives, the evidence for Intelligent Design is either supposed to remain undetectable or it is supposed to be so obvious that the natural world screams, "Design!" However, the actual evidence for design may exist in such a way that neither expectation will be satisfied, meaning that both extremes of perspective ensure that the Rabbit remains neglected. If the Rabbit is supposed to scream, it will be dismissed unless we all hear it screaming. If the Rabbit is supposed to be invisible, the Duck is the only thing to see. Since there is plenty of room between silence and screaming, perhaps we should explore within this middle ground if we are to assess suspicions of Intelligent Design. The fingerprints of design may be subtle, rather than extraordinary, but not so subtle that they are invisible.

In the search for the fingerprints of Intelligent Design, it is useful to identify and separate two types of evidence that are being evaluated and discussed. First, there is Epistemological Evidence, the demand or expectation of extraordinary evidence or data that would presumably convince even a hardcore skeptic to agree with the opposing perspective. Some possible examples include:

- A critic of Intelligent Design states he will believe in it if he can see the designer designing something.
- A tobacco company president is willing to believe smoking causes cancer if everyone who has ever smoked can be shown to have developed cancer.

- A creationist is willing to believe in evolution if a monkey exposed to continual x-rays develops the ability to talk to humans about God.

While such extraordinary data may in fact convince a skeptic to change their point of view on an opposing perspective, this kind of extreme evidence rarely occurs for any event in our world. The bulk of the actual evidence in support of *any* claim or event is typically much more subtle in reality. Therefore, it is necessary to consider whether the requested evidence is not only consistent with reality, but whether such "convincing" evidence would or could in fact result from the investigation. For example, would exposing a monkey to x-rays in fact result in a talking monkey, regardless of to whom it was talking? Exposing a monkey to x-rays would provide us with an x-rayed monkey, but why think that the truth of evolution means that such a monkey should talk? While x-rays will induce multiple mutations in the monkey's genome, there is no logical connection between such an experiment and the truth of evolution.

Most demands for Epistemological Evidences are often based on a variety of faulty assumptions. For example, it is sometimes acknowledged by skeptics that finding a copy of the book of Genesis encoded in a DNA molecule would be convincing evidence of Intelligent Design. However, the request for this type of evidence is based on several assumptions which do not necessarily follow from the concept of Intelligent Design. Seeking such a message in the DNA assumes that if a designer bio-engineered and deposited cells on this planet billions of years ago, such a designer intended for mankind to discover this message at some point in time. It assumes a designer who chooses to mark his handiwork by shouting biblical verses from biological molecules. It assumes that the designer chooses to communicate with mankind in a strange, subtle manner that can only be viewed by molecular biologists in the Twentieth Century and beyond. It assumes that such a designer, wanting to be acknowledged in this fashion, would not use other methods such as less subtle clues or clear evidence of design that defy mankind's natural explanations. It also makes certain assumptions about the nature and personality of such a designer. What type of designer would endow the original cells with such a message? Without evidence that there is a basis for making such assumptions about the designer, why would it be logical to demand that the truth of Intelligent Design be dependent on the discovery of such a message in the DNA?

Demands for Epistemological Evidence are also commonly disconnected from the truth of a proposition. For example, if the original life forms were designed and deposited on this planet billions of years ago, the demand for a DNA-based Genesis text is intrinsically flawed since non-selectable messages in the genome would have decayed into oblivion a long, long time ago; natural selection would not prune away any of the mutations that served to erase the message. Since a designer of such complex biological systems could reasonably be expected to be aware of this fact, there is no reason to think the designer would have bothered to insert such a message in any genome.

Yet let us assume the designer does want to communicate in such a way and was trying to communicate with a special group of Twentieth Century scientists. How would this be accomplished? As an illustration of the problems involved, I have encoded a portion of the text from Genesis, the first book of the Bible, in the language of nucleic acids, and the following is the fragment that contains the message:

```
G G C G U G A A C A A U G U C C C A U G A G A C -
G U A U G C A C U G C U G A A A C C A G U -
G A U G C C A A G U A A U G U C G A G A A A C U G C U U -
U C A C A U U C U C U U U U A G A U G U G C C A G U G
C C C C A U G A C C G A C G U A U U C U G C C C A A U G -
G A C G C G U U U C U A C A A U U A A C A C A C U G C C C C A U -
G U A A U U C C A C A U U C A A G U C C U U U U C C A U U -
U C U U C C A C U A
```

Assuming this message existed within DNA molecules and assuming that a scientist was likely to have sequenced it, how is it possible to recognize that this is a message and how is it possible to decipher the meaning of the encoded message? I propose a challenge: What verse from the book of Genesis is encoded in the above message? If you figure it out, be sure to let me know. I encoded this message years ago and cannot remember what I encoded.

Note that attempts to decode this message are accompanied by additional knowledge, providing an advantage that would not be available to the average research scientist. There is factual knowledge that a message is present, that it is in the English language, and that the message is from the book of Genesis. So what is the message in the code?

Deciphering this message requires that a code be perceived and interpreted. The problem is that all codes are conventional. Just because I can assign a nucleotide sequence to represent a letter of the English alphabet does not mean you are able to decode it without knowledge of the convention I used. If such a message as this is not easily decoded, why would it be logical to assume that a scientist could recognize and decode a message written by a non-human designer?

Even if we were to find some message encoded in a genome, it is entirely possible that rather than be convinced by such "evidence" critics of Intelligent Design may simply enhance the stringency of their demands. One might argue that all that has been demonstrated is that some intelligent agent encoded a message in the genome and this does not extrapolate to mean that anything else in the cell was designed. It is not at all clear that this or any other type of data, however strong or supportive of Intelligent Design, would ever satisfy the demands associated with the expectation of Epistemological Evidence.

Rather than chasing down some form of extraordinary evidence just to convince a skeptic, the investigator should give priority to a type of evidence that I call Ontological Evidence, which is data that logically would be expected to exist if a hypothesis is true. These would be facts about the world that exist because of the existence of some previous phenomenon or event. For example, if it is true that humans and monkeys recently shared a common ancestor, this does not mean that we should be able to get monkeys to talk by massively mutating their genome. It only means, for example, that a high-resolution focus should turn up significant similarities between humans and monkeys at all levels of biological analysis. This is because the truth of common ancestry predicts such similarities. Neither should we expect to catch the designer in the act of designing if life itself was designed billions of years ago. We expect instead that a high-resolution focus should turn up significant similarities between living cells and artifacts at all levels of biological analysis.

A focus on Ontological Evidence may not erase the Duck from our perceptual field, as that would be the job of Epistemological Evidence. The focus on Ontological Evidence will instead help to prevent us from neglecting the Rabbit which in turn will assist us in better perceiving the Rabbit on its own terms. If such a focus can eventually generate a positive record of results, creating a better understanding of life and evolution, the Rabbit will emerge as a full co-partner with the Duck and eventually be allowed admittance into the science lab.

References

1. Copley, S. D., 2000. "Evolution of a Metabolic Pathway for Degradation of a Toxic Xenobiotic: The Patchwork Approach." *Trends in Biochemical Sciences*, 25:261-265.

2. The following description is simplistic, as I am merely trying to convey the most relevant points from this example of evolution.

3. PATN Patent Bibliographic Information. http://www.nalusda.gov/bic/Biotech_Patents/1994patents/05364787.html; last accessed 07/08/04.

4. Dawkins, R., 1986. *The Blind Watchmaker: Why the Evidence of Evolution Reveals a Universe without Design*. W.W. Norton & Company, New York.

5. Dawkins, R., 1996. *Climbing Mount Improbable*. W.W. Norton & Company, New York.

6. BBC News. "GM Goat Spins Web Based Future." August 21, 2000. http://news.bbc.co.uk/1/hi/sci/tech/889951.stm; last accessed 03/02/07.

7. Berra, T.M., 1990. *Evolution and the Myth of Creationism*. Stanford University Press, Stanford, California, pp. 118-119.

8. McDonald, J.H., 2002. "A Reducibly Complex Mousetrap" http://udel.edu/~mcdonald/mousetrap.html; last accessed 07/12/04.

9. Monastersky, R. "Seeking the Deity in the Details." *Chronicle of High-*

er *Education*, December 21, 2001. http://chronicle.com/free/v48/i17/17a01001.htm; last accessed 03/02/07.

10. Jastrow, J., 1899. "The Mind's Eye." *Popular Science Monthly*, 54:299-312.

11. Richards J.H. Jr., 1999. "Psychology of Intelligence Analysis." https://www.fas.org/irp/cia/product/facttell/csi_info/psychology.html; last accessed 07/03/06.

12. Chandler, D. "Visual Perception 5." http://www.aber.ac.uk/media/Modeules/MC10220/; last accessed 07/15/04 and Brewer, W.F. and Treyens, J.C., 1981. "Role of Schemata in Memory for Places." *Cognitive Psychology*, 13:207-230.

13. Bourne, L.E. and Ekstrand, B.R., 1982. *Psychology: Its Principles and Meanings*, 4th ed. Holt, Rinehart and Winston, New York, p. 63.

14. Brugger, P. and Brugger, S., 1993. "The Easter Bunny in October: Is It Disguised as a Duck?" *Perceptual Motor Skills*, 76:577-578.

15. This picture can be seen at: http://www.aber.ac.uk/media/Modules/MC10220/Images/specs.gif.

16. As described by Chandler in reference 12.

17. This picture can be seen at: http://www.cia.gov/csi/books/19104/fig2.gif.

18. Interview With Carl Sagan. *Nova Online*. http://www.pbs.org/wgbh/nova/aliens/carlsagan.html; last accessed 07/19/04.

19. Miller, K., 1999. *Finding Darwin's God: A Scientist's Search for Common Ground Between God and Evolution*. Cliff Street Books, New York, p. 241.

CHAPTER 7

DESIGNING EVOLUTION

M ight evolution itself have been designed? At first glance, the idea would seem ridiculous. When things are designed, they are designed to carry out an objective, yet there is no obvious evidence that evolution reaches for some distant goal. Instead, evolution by natural selection is inherently myopic, where features that impart an immediate reproductive advantage end up being disproportionately propagated. That is it. End of story.

As a process, evolution is significantly influenced by contingency. Side-stepping obvious stochastic processes such as genetic drift, natural selection is said to be a non-random process. While it is true that a genetic trait conferring a selective advantage will spread throughout a population of organisms in a deterministic fashion, whether the trait will confer a selective advantage is often due to chance. Recall the PCP degradation story from Chapter 6. The mutation that allowed PCP to be degraded would be deleterious in an environment without PCP. Thus, whether that mutation would spread by natural selection was dependent on the mutation occurring in an environment where PCP existed. And whether that mutation occurred in such an environment was simply a matter of historical contingency. In fact, evolutionary history is so permeated with contingency that many biologists would describe it as completely unpredictable. Evolutionary biologist Stephan Jay Gould drove this point home with the metaphor of replaying the tape of life. Put simply, if we could rewind natural history and start again at some distinct point in the distant past, what would replay would be a very different evolutionary story. This is because our particular natural history is so loaded with chance events that there is no reason to think the exact same set of chance events would play out again.

In what way can all this chance be reconciled with teleology and the design of evolution? One option is purely theological. Without violating any law of nature, God could have introduced various specific mutations into evolutionary history to elicit the intended result. Because God is omniscient and omnipotent, He would be easily able to choose the right places for the right mutations. And as far as we know, every significant mutation in the lineage that led to the evolution of *Homo sapiens* may have been caused by God. That our science would not be able to detect such events is not meaningful from the theological perspective. While we could not consider this a scientific explanation, neither could we say it was false.

Since we have no independent experience with a designer that is both omniscient and omnipotent, the effects from such a cause are not easily investigated. To more effectively infer design, in an empirical, investigative sense, we will restrain our hypothesis to invoking a human-like intelligence. If the intelligent cause is completely unlike human intelligence, how would an investigation recognize the signposts of its intervention? If the intelligence is completely unlike us, it would not think or design as we do. As long as the hypothesized agency is human-like, we can more safely extrapolate from our own experience with our own intelligence and design. And such extrapolations make it possible to formulate testable hypotheses. But could a human-like intelligence really design evolution? Because of the inherent contingency and unpredictability associated with evolution, a human-like intelligence would not know where to place the mutations nor account for their effect across deep time. Furthermore, it is not clear whether a human-like intelligence could even manipulate a biosphere across a time span of billions of years.

If we are to build on our Intelligent Design suspicion, it is necessary to do so modestly. We will therefore add another methodological constraint and propose a single act of intelligent intervention—the design of the first cells that inhabited our planet. There are several reasons for proposing this constraint.

First, there is the issue of *significance*. The most significant unanswered question in biology is the origin of life. How did life first appear on this planet? Not only has this question escaped a non-teleological explanation for decades, it is the most crucial question in biology. The origin of life speaks to the essence of life, and that, in turn, builds context for the rest of biology, including evolution. All else follows from the initial states provided by the original cells and the context they set for subsequent evolution. In comparison, the rest of biology is a footnote.

Second, there is the issue of *testability*. While there are immense—if not insurmountable—problems in assessing and testing for design in the form of omnisciently-guided mutational tinkering across deep time, the notion of a human-like intelligence designing a living cell is not nearly as troublesome. Scientists are currently making their first steps toward designing life, and such an objective does not appear impossible over the next century or so (a small blip considered against the backdrop of our ancient universe). Constraining Intelligent Design to the origin of the first cells makes it easier to extrapolate, and thus test, our own experience with design and life. As we acquire experience by designing artificial life forms, this experience can inform our hypotheses about life's design.

Third, there is the *evidence*. Thus far, the various clues discussed in Chapters 3-5 are all biological universals, features shared by all living things. If the first life forms were designed, and all of today's species are the descendants of these originally designed cells, the universality of these clues does not merit inferring design beyond the first life forms. Thus far, the clues only point to the design of life.

Fourth, there is the issue of *parsimony*. By constraining our design inference to the origin of life, we pay tribute to Occam's Razor and the track record of success generated by the non-teleological approach. The Razor is essentially a useful rule of thumb that tells us to choose the simplest explanation, because it is most likely to be true. Those who find the clues for life's design to be insufficient for generating a suspicion of design will, of course, use the Razor to completely cut away design. However, those who do entertain the suspicion of Intelligent Design, because of the clues, can pay tribute to the Razor (and the success of the non-teleological approach) by constraining the design inference to the origin of life. Such a position is a compromise between the Razor and the direction the clues point.

Last, there is the issue of *practicality*. If we hypothesize the design of life's first cells, we are near or at the level of the bacteria. Bacteria are the simplest life form on this planet and thus the easiest to study. As such, science has already produced a very robust knowledge base about bacteria, giving us plenty of material to explore from a teleological perspective.

These five reasons, taken together as a synergistic whole, help us appreciate that the hypothesis of life's design is rooted in rational consideration.[1] While these reasons constitute a methodological constraint on our design inference, they should not be mistaken for a dogmatic rule. If, for example, evidence merits the inference for a further intelligent intervention, we should feel free to follow through on it. The key is the need for further evidence.

PUTTING DARWIN TO WORK

So let us propose the design of the first cells. The first question many would ask is this: why did a designer design the first cells? What was the purpose? This question is primary because of a basic principle among human designers—they design for a reason. From a human perspective, there is always some objective behind the activity of designing. In observing living cells and organisms, there is indeed a clear purpose behind their design. Franklin Harold points it out: "Living things clearly have at least one purpose, to perpetuate their own kind."[2] So why does life continually reproduce itself? From the non-teleological perspective, reproduction is a brute given and the cornerstone of Darwinian evolution. From the teleological perspective, reproduction is the means by which we can carry design into the future without the need for continual interventions on the part of the designer. The text of the New Testament, for example, was carried thousands of years into the future because scribes would make faithful copies on a regular basis. Reproduction thus puts design over deep time into the hands of a human-like designer. Not only do human designers typically design with the intent of having their designs persist, but the ability to propagate design through reproduction removes the need to continually intervene over time. When viewed from this perspective, the purpose of life's design had to do with the future. The design was intended to reach beyond the original life forms.

The DNA molecule itself also reaches into the future. DNA is replicated just prior to the reproduction of the cell. This is because the DNA contains the necessary information that will be needed by the new cell. DNA consists of two independent chains of nucleotides that wind around each other to form the double helix. Each chain is held together by covalent bonds between the sugar and phosphate groups of the nucleotides, while the two chains are held together by hydrogen bonds between the complementary nitrogenous bases of the nucleotides on each strand. The sequence of nucleotides in each strand stores the code-script for the construction of RNA and protein. But why are there two strands? Surely we could code all the RNA- and protein-forming information on a single strand of DNA. In one of the most understated observations ever made in science, James Watson and Francis Crick, after outlining the double helix model, noted: "It has not escaped our notice that the specific pairing we have postulated immediately suggests a possible copying mechanism for the genetic material."[3] The fact that DNA exists as a double helix of two nucleotide chains foreshadows the manner in which the structure of DNA is perfectly suited for replication. To replicate DNA, all you need to do is unwind the two strands and then use each strand as a template for the synthesis of a new, complementary strand. In one molecule, there are two perfect solutions for two design problems—coding the machinery of life and perpetuating the information across time. A more beautiful molecular expression of the form-function relationship would be hard to imagine. Seen from this vantage point, the very structure of DNA is evidence that indicates life was designed to reproduce.

From the larger biological perspective, this means the original design anticipated evolution. This follows from the simple fact that mistakes in replication, in the form of mutations, are essentially built into the fabric of physical reality. As Ken Miller explains:

> The DNA molecule is structured in precisely a way that makes the behavior of individual atoms, even individual electrons, significant. When a mutation, a mistake in the copying of DNA, occurs, there are no intermediate chemical forms. One of the four DNA bases is changed completely into another base, and that change has a direct (and possibly permanent) effect on the code-script of the gene. As a

result, events with quantum unpredictability, including cosmic ray movements, radioactive disintegration, and even molecular copying errors, exert direct influences on the sequences of bases in DNA.[4]

Since reproduction entails mistakes in replication, variation is ensured. For example, even if the original cells were all genetically identical (clones), sooner or later variants would appear as a consequence of mutation. Once variation appears, Darwinian evolution kicks into gear. If the variant does not affect the ability to reproduce, the mutation is neutral and whether the variant spreads throughout the population or is lost from the population is a matter of chance. If the variant hinders reproduction, it will be eliminated from the population. If the variant enhances reproduction, it will spread throughout the population, perhaps replacing the original version. Any designer attempting to perpetuate a design across time by using the strategy of reproduction must factor for Darwinian evolution. And this poses a serious problem for our attempt to perpetuate design.

A core element of the non-teleological perspective of evolution is that mutations are random with regard to fitness. This means that mutations are not inherently forward- or outward-looking. Instead, a mutation simply occurs in a random fashion (a genuine mistake) and whether or not it benefits the organism depends on contingency, for as far as we know, evolution does not create targeted mutations to solve specific problems. For example, if there was some mechanism by which the PCP molecule itself could trigger the specific mutation that elicits the expression of *continue* (see Chapter 6), we would have a powerful indicator of a teleological mechanism at work. In such a case, the cell would be selectively mutating regions of its DNA that it needs to retool in order the meet the challenges of the environment. But that is not how it happens. What you have instead are a large number of cells each mutating their genomes at random. The population of cells is effectively playing the lottery. The one genome that happens to mutate the "right" spot wins the prize, as this genome is at a selective advantage in comparison and will then spread its progeny throughout the population. The problem is that the lottery winners, over time, cannot be predicted and such winners may explore trajectories that not only were not intended by

DESIGNING EVOLUTION

a designer, but may actually hinder the ability to design across time using reproduction. All of this unintended evolution can thus be considered noise. If a designer is trying to use reproduction to perpetuate a design far into the future, how does one control for all the noise that Darwinian evolution will produce along the way? What would prevent this noise from drowning out the signal of design? How can a designer solve these problems?

One strategy is to design reproduction such that random mutations cannot occur. But since random mutation is built into the quantum fabric of reality, this option does not exist for our human-like designer.

Another strategy is to design organisms such that all mutations are always deleterious. For example, it might be possible to design life using a set of amino acids that are all quite different and using a genetic code that works in a way that is contrary to the Universal Optimal Code discussed in Chapter 4. With this code, all mutations could result in amino acid substitutions such that all changes are deleterious. In this case, Darwinian evolution would be used to eliminate every variant that popped into existence, ensuring that only the designed states could survive and propagate. This solution renders these designed cells fragile and unable to respond and adapt to all the contingencies of the environment. These cells would likely die at some point, and with their extinction, the whole design contained within them would be gone forever. Variation itself is necessary in order to propagate the rest of the design across time and changing environmental conditions. Attempts to eliminate the ability to produce variants would eliminate the propagation of the design.

Rather than working against mutation and Darwinian evolution, using a more subtle, yet ingenious plan, an intelligent designer might seek to enlist and exploit random mutation and natural selection. If we are faced with an obstacle that is too hard or costly to eliminate, we can turn the obstacle into something that serves our end. One clue that this approach may be at work stems from the writings of Ken Miller who, after describing how DNA is inevitably mutated, observes that "life is built around a chemistry that provides an amplifying mechanism for quantum events."[5] In other words, the DNA molecules may have been designed to tap into the indeterminate nature of quantum reality, allowing organisms to constantly sample, at random, from an immensely large pool of variants. Life was designed not only to reproduce, but to spawn variants on a theme.

At this point, let us return to the principle of mutations being random with regard to fitness. Does this really speak against the design of life and evolution? Say we expose a population of bacteria to an antibiotic. Someone might think that if bacteria and evolution were designed, the bacteria would be able to mutate only those nucleotide positions that would thwart the activity of the antibiotic. But how would you design that? Each cell would have to be endowed with an elaborate computer that would process all the data about the environment. The computer would then map all this information to a complete abstract representation of the dynamic biochemistry of the cell. From there, the computer would determine the nature of the threat of the antibiotic, its biochemical mechanism, and then realize the problem could be solved by mutating a particular position within a particular gene. Then the computer activates a pathway that precisely targets a specific "A" in a sea of A's, T's, C's, and G's. Is this even feasible? If so, is it feasible for a bacterial cell to contain such a computer? How much energy would it take to run it and faithfully propagate it for billions of years? How would the computer be propagated without losing its ability to function across deep time?

Now let us take the problem out of the lab where a single species is being challenged with a single variable. Imagine an animal living in a forest. Can a computer ever capture all the information about the dynamic, contingent environment? Including the feeding behavior of, say, a recently introduced predator? Is this feasible?

Maybe a designer developed a better solution: Let the population of cells be the computer. This population can then be thought of as a neural network, where all cells are connected, at the very least, through the same genetic program called "survive." There is no need to install a computer in each cell that monitors the environment and programs specific changes in the genome in response to environmental challenges. That objective is carried out by the population of cells, where different solutions to an environmental challenge are put on the table through a random mutagenic walk, and the solution that works ends up changing the population. Variation among a population followed by natural selection is exactly the type of strategy a designer might employ when endowing cells with the ability to adapt and learn against the backdrop of a sea of contingency.

As we speak, scientists around the world adopt exactly these two strategies as they attempt to design new drugs and biological molecules.[6] Let us say you want to design a new protein that will bind to another protein that already exists (call it A). One strategy is called "rational design." Here scientists draw upon their biochemical knowledge and information about protein A and use this insight to engineer the new protein. The second strategy is referred to as "*in vitro* selection." Here, one would use protein A as a form of bait to fish for a partner among a large pool of random variants. The experiment is designed to pull out the proteins that happen to bind to protein A with sufficient specificity and strength. To do this, simply expose the random population to protein A (the bait) and those that just happen to bind A will get pulled out. Once you isolate and amplify protein A's new-found partner, you can then refine their interaction by introducing individual mutations into the partner. Both strategies have spawned their own successful track record and many scientists view these two approaches as complementary.

The twin strategies employed to design new biomolecules perfectly maps to the thesis of design and evolution. Rational design is an approach that can be implanted through intelligent intervention. But because our methodological constraints hold design to the origin of the first cells, giving us a single window for intervention, this approach is not available for any biotic changes subsequent to the original design. That leaves us with the option of selecting from a pool of variants, like *in vitro* selection. Once again, the hypothesis of a human-like designer returns us to Darwinian evolution.

Yet the design problems associated with lottery winners still remains. Because the variants are randomly generated, and the lottery winners win merely by coming up with something, anything, that "works," we cannot predict the winners or the effects they will cause. The million dollar question is this: can a designer use Darwinian evolution to accomplish a biological objective beyond "survive and reproduce?" Does the very strategy that is so useful in perpetuating design ultimately erase it?

Despite the fact that the blind watchmaker has no vision or foresight, and does not plan for the future, it can be guided. In fact, perhaps the blindness of selection is exactly what makes it vulnerable to guidance from an intelligent source. For example, in their review of one form of *in vitro* selection (known as phage display), George Smith and Valery Petrenko observe:

> Imagine, then, the applied chemist, not as designer of molecules with a particular purpose, but rather as custodian of a highly diverse population of chemicals evolving *in vitro* as if they were organisms subject to natural selection. *A chemical's "fitness" in this artificial biosphere would be imposed by the custodian for his or her own ends.* For instance, the population might be culled periodically of individuals who fail to bind tightly to some biological receptor; the population would then evolve toward specific ligands for that receptor . . . . *Progress toward the custodian's chosen goal* would in a sense be "automatic": once appropriate selection conditions are devised, no plan for how the system is to meet the demands of selection need be specified.[7] (emphasis added)

Since selection is blind, a seeing and intelligent investigator can step in and become the one who defines fitness. No law is violated by such an act. Smith's and Petrenko's description is simply the molecular version of artificial selection, which is the process of intentional modification of a species by encouraging the breeding of certain traits over others. Artificial selection depends on an intelligent agent intervening from outside the system. But might it be possible to design cells with intrinsic "selectors" that mimic the role of the custodian introducing goals? If so, we can really get a feel for how deep this rabbit hole is going to go. In some cases, what we may think of as natural selection could really be more like artificial selection from a temporal distance.

FRONT-LOADING EVOLUTION

Since the design of the first cells entailed the propagation of design through reproducing entities, and reproduction entails evolution, a truly intelligent designer would anticipate evolution. Yet this poses a serious problem: How does one design future states through the present? One possibility is *front-loading* future states into the present design. Front-loading is the investment of a significant amount of information at the initial stage of evolution (the first life forms) whereby this information shapes and constrains subsequent evolution through its dissipation. This is not to say that every aspect of evolution is pre-programmed and determined. It merely means that life was built to evolve with tendencies as a consequence of carefully chosen initial states in combination with the way evolution works.

Front-loading does not allow for a prediction of specific outcomes, at a specific time and place, but does allow that specified outcomes can be made much more likely. A rough analogy to the concept of front-loading is the Las Vegas casino. As long as enough people gamble in the casino, it makes a profit. Yet the profits are derived by people playing games of chance. We cannot predict that a given casino will enjoy a specific profit at a specific time. But we can predict that the casino will profit, because the rules inherent in the games of chance favor the casino. In other words, it is the rules behind the games of chance that front-load profits for the casino.

Front-loading, by definition, is about designing the future through the present. It is about imposing some kind of constraint on evolution, or more simply put, it is *using evolution to carry out design objectives*. Since evolution would proceed outward from the originally designed cells, evolution may have been endowed with various sequences and structures to increase the odds that certain future states would be found through a random search stemming outwards from this front-loaded state. These sequences and structures might act like the rules of the casino, where the initial design events may express themselves throughout their subsequent history, acting as the surrogates for the artificial selector.

The most obvious question to ask at this point is this: what was front-loaded? Since the investigation begins with the initially designed cells, if the evolutionary mechanisms were designed to exploit the front-loaded state, just how far out do these dynamics spread before being completely diluted by the noise of non-teleological processes? The possible outcomes of the originally front-loaded states are many. To name just a few, the evolution of:

- Multi-cellularity
- Plants, fungi, and animals
- Plant-like, fungi-like, and animal-like creatures (creatures that function as analogs to what exists)
- Invertebrates and vertebrates
- Invertebrate-like and vertebrate-like creatures
- Mammals
- Mammal-like creatures
- Humans
- Human-like creatures

Another way to look at it is by starting with what exists. The design objective behind the front-loading of evolution may have entailed the emergence of our specific biosphere (humans, platypus, and jellyfish, etc.), a subset of our specific biosphere (humans, platypus-like, and jellyfish-like creatures, etc.), an analogous biosphere (human-like, platypus-like, and jellyfish-like creatures, etc.), or a subset of the analogous biosphere (jellyfish-like creatures amid other things non-teleological processes spawn). The front-loading of evolution does not necessarily mean the originally designed creatures were endowed with the information to form mammalian brains and glands. It could mean the original information made it more likely that something akin to mammalian brains and glands would eventually appear. Or it could be even more modest and simply mean the deck was stacked such that the appearance of multi-cellularity was highly likely. Whatever the objective, it remains essentially teleological. We all understand the basic principle of using the past to make sense of the present. The Gestalt shift involved in the consideration of front-loading allows us to contemplate a reversal of this thinking, where in certain cases, the present makes sense of the past. We get a better understanding of the past by understanding its future.

UNPREDICTABLY PREDICTABLE

While a particular course of evolution may be inherently unpredictable, not everything about evolution is unpredictable. One thing we can clearly predict about evolution is that it will borrow from pre-existing states. Evolution rarely designs from scratch. Instead, most biologists think of evolution as a tinkerer, where it tweaks and modifies what it has been handed and seeks to maximally exploit such tinkering. Second, not only does evolution borrow from pre-existing material, it borrows from within a pre-existing architecture. For example, if we designed cells 3.5 billion years ago, we could very well predict something about their descendents 3.5 billion years later—they would be using the same genetic code and the same set of amino acids to construct their machines. We could predict this because such features are deeply embedded in the architecture of the cell and help define the essence of the cell and life. This means that as the cells evolve over time, they will carry these aspects along with them. Evolution really does not have the "choice" of eliminating and replacing them with another radically different code and set of amino acids, as that would be akin to selecting against life itself. It is far easier to simply use what you have and build on that.

Again and again, scientists are finding that current structures are expressions of ancient things. Since humans evolved recently and humans are most interested in humans, let us consider them. A modern triumph of biology was the sequencing of the human genome, whereby the actual sequence of 3.1 billion nucleotides was spelled out. The sequenced genome provided many interesting insights, especially when compared to the previously sequenced genomes of worms and fruit flies. The *New York Times* reported, "The human genome, besides being only just out of the worm league, seems to have almost too much in common with many other kinds of animal genomes."[8] Australia's *Sydney Morning Herald* reported, "What sets us apart from flies and worms is the complexity of our proteins. Our extra genes do not make lots of new kinds of proteins. Rather, they reshuffle the different bits of old protein in novel ways . . . ."[9] It was determined that while flies have 13,000 genes and nematode worms have 18,000, the human genome has approximately 30,000-40,000 genes. The scientific journal, *Nature*, commented on the source for most of these new human genes:

> Furthermore, the additional genes are not primarily the result of invention of new protein domains. We have many of the same protein families as flies and worms, although we have more in each

family. The additional genes come from reshuffling the number and order of protein domains, analogous to making new cars out of old parts.[10]

Biologist David Baltimore makes essentially the same point:

> Where do our genes come from? Mostly from the distant evolution-ary past. In fact, only ninety-four of 1,278 protein families in our genome appear to be specific to vertebrates. The most elementary of cellular functions—basic metabolism, transcription of DNA into RNA, translation of RNA into protein, DNA replication and the like—evolved just once and have stayed pretty well fixed since the evolution of single-celled yeast and bacteria. The biggest difference between humans and worms or flies is the complexity of our pro-teins: more domains (modules) per protein and novel combinations of domains. The history is one of new architectures being built from old pieces.[11]

Despite the hundreds of millions of years of evolutionary tinkering in the three lineages that led to humans, flies, and worms, much commonal-ity remains. In fact, when the mouse genome was sequenced and compared to the human genome, Eric Lander, Director of the Whitehead Center for Genome Research at MIT, commented, "as far as I can tell, [there's] no significant difference between mouse and human. . . it's basically the same set of genes, just tinkered with in little ways."[12] This is equally true when genomes from different types of plants were compared:

> We wanted to know if woody and herbaceous plants evolved dif-ferent genes that account for their diversity, or if they use the same genes in different ways," said Sederoff [Ronald Sederoff is Distin-guished University Professor of Forestry at North Carolina State University] "Our research strongly suggests the latter."[13]

So evolution has been working with basically the same set of components within the same basic system architecture. The work it does has been prima-rily reshuffling and tweaking the original toolkit.

Front-loading is plausible because, across all forms of life, cells share the same basic architecture and components. A designer with an eye to the future will know that this architecture and these embedded components are likely to remain intact. And even if a specific component were to be lost in one lineage, it may very well remain in many or most of the other lineages. The theme is driven home when we compare the human genome to that of a very simple single celled creature—yeast. When comparing a yeast genome with the human genome (and all other eukaryotic genomes), *The Scientist* reported:

> The researchers identified highly conserved genes important for eukaryotic cell organization, including those required for the cytoskeleton, the compartmentation of the cell, and processes within the cell, including cell-cycle control, proteolysis, protein phosphorylation and RNA splicing. They suggested that these genes might have originated with the appearance during evolution of eukaryotic life forms whose cells contain nuclei.[14]

It is not just the striking similarity in the sequences of these genes that is remarkable, but we also have a plentiful supply of laboratory experiments demonstrating that the components from human cells, for example, are interchangeable with their homologs in yeast. Consider a special set of genes involved in regulating the cell cycle, the ordered series of events that coordinate the growth and division of cells. The cell cycle genes not only coordinate DNA replication with growth and cell division, but also employ circuitry that senses and answers at least three basic binary questions before the cell is licensed to replicate. Are there enough nutrients in my surroundings? Am I big enough? Is my DNA damaged? If the answer is Yes, Yes, and No, the cell will commit itself to dividing. Even though yeast and humans have diverged from each over a billion years ago, where each lineage has experienced its own unique history of contingent evolutionary challenges, much of the basic cell cycle machinery from human cells can replace that found in yeast.[15] The same is true of components that control the organization of the cell's cytoskeleton,[16] RNA splicing,[17] protein degradation,[18] protein synthesis,[19] and the regulation of gene expression.[20] Or consider the RNA polymerase, the multi-component molecular machine that synthesizes the RNA using DNA as a template. One team of researchers sought to replace individual components of yeast RNA polymerase with their corresponding components from human cells. They concluded:

> Overall, a total of six of the seven human subunits tested previously or in this study are able to substitute for their yeast counterparts *in vivo*, underscoring the remarkable similarities between the transcriptional machineries of lower and higher eukaryotes.[21]

Even though evolution is supposed to be inherently unpredictable, as we can see, it has occurred within a very predictable biological matrix.

SELECTING YOUR SURROGATES

If we return to the *in vitro* selection procedures, recall that the researcher acts as a custodian over a large population of random molecules, essentially fishing out what he is looking for by providing the right molecular bait. The fishing metaphor is useful. When fishing, certain baits work better at catching certain types of fish. A fisherman trying to catch trout can front-load the successful accomplishment of his objective by choosing the right fishing spot and the right bait. The lab logic is not much different. Consider one set of experiments where researchers were looking for a protein that could bind the molecule ATP.[22] They generated 6×10^{12} random proteins (each protein was about eighty amino acids in length) and incubated them with an inert substance that was attached to an ATP molecule. They took their pool of randomly generated proteins and essentially mixed it with the ATP, washed away the unbound material, retrieved the bound material, and then used the bound material to start the cycle over again. Basically, they attempted to purify this random population such that only those sequences able to specifically bind ATP remained. After eight rounds of this cycle, the fraction of random proteins that could bind ATP rose from 0.1 to 6.2 percent. At this point, the researchers decided to take a look at the sequences that were binding and found the binders to be dominated by four distinct families of proteins (none showed similarity to each other or any other biological protein). These four classes of ATP-binders bound ATP very weakly (in other words, the binders were about twenty times more likely to exist in an unbound state than bound to ATP). The researchers then switched gears. They used a common method to introduce single mutations into the amino acid sequence of the ATP-binders for three consecutive rounds, at a mutagenic rate of 3.7 percent per amino acid for each round. After these three cycles of mutagenesis, the researchers went back to the original procedure and found one of the four classes to predominate, having a modest improvement in binding.

The whole experiment is an intelligent use of chance. First, you fish out the proteins that weakly express a function you are trying to find, which is easily accomplished by using the function itself as bait in the pool, cleansing away all the other sequences that do not meet your criteria. Once the candidates are isolated, you start over with them, but this time, the bait is more complex, as it is not merely the function, but also includes the sequence of the binder. The mutation steps that followed were built around a strategy that kept most of the identified sequence constant while tweaking on its periphery. The result was the isolation of a protein with improved function.

Life's designer may have also made intelligent use of chance. Only in this case, the "bait" was not a simple molecule like ATP, nor a single complex of ATP and a protein. Instead, the bait could have been the entire cell, or set of heterogeneous cells. What the blind watchmaker could subsequently find was then constrained by the carefully chosen initial conditions. Just as the researchers, as artificial selectors, set up their *in vitro* selection experiment such that it was rigged to find ATP-binding proteins, so too may life's initial conditions have been rigged by the design of the cell's architecture and the choice of which components to employ. In such a case, this chosen state would then act as the surrogate for the artificial selector.

What type of proteins might a designer choose when designing the first evolution-ready cells? Imagine a hypothetical protein built from 100 amino acids that elicits function F. In a rather simplified manner, let us think of proteins as containing information. Say, for example, that in order to elicit F, a specific sequence of all of the 100 amino acids is needed, such that a single mistake, at any place in the sequence, eliminates F. We can think of such a protein as a high-information protein, because in order to elicit F, the amino acid at each of the 100 positions must be specified. At the other extreme end of the scale, imagine we can get F without specifying any of the 100 positions. We can consider this a low-information protein, as the function F is not dependent on the sequence. Any sequence of 100 amino acids would elicit function F. So there are two extremes of information content: one where all 100 positions must be specified and one where none of the positions needs specifying. From here, we think of a continuum, where F depending on the specification of ninety positions is toward the high end and F depending on only 10 positions is toward the low end. What type of proteins should be used to front-load evolution? High-information proteins or low-information proteins?

The answer is neither, as reliance on proteins that draw solely from both ends of the information content continuum can be counterproductive to front-loading. Consider the high-information proteins. Imagine a cell that is constructed such that every amino acid in every one of its proteins was essential. This is a terrible design. The cell might be a marvel to look at, but it would also be incredibly fragile. A *single* amino acid substitution, as a consequence of mutation, in *any* one of the cell's components would be fatal. Since mutation is inevitable, the cell has been designed such that it cannot propagate over any serious period of time. If every position in every protein is essential for the cell's survival, then there is no room for adaptation. Every single mutation would be deleterious and selected against. The cell would be like an ice sculpture of a hammer—frozen, fragile, and useless.

At the other end of the spectrum are cells built around low-information proteins. Suppose a cell is constructed whose protein functions do not depend on the sequence of amino acids. Is this a plausible design strategy? First, such a design is probably not possible. If protein function was completely independent of amino acid sequence, it would stand to reason that the number of protein functions that exist would be extremely limited and insufficient to carry out the activities of life. All proteins, with all kinds of different sequences, would have the same functions. The only thing that might distinguish them would be their different sizes.

Second, low-information proteins may be ineffective at carrying out certain design objectives over time. The function of front-loading is to enlist the service of the blind watchmaker in fulfilling the objectives of the design. But with low-information proteins, the designer ends up competing against the blind watchmaker in an attempt to propagate the design signal through the noise. This is because it would be easy for chance to generate such proteins. Consider a 100 amino acid protein where only five positions need to be specified to elicit the function. Since there are twenty different amino acids, there is a one in twenty chance for each amino acid to end up at the right place. The chance of this appearing with all five is 3.125×10^{-07}. It has been estimated that there are 5×10^{30} bacteria on our planet.[23] If an average of 2000 different proteins per cell is assumed, that is 1×10^{34} bacterial proteins. Even though the global pool of bacterial proteins is redundant (due to evolutionary descent) and not truly random, it is likely large enough to spawn a protein that depends on only five amino acids being properly specified. Since low-information proteins could easily be generated by chance, the blind watchmaker is likely to replace a designed protein with something that was subsequently generated by chance.

Third, there is no need to design functions that depend on such low-information proteins. Since they are easily generated by chance, life's designer could rely on chance and the blind watchmaker to spit them out on a continual basis.

Given these considerations, a front-loading designer would probably opt for mid-level information proteins. By moving away from the high end of the spectrum, the designer imparts robustness to the components. The proteins can tolerate insults yet still carry out their objectives. Furthermore, since the components must propagate over great spans of time, one might expect most components to eschew the high end of the information spectrum. Yet to keep the design signal from being drowned out by evolutionary noise, the designer should choose various proteins that also eschew the low end of the spectrum. Perhaps there is an optimal information level that functions to carry the signal across time, yet is robust enough to resist deleterious mutations incurred along the way.

What type of proteins does life use? We can begin to address such a question because scientists have determined the sequence of over 100 bacterial genomes, making it possible to compare all the protein toolkits. Let us begin with *Escherichia coli*, a bacterium that has been the workhorse of microbiologists and molecular biologists for decades. *E. coli* contains 4247 protein coding genes.[24] When the genome from *E. coli* is compared to that of another bacterium, known as *Salmonella typhimurium*, 3643 of *E. coli*'s genes have a close match in *Salmonella*.[25] These 3643 shared proteins all show more than 40% similarity in amino acid sequence. When the shared proteins are compared with each other, and scored in terms in their sequence similarity, the results are shown in Figure 7-1a.[26] Almost 60 percent of the shared proteins have an amino acid sequence that is more than 90 percent similar. In fact, close to 75 percent of the proteins have an amino acid sequence that is more than 80 percent similar. This would seem to indicate that most of the proteins used by these two species of bacteria are high-information proteins, as it looks as if more than 80 percent of the amino acid positions are resistant to mutation. But this would be misleading, as *E. coli* and *Salmonella* are very

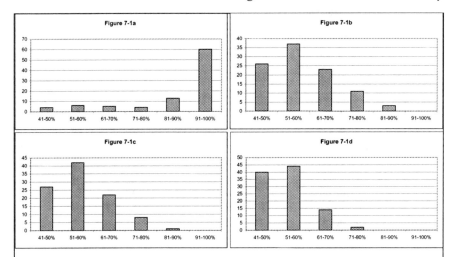

Figure 7-1. Frequency of Conservation among Shared Proteins. Graph "a" represents a comparison of *E. coli* proteins that are similar to *Salmonella* proteins. The X-axis groups proteins according to the percent of amino acids shared and the Y-axis represents the percent of proteins that display the given amino acid sequence similarity. Graph "b" compares *E. coli* proteins with those from four other proteobacteria. Graph "c" compares *E. coli* proteins with seven other eubacteria. Graph "d" compares *E. coli* proteins with four other archaebacteria.

closely related, having diverged from each other about 120 million to 160 million years ago.[27] There simply may not have been enough time to change the non-essential amino acids, so the 80+ percent sequence similarity is not a good indicator of functional requirement.

So let us track further back in time and give the mutations more opportunity to erase. Both *E. coli* and *Salmonella* belong to a very successful group of bacteria known as proteobacteria, which must have come into existence long before the common ancestor of *E. coli* and *Salmonella*. This group of bacteria is so diverse that microbiologists break it up into groups known as alpha, beta, gamma, delta, and epsilon. *E. coli* and *Salmonella* belong to the gamma division. So what happens when we compare *E. coli's* proteins to those of bacteria representing each of the other four divisions? In this case, we find 1549 of *E. coli's* proteins among these four groups.[28] The results are shown in Figure 7-1b. The largest group of shared proteins shows 51-60 percent sequence similarity. In fact, 70 percent of the shared proteins have 41-70 percent sequence similarity. The bulk of the shared bacterial proteins thus seem to be the mid-level information proteins we expected from the hypothesis of front-loading.

But what if we tracked even further back in time to see the results of mutation? Proteobacteria are just one group among all eubacteria and must have diverged from common ancestral strains even earlier. So let us compare *E. coli's* proteins to the proteins expressed by various members of the most distantly related bacteria, such that we are effectively back to the last common ancestor of all eubacteria. Here I used seven extremely different bacteria that, on average shared 1393 of *E. coli's* proteins.[29] Those results are shown in Figure 7-1c and, remarkably, the pattern is almost exactly the same as that seen with proteobacteria. The most common set of proteins are those that share 51-50 percent sequence similarity, and 64 percent of the shared proteins have 51-70 percent sequence similarity.

Finally, what if we compared *E. coli's* proteins to the most distantly related group of bacteria of all? This group, known as archaebacteria, typically exists in extreme environments and is believed to have diverged from eubacteria billions of years ago, not far from the origin of life itself. Four distantly related members of archaebacteria were used that, on average, express 868 of *E. coli*'s proteins.[30] Given the tremendous difference between *E. coli* and archaebacteria, it is not surprising they share only 868 proteins. Yet as Figure 7-1d demonstrates, the most common group of shared proteins is that which has 51-60 percent sequence similarity. Whether the proteins from *E. coli* are compared to those of other proteobacteria, all eubacteria, or even archaebacteria,[31] it appears the bulk of shared proteins are mid-level information proteins, just as we might expect if front-loading has occurred. The functions these proteins elicit are apparently dependent on roughly half the amino acid positions being constrained, while the other half are free to mutate, conferring a degree of robustness.

If cells were designed to front-load evolution, a heterogeneous mix of low-, mid-, and high-level information proteins may have been utilized to balance the demands of flexibility and versatility with an attempt to propagate a design signal. While a genome loaded with high-information proteins would render cells fragile, a genome could be peppered with carefully chosen high-information proteins that would significantly constrain and even steer evolution for an extremely long period of time.

Eukaryotes provide a nice illustration of maximally exploiting a relatively small set of high-information proteins. Consider three different proteins that are universally found among eukaryotes: histone, actin, and ubiquitin. If the amino acid sequence of these proteins from humans and baker's yeast are compared, we find a stunning lack of change since the two split over a billion years ago. With histone H4, 90 percent of the positions contain identical amino acids and with another histone protein, H3, 83 percent are the same. A similar situation exists with actin, where 88% of the positions have identical amino acids. Finally, ubiquitin is the most impressive, where 96% of the positions have the same amino acid. All of these proteins play important and wide-reaching roles in the cell. The two histones associate with the DNA and package it in a condensed form. As such, not only do they play crucial roles in organizing the DNA, they regulate access to the DNA, thereby influencing gene expression. Actins are important cytoskeletal proteins, playing a role in organizing the contents of the cell and even participating in cell movement. Ubiquitin is a molecular tag that is attached to other proteins, marking them for destruction. This protein thus plays a role in the general economy of protein content and is crucially involved in such tasks as cell division, removal of defective material, gene regulation, and even the development of embryos. These three proteins contribute much to the identity of the eukaryotic cell and have likely shaped its evolution in profound ways.

MULTI-TASKING

It is time to face the most serious problem for the hypothesis that evolution is front-loaded—*noise*. We have seen there are ways we can generally direct evolution as a consequence of carefully choosing our starting material and original architecture. In one sense, if life is designed—and designed quite well—some amount of front-loading is inevitable and is a direct consequence of the designed solutions that are implemented. I will call this passive front-loading. With passive front-loading, ancient designs are retained for billions of years, even expressing themselves in new contexts while not being significantly improved upon by this immense span of evolutionary tinkering. Extremely useful, high-information proteins and protein complexes, along with the cell's basic architecture and the genetic code constitute passive front-loading, as a designer could count on them being present in the descendants of the originally designed state. On the other hand, front-loading may entail anticipation at the hands of the designer. I will call this active front-loading. With active front-loading, the original life forms are designed to reach for some particular future state. Active front-loading may play off the passive front-loading, and involve some "unpacking" of a previously hidden design.

Since the history of evolution is one filled with contingency, it would seem that we can no more design evolution such that mammals would appear about 200 million years ago and radiate into our more familiar groups about 65 million years ago (after dinosaurs went extinct) than we could design human history such that Michael Behe would win the Pennsylvania lottery on January 8, 2008. But then again, front-loading does not need to specify a time and place in the future. And the actual intended outcome of the front-loading remains an area yet to be explored and investigated. So let us consider a heuristic example that may clarify some ways a designer could reach into the future amid the evolutionary noise.

How might it be possible to indirectly design a mammal-like organism by designing single-celled life forms? Because of their size and metabolism, mammal-like organisms are going to require many things not necessary to single-celled organisms, for example, plenty of oxygen to drive the electron-transport chain (something that was also designed and expected to be passed on due to passive front-loading). So part of the design problem is providing a means of delivering this oxygen to all the cells of a multi-cellular creature while you are crafting a uni-cellular creature. This would include something akin to blood and a means of delivering the blood. It is a hard problem, but we have to start somewhere.

Because of your extensive understanding of protein biochemistry, say you have found or designed something like globin, a spectacular blood protein that serves the purpose of oxygen delivery almost perfectly. Globin, which is used only in the red blood cells, has the ability to reversibly bind oxygen, making it useful for picking up oxygen, delivering it, and unloading it. So you endow some of your original life forms with globin to be used millions of years later in the blood of some mammal-like organism. Now you face the full brunt of the design problem. Unless globin serves your original microbes, it is functionless. If it is functionless, natural selection will not remove the mutations from the population of microbes. Effectively, your globin gene could be called junk DNA and would decay rapidly into oblivion. So how do you preserve the globin for hundreds of millions of years so that it is present when the biosphere is ready to evolve mammal-like organisms? Worse yet, how do you design the machinery for blood vessel formation in a single-celled organism without blood or blood vessels? Do not despair, there are strategies.

In his book, *The Mechanical Design Process*, engineer David Ullman discusses the fact that a single component of any design may carry out multiple functions. To illustrate this, he uses something as mundane as a bicycle's handlebars:

> They are a single component that serves many functions. They allow for steering (a verb that tells us *what* the device does), and they support upper-body weight (again, a function telling what the han-

dlebars do). Further, they not only support the brake levers but also transform (another function) the gripping force to a pull on the brake cable. The shape of the handlebars and their relation with other components determine *how* they provide all these different functions.[32]

This basic fact about design could be exploited to partially solve our design problem. We could simply design proteins with the capability or potential to carry out multiple functions. The proteins could be designed such that one function serves uni-cellular life while another function serves a multi-cellular task. As long as the multiple functions are encoded by the same sequence of amino acids, selection will maintain the sequence necessary for uni-cellular life, thus indirectly preserving the multi-cellular function to be exploited when multi-cellular states appear.

Consider a protein known as platelet-derived endothelial cell growth factor (PD-ECGF). This protein is an extra-cellular protein, meaning it is produced in the cell, but exported outside the cell to fulfill its function. It is classified as a growth factor (it promotes the growth and development of other cells) and its basic biological function is listed as "cellular communication and signal transduction."[33] In humans, it is expressed in the liver, placenta, the lining of the uterus, skin cells, and platelets (specialized cells that circulate in the blood and help clot the blood when needed). PD-ECGF specifically functions as a signal to stimulate blood vessel growth and maintenance of the blood vessel linings. How in the world could you design PD-ECGF and place it in a uni-cellular organism without having it mutate into oblivion before blood vessels evolved? PD-ECGF is actually a common metabolic enzyme known as thymidine phosphorylase,[34] found in eubacteria, archaebacteria, and eukaryotes. The enzyme plays a basic housekeeping role in modifying the nucleotides used by DNA. It is a little over 300 amino acids in length and 46 percent of the positions contain the same amino acids in the proteins from *E. coli* and humans (another mid-level information protein). The solution in this case is simple. Express the protein inside the cell and it functions in the metabolism of nucleotides. Express it outside the cell and it can act as a signal to promote the growth of blood vessels. Since all cells require nucleotides, PD-ECGF's potential activity has always been with life.

The PD-ECGF story is not atypical. In fact, Constance Jeffery of the University of Illinois at Chicago refers to such proteins as moonlighting proteins.[35] T. Ramasarma, from the Department of Biochemistry at the Indian Institute of Science, prefers to call them multi-functional proteins.[36] Shelley D. Copley, an associate professor of molecular, cellular, and developmental biology at the University of Colorado, notes, "Moonlighting is a clever mechanism for generation of complexity using existing proteins without requiring expansion of the genome."[37]

Consider gephyrin, a protein that is expressed in the lungs, kidneys, liver, spinal cord, and brain.[38] Its function in the brain is well-known, where it anchors various receptors involved in the transmission of signals between brain cells. Gephyrin itself is a protein that is inserted into the membrane and can interact not only with other receptors, but also various components of the cell's cytoskeleton. Gephyrin also functions as an enzyme that synthesizes something known as the molybdenum co-factor (Moco), an important component of many different metabolic enzymes.[39] Gephyrin can even substitute for the normal Moco activities found in plants and bacteria! Copley describes gephyrin's function as follows:

> The function of gephyrin at post-synaptic membranes is likely to be unrelated to its catalytic abilities; rather, it appears that the structure of gephyrin is ideally suited for forming a regular scaffold on which other proteins may assemble.[37]

Then there is the SMCD protein, involved in sticking replicated chromosomes together just prior to cell division. When secreted from mammalian cells, it is known as bamacam, a protein that plays a core role in the extra-cellular protein environment of tissues.[40]

Yet another example of a moonlighting protein is the enzyme, phosphoglucose isomerase (PGI). This enzyme plays a crucial role in the widespread metabolic pathway known as glycolysis, found in creatures ranging from bacteria to humans. But when it is secreted from cells, it acts as a signal involved in many important roles in animals. PGI can stimulate certain white blood cells to produce antibodies, stimulate nerve growth, and stimulate cell migration.[40]

Another glycolytic enzyme, phosphoglycerate kinase, produces angiostatin, an inhibitor of blood vessel growth, when secreted.[41] Another glycolytic enzyme, pyruvate kinase, can bind a hormone produced by the thyroid gland, T3, apparently allowing the hormone to influence metabolism.[42] The glycolytic enzyme enolase also moonlights as an essential component of a molecular machine that shreds unneeded or defective RNA.[43] What is more, enolase, along with a whole set of other metabolic enzymes, also function as crystallins, proteins expressed in the lens of the eye that help focus light.[41] Another enzyme, fumarate hydratase, an enzyme in the Krebs citric acid cycle can also function to suppress the formation of tumors.[40]

The list of moonlighting proteins is quite impressive and getting larger every day. Ramasarma provides a list of fifty-six examples.[36] What is remarkable is that there is no solid method or test for identifying moonlighting proteins, as scientists have largely discovered them through serendipity. The hypothesis of front-loading would predict these fifty-six examples are just the tip of the iceberg. In fact, because of their telic utility, a front-loading perspective predicts that multi-functional proteins will turn out to be commonplace.

The multi-functional nature of many proteins can be unlocked across time. A designer could implement one of the protein's functions in service of uni-cellular life, while the other functions remain "in-waiting" for the appearance of the proper context for their expression. We know, for example, the multiple functions of various proteins are often unleashed as a function of location. A different function can be unlocked by localizing the protein in a different place in the cell,[44] by localizing the protein outside of the cell, or by localizing the protein in a different type of cell. For example, a protein may function differently depending on whether it is expressed in a skin cell or a nerve cell. The different locations simply provide the arena for the alternative functions to express themselves. Thus, it is not unreasonable to hypothesize that a protein designed to fulfill the needs of a protozoan would also contain a design to serve the needs of a muscle cell billions of years later. As long as the multiple functions are linked by structure and sequence, the alternative function will always be available to evolution. In fact, the inherent alternative function may serve as the "bait" to fish out other useful variants (as in the *in vitro* experiments) in a manner that fully unleashes the alternative function.

DESIGNED TO REDESIGN

A design theme that emerges from multi-functional proteins is the potential to bury secondary designs within a primary design. Then, when the proper context arises, the secondary design emerges in either a fully functional form or as bait to fish out components offered up by a random walk. Functions designed for the future are deposited and then carried into the future. Evolution is rigged. Yet buried designs have deeper implications. A designer could, for instance, design a protein with one function such that another particular function, or specific set of functions, are easily accessible by a random walk of mutations. The first function may serve the original state while the later ones become useful in a more complex state. In a sense, the gene itself is rigged to evolve other specific interactions, resulting in the emergence of other functions at a later time.

There are at least two problems when trying to channel the evolution of a gene and its products. First, we must still cope with the manner in which mutations, over time, may erase the positions needed to predispose the original gene toward reaching its intended future state. Second, since the new functions must be unleashed by mutational changes (rather than being inherent as with moonlighting proteins), how can we increase the chance that such mutations would occur when needed?

Both of these design problems are solved by a process that just happens to be a major driving force of evolution—gene duplication.[45] In fact, gene duplication appears to be the primary means by which evolution spawns new functional proteins and new body plans. The principle behind gene duplication is straightforward (see Figure 7-2). Imagine a gene that codes for a protein that carries out some essential function, A. There are several mechanisms that can eventually make a carbon copy of the gene (by itself or as part of a group). Now that there are two copies of the gene, the hands of evolution are untied. The original gene can continue providing the needed function A as before. But the new copy is free to acquire mutations. If the mutations destroy the functional capability of the gene's product, then the copy will simply decay into non-existence. But if a mutation confers some shift in function (or even a new function) that is beneficial, selection will retain and propagate this copy.

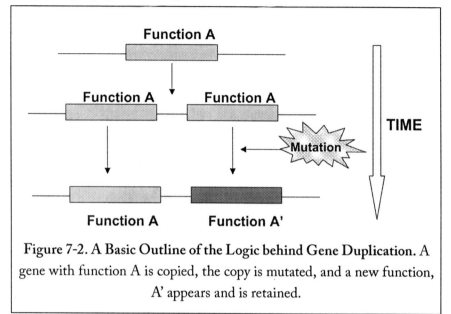

Figure 7-2. A Basic Outline of the Logic behind Gene Duplication. A gene with function A is copied, the copy is mutated, and a new function, A' appears and is retained.

Gene duplication, over time, can take a single gene and turn it into a family of related genes, often carrying out similar but refined functions. One among many such families is the kinesin family. Kinesins are motor proteins that use ATP to generate mechanical force, often shuttling cargo back and forth within cells. They are both specific to and ubiquitous among eukaryotes. Gene duplication has split an original kinesin sequence into some ten distinct families, each carrying out specialized roles.[46] When it comes to multi-functional proteins, the duplication event, followed by divergence, could separate an original protein with functions A and B and create two proteins, one optimized for function A and the other optimized for function B. For example, gene duplication has exploited the multi-functional state of the crystallins much in this fashion.[47]

Gene duplication solves the design problems cited above simply because cells can retain the core designed state while the duplicate is free to mutate and explore new solutions. As long as the original is effectively retained,[48] the pathway to the new function is retained and propagated. It is a beautiful solution for a front-loading designer. In one process, we both propagate the original design and set things up to unpack secondary designs without erasing the original design. Stability and change, all in one package. As an added bonus, the influence of contingency is dampened. It does not matter if some or many gene duplication events drift off in unintended fashion (most will merely tweak the original function or decay away). The beauty of gene duplication is that it explores sequence space *while retaining and propagating the original sequence.* As long as the original sequence is essentially retained somewhere, someplace, evolution gets to "try again" over and over and over in its rigged search for some future design. In other words, if a designer wanted a secondary design to unpack itself in an animal cell, duplication of the original sequence is bound to happen in all cells, including animal cells. When it eventually occurs in an animal cell, the stage is set to unpack the secondary design. If it fails, we need only wait until the next round of duplication and mutation occurs. It is the intelligent use of chance.

Allan Force, from the Virginia Mason Research Center, adds another twist to the story of gene duplication that reinforces its great potential for front-loading.[49] Force and co-workers begin by considering not only the gene, but also the upstream regulatory modules that control the gene's expression (time and place-dependent). They then propose that after gene duplication, no new function emerges, but instead "subfunctionalization" occurs where one regulatory module may be lost in one gene, while another regulatory module (but not the same one) is lost in the other gene. As a result, the organism now requires both copies of the gene to ensure it will be expressed properly. As a nice example, they cite the gene pair eng1 and eng1b from zebrafish. Eng1 is expressed in the pectoral appendage bud, while eng1b is expressed in a specific set of neurons in the hindbrain. Yet examination of the unduplicated gene (En1) in different animals (mice and chicken) is expressed in both the pectoral appendage buds and hindbrain ganglia. Thus, gene duplication did not give rise to novel functions, but instead simply partitioned the functions associated with the original gene (eng1 lost the ability to be expressed in neurons and eng1b lost the ability to be expressed in the hindbrain). Since expression is needed in both places, zebrafish must keep both genes. Subfunctionalization, through gene duplication, clearly is a process quite friendly to front-loading, as it is consistent with an originally designed complex state that can be teased apart over time in a manner that channels evolution.

Flexibility

Another way to facilitate the front-loading of evolution is to design life such that it is effectively modular. Modularity is an important concept in robotics, computer programming, and engineering. For example, Hunt Engineering, a hardware supplier that designs solutions for imaging, RADAR, SONAR, communications, and other processing intensive applications, describes their approach as follows:

> We use a **modular** approach wherever possible so that we can **re-use** technology that we develop in a very wide variety of systems. All of our modular products are designed to be as **flexible** as possible so that they might address the needs of many different customers.[50] (bold not added)

Thomas Hansen, from Florida State University, explains:

> Indeed, modularity is a basic principle of good programming. Engineers have learned to design robust and flexible programs by dividing the task up into a set of modules, subroutines or objects, with simple well-defined interfaces.[51]

Modules can be viewed as building blocks or subsystems that function with a degree of independence from the overall system. If life was designed, and our analogy to human design is substantial, then we would predict life would be modular. And there is plenty of evidence that indicates it is.[52] A striking example was mentioned above—we can take the human cell cycle machinery and plug some of it into the architectural context of a yeast cell and still get function. But how does modularity help our designer front-load evolution?

Modularity enhances evolution and thus the perpetuation of design. Since life is built around discrete modules that interface with each other, it is possible for selection to fine tune one module independent of the others. The alternative is to have every component linked with every other component in such an intricate manner that changes in one component may resonate in deleterious fashion with multiple other components. Because of modularity, the blind watchmaker can expand and/or tailor individual modules to meet the specific needs of the organism with minimal effect on the remainder of the organism's physiology.

Even though the actual specific objectives of front-loading are not known, a survey of the possibilities outlined earlier in this chapter all have one thing in common—they begin with a pool of uni-cellular life forms and reach for a more complex state. It is thus reasonable to hypothesize that complexity was front-loaded. Whether it is the complexity of a mere multi-cellular state or the complexity of a more specified mammal-like creature, the common theme of increased complexity emerges. And that raises another design problem for our front-loading designer.

Ronald Fisher was probably the first scientist to help merge the science of Mendel's genetics with Darwin's Theory of Evolution. Yet he helped highlight a problem with the evolution of increased complexity. Evolutionary biologist H. Allen Orr, from the University of Rochester, explains it as follows:

> In his classic discussion of adaptation in *The Genetical Theory of Natural Selection*, Fisher calculated the probability that random mutations of a given phenotypic size would be favorable, famously showing that this probability falls rapidly: Small mutations are reasonably likely to be favorable, but large ones are not. Indeed very large mutations suffer vanishingly small chances of being advantageous. But Fisher further showed that mutations of a given size are less likely to be favorable in complex than simple organisms. The reason is intuitively clear: A random mutation of some size is more likely to disrupt (not improve) a complex than simple organism for the same reason a random change of some size is more likely to disrupt (not

improve) a complex than simple machine. Changing the length of an arbitrary mechanical part by one inch, for instance, is more likely to derail the function of a microscope than a hammer.[53]

Orr then analyzed Fisher's argument in more mathematical detail and reached the same conclusion. "Given the same size mutations and the same total strength of natural selection, complex organisms cannot adapt as quickly as simpler ones," he writes, and describes this as the "cost of complexity." This should not be interpreted to mean that complexity cannot evolve. As Orr explains:

> It must be emphasized, however, that the cost identified here need not preclude the evolution of more complex forms. The point is merely that organismal complexity *is* attended by costs of calculable magnitude. But there may well be other, and perhaps more than compensatory, ecological advantages to complexity (e.g., the ability to invade specialized niches) that are not reflected in such population genetic calculations.[53]

However, the ability to invade specialized niches would not be a particularly useful strategy for a front-loading designer to depend upon. Not only are specialized niches often heavily dependent on contingency, they tend to be dead-ends in evolution. For example, one study of bacterial evolution in the lab showed "niche specialization may come with a cost of reduced potential to diversify."[54]

One way to address the cost of complexity is through modularity, which essentially simplifies an organism. Instead of having fifty genes (for example) smeared across the genome all contributing to a trait (while also contributing to dozens of other traits), a genetic module devoted to the trait becomes less entangled and convoluted, thus less complex. Orr himself raises this as a possible solution, arguing that by "bundling" characters, you effectively reduce the number of independent characters in an organism. He also notes that Gunter Wagner, from the Department of Ecology and Evolutionary Biology at Yale University, has made a strong case that modularity imparts just this advantage.

When we combine the features of multi-functional proteins, gene duplications generating new functions and teasing apart old functions, along with the modular essence of life, this opens the door for another powerful means of generating evolutionary novelty—cooption. This is essentially a change in function by finding a *new* use for an existing feature. As intelligent beings, we constantly make use of cooption. For example, during one summer, I put a new roof on my house. Like many others before me, I used a garden tool to rip off the old shingles—the shovel. In other words, while the shovel is designed for digging up dirt, it is extremely useful for the purpose of roofing. Not only does it scoop up old shingles, but because of its design, it provides the useful leverage for prying the shingles and nails from the wood of the old roof. While this type of cooption, by chance, is not uncommon in our experience, engineers can build with cooption in mind, as one advantage of the modular design is that it allows designers to reuse the modules in different contexts.

In biological evolution, cooption is believed to have been very important. As the great evolutionary biologist Ernst Mayr noted, "Most evolutionary changes take place without the origin of new structures. Even when we compare birds or mammals with their strikingly different reptilian ancestors, we are astonished at how few are the truly new structures . . . . By far the most important principle in the interpretation of the origin of new structures is that of the "change of function."[55] Cooption goes by many names, including co-optation, recruitment, and functional shift.

If cooption is the action verb, the trait generated by cooption is said to be an exaptation.[56] The teleological flavor inherent in cooption can be appreciated from the fact that the term exaptation was intended to replace an older term, namely, preadaptation. As biologists Maria Ganfornina and Deigo Sanchez point out, "The term preadaptation itself has often been criticized because of its teleological connotation."[57] If one trait is preadapted for another nonexistent trait, one gets the impression that the future was somehow planned. Yet a teleologist can hardly consider this a substantive criticism. Might there be some exaptations that are true examples of preadaptations? It is not necessary for a teleologist to explain all cooption events as exaptations, but there surely may be examples where certain cooption events were rigged to happen.

Cooption is clearly a mechanism that a front-loading designer would exploit. The phenomena of new functions emerging from old functions can be understood and designed to eventually happen, especially with the help of modularity, multi-functional proteins, gene duplication and divergence. And what makes it all the more plausible is the lack of diversity among the cellular components and functions of life. Ganfornina and Sanchez point out a well-known fact in biology, re-emphasized by the sequencing of genomes (see above):

> . . . the immense biodiversity we see around us is generated from a set of conserved building blocks. Generation of building blocks *de novo* seems to be rare after the initial set originated early in the history of life. Instead, life invents by modification, duplication, and functional changes of the available blocks.[57]

Paleontologist Simon Conway-Morris echoes the same theme:

> . . . the diversity of life is, in molecular terms, little more than skin deep. Most, perhaps all, of the basic building blocks necessary for organismal complexity were available long before the emergence of multi-cellularity.[58]

Conway-Morris also adds the concept of "molecular inherency," where "a gene known to be of major importance in organogenesis in a higher animal also occurs in a more primitive group." All of this speaks to front-loading, where cooption exploits and draws out the potential of the front-loaded state. Perhaps the phenomenon of cooption is not always an evolutionary "free-for-all" but instead occurs under high-order constraints. For example, Conway-Morris quotes two other scientists who "gently question received orthodoxy by reminding us that cooption of genes might be analogous to plugging of particular computer 'chips' into a new program." The "program" itself may not be the product of cooption, but was instead designed to make use of cooption. The abstract of one scientific review paper on cooption ends as follows:

> We integrate this information with recent models of gene family

evolution to provide a framework for understanding the origin of co-optive evolution and the mechanisms by which natural selection promotes evolutionary novelty by inventing new uses for the genetic toolkit.[59]

But is natural selection always "inventing" new uses? Or has life been designed such that natural selection might find uses that were rigged to emerge? And if life finds the new uses in an approximate context they were designed to be useful in, natural selection would simply lock into place what was previously buried inside life.

At this point, let us finally return to the design problem of preserving that globin sequence for millions of years such that a mammal-like creature would be able to exploit it to deliver oxygen to its tissues. How do you preserve the globin for hundreds of millions of years so that it is present when the biosphere is ready to evolve mammal-like organisms? Well, there are three possible ways of doing this. First, you could give globin a function in microorganisms so that it would be propagated. Second, you could employ a protein very similar to globin in microorganisms, meaning it would be easy to evolve globin eventually through gene duplication and divergence. Third, you could use both strategies.

Globin occurs in all the kingdoms of living organisms, even though its distribution is episodic among the non-vertebrate groups in contrast to vertebrates. In bacteria, it is used for oxygen sensing and to control nitric oxide levels. Also, in some cyanobacteria, it is used to increase the efficiency of oxygenic photosynthesis. Yet the episodic distribution among microorganisms indicates that globin is not essential for microbial life, like it is for vertebrate life. Second, globins and certain cytochromes (proteins important in metabolism) have similar structures. Both bind a complex chemical factor called heme. Globins use the heme to bind oxygen while the cytochromes use the heme to bind electrons. If the designed globins were lost, they could be plausibly regenerated through duplication and divergence of the cytochromes.

The crucial point is that if a designer introduced cytochromes/globins into the original cells, they would not be surprised at all to find that a mammal-like creature, evolving billions of years later, also "just happened" to have built their circulatory systems around it. In fact, this may very well be what their models would have predicted.

The story gets more interesting when we consider the mammalian circulatory system. Its business end is gas exchange, where the blood brings oxygen to the tissues and picks up carbon dioxide from the tissues. There are three basic components to such gas exchange—flow of blood to the tissue, release of oxygen from the blood, and use of oxygen by the tissue cells. What is intriguing is that each one of these three basic steps is built around the heme-binding domain of a similar protein. First, the globins can bind and release the gas nitric oxide, where the release of this gas regulates blood flow through altering the contracted state of the vessel walls. Second, the globins also bind and release oxygen to the tissues. Third, the cells of the tissues use the oxygen in an essential metabolic process called the electron transport chain, which involve the cytochromes. Molecular properties, which can be designed, may serve to "guide" organismal evolution more than appreciated. In this case, the properties of designed proteins in bacteria have channeled evolution such that this three-component gas exchange would eventually emerge in a mammal-like creature and function as it does. The design of a protein may have front-loaded the appearance of a particular type of organ system that handled gas delivery and exchange.

Chance Favors the Prepared Genome

The genetic code itself may also have been used to front-load evolution. Because it is deeply buried in the matrix of life, such that the blind watchmaker would use rather than replace it, a front-loading designer has the assurance of its continued existence. We have seen that the genetic code works exceedingly well in preventing deleterious changes from occurring, thus enhancing the perpetuation of design and a passively front-loaded state. But could the code itself participate in the unpacking of buried designs?

While mutations are random with regard to an organism's fitness, they are not purely so. One way to appreciate this is to survey nucleotide changes in pseudogenes. These are thought to be functionless pieces of DNA, often the products of earlier gene duplications, in the process of decay. Since they are functionless, the variants that appear are not being pruned away by selection, thus providing us with a decent view of all the random changes happening to the DNA. If, for example, all mutations were equally likely, then the various A's, G's, C's and T's should be changed with a relatively equal frequency. But this is not the case. Consider Table 7-1, which shows the relative mutation rates involving each of the four nucleotides measured in sixteen different mammalian pseudogenes.[60] What we see is that the majority of substitutions are either a C being changed to T or a G being changed to A. This is actually the same mutation, as DNA's double helix means any given nucleotide is paired with another (where C pairs with G and T pairs with A). If the C changes to T, then the copying mechanisms of DNA mean the new strand will have an A instead of a G at the opposite position (since the A is needed to pair with the new T). The predominance of C-to-T mutations is seen in many other analyses using DNA from many different sources.[61] C-to-T mutations are clearly among the more common type of mutations and, in fact, may be the most common.[62]

Table 7-1. Relative Substitution Rates (%) In Mammalian Pseudogenes				
	Original Nucleotide			
Mutant Nucleotide	A	T	C	G
A	-	4.4	6.5	20.7
T	4.7	-	21.0	7.2
C	5.0	8.2	-	5.3
G	9.4	3.3	4.2	-

Why is the C-to-T mutation, technically called a transition, so much more common than most other base substitutions? The mutation occurs because the cytosine base is especially prone to a spontaneous chemical reaction known as deamination. In other words, the laws of chemistry impose a distinct trend on the mutation of DNA. A front-loading designer may have chosen the cytosine base for just this reason, as it would mean that any codon containing C would be more prone to mutation than codons lacking the base. Since codons code for amino acids, this might mean that certain amino acid substitutions were also more likely during evolution. Might the genetic code have been designed such that preference was given to certain amino acid substitutions, imposing yet another direction on evolution? The bias toward C-to-T transitions could be used to exploit a front-loaded state. For example, protein X could be designed to fulfill function A, but buried in the sequence of X is the potential for function B (that is, function B is nearby in sequence space relative to sequence X/function A). A gene duplication, followed by exposure to the C-to-T mutational "stream," could unlock function B, if the original sequence X was specifically designed to be unlocked by such mutations. Chance favors the prepared genome.

With the front-loading hypothesis in mind, I decided to see how the genetic code would handle the C-to-T mutations. There are thirty-seven codons that contain at least one C. A single C-to-T transition expands this set to forty-eight codons (since some of the original codons had two or more C's). For example, the codon CCA generates CTA and TCA as a result of cytosine deamination. Of the forty-eight substitutions, seventeen do not change the amino acid that is coded. These are silent and can be ignored. Among the thirty-one changes, three convert the amino acid codon into a stop codon. This would cause the ribosome to prematurely halt synthesis of the protein. Finally, twenty-eight substitutions result in amino acid changes. So what happens when the amino acid is changed as a result of the C-to-T mutations in the gene?

If we focus on these twenty-eight substitutions, the pool of codons containing at least one cytosine code for eight of the twenty amino acids. The pool resulting from the twenty-eight C-to-T transitions contains nine amino acids. When the two pools are compared, a striking difference is noted (see Figure 7-3). The amino acid pool used by the mutant sequences is far more hydrophobic than the original pool. Recall that the twenty amino acids differ in several chemical respects. Some amino acids are hydrophobic, or oily, while others are hydrophilic and readily dissolve in water. Over the years, scientists have measured the hydrophobicity of amino acids using all sorts of methods and arranged them on a scale ranging from most hydrophobic to least (most hydrophilic). There is often a good bit of disagreement among parts of the scales, as the results often depend to some degree on the method of analysis. Nevertheless, if you average all the positions from forty-three different scales, you get a mean Hydrophobicity Scale with the

following progression from most to least hydrophobic—IFLVMWCYAH-
GTPSRNQEDK (where each letter of the alphabet represents one of the
twenty amino acids).[63] In this case, the most hydrophobic amino acid is
isoleucine (I) and the most hydrophilic amino acid is lysine (K).

If you look at Figure 7-3, the scale is represented twice. The amino acids
highlighted in the upper row are those coded by C-containing codons. The
amino acids highlighted in the bottom row are those coded after the C has
been converted to T by deamination. Note that the original pool (from the
top row) is predominantly represented by hydrophilic amino acids, but with
a somewhat disordered arrangement. But look what happens as a consequence of the C-to-T mutational stream. The pool is essentially converted to
an ordered cluster of the eight most hydrophobic amino acids! Notice also
(from the connecting arrows) that each change is associated with an increase
in hydrophobicity. We can therefore call this the Increased Hydrophobicity
Effect (IHE). The sole exception is the proline (P) to serine (S) substitution,
which I shall explain in a moment.

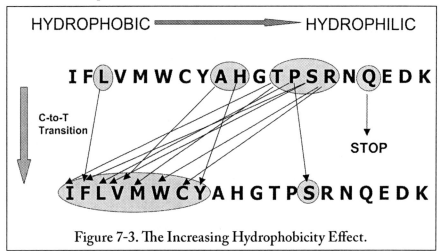

Figure 7-3. The Increasing Hydrophobicity Effect.

What might be the significance of the IHE? Hydrophobic amino acids
have long been recognized as an essential driving force in protein folding,
where the linear strand of amino acids is folded into its distinct three-dimensional form. When proteins fold, they experience what is often called
a hydrophobic collapse, such that the oily amino acids tend to get buried in
the center of the protein while the hydrophilic amino acids tend to populate

its surface. A protein's three-dimensional structure can be viewed as having different levels of organization. For example, a stable complex of two distinct amino acid chains is referred to as the quaternary structure, where the two proteins interact via contacts on their respective surfaces. The distinct three-dimensional shape of a single amino chain is the tertiary structure. The tertiary structure, in turn, is built from an arrangement of lower-level secondary structures, including alpha helices (coiled structures), beta sheets (folded structures), and coils (disorganized linear strands). Since the IHE replaces hydrophilic residues with hydrophobic residues, and hydrophobicity is the driving force of protein folding, the IHE is a possible candidate for a built-in protein redesign mechanism. For example, it is known that a simple binary pattern of hydrophobic and hydrophilic amino acids can create a *de novo* alpha helix.[64] Almost every one of the substitutions swap from a pool that is largely indifferent to secondary structure, replacing it with a pool that is often involved in alpha helix and beta strand formation.[65] Furthermore, the new pool includes cysteine (C), raising the possibility that new interactions, called disulfide bonds, could form to help stabilize a modified form.[66]

But what about the proline (P) to serine (S) substitution? Remarkably, the same theme of protein redesign explains this change. Proline has long been known to be an amino acid that disrupts the alpha helix, while serine is indifferent to the formation. Thus, the only substitution that happens to violate the flow of increased hydrophobicity just happens to eliminate a serious hindrance to alpha helix formation. Finally, the IHE may be a mechanism that allows the proteins to stick together and form larger complexes, as there is plenty of data that support an important role for hydrophobic interactions as stabilizing forces that hold distinct proteins together.[67]

Such considerations allow for a provocative hypothesis: a set of originally designed proteins may have been designed such that they could exploit the effects of C-to-T transitions, in essence channeling original designs in a direction to increase the chances that a buried, secondary design is extracted. For example, proteins that played essential roles in the evolution of multicellularity may have been spawned from the IHE. This hypothesis makes a prediction that can be tested. For example, if the multi-cellular state was front-loaded with life's design, we would expect to find that conserved, multi-cellular-specific proteins have crucial FLIYWVMCS amino acid residues that can explained by C-to-T transitions relative to their ancestral state.

There are some remarkable features of this pattern of substitutions mediated by cytosine deamination. First, it occurs within a code that is optimized to minimize the effect of mutation. That is, while the code is typically working to prevent radical mutations, a specific segment of the code, reachable through one of the most common mutations, seems to amplify the existence of radical mutations. It is as if the code has built both a fence around mutations and a specific gate through which they can exit. What is more, cells have machinery that can work to both correct C-to-T mutations (an enzyme called uracil glycosylase) or to accelerate their occurrence (the enzyme cytidine deaminase). Might it be possible that such machinery itself could be controlled by the cell, such that the cell has the ability to turn the IHE on and off? For example, the cytidine deaminases play an important role in generating antibody diversity.[68]

Second, because of the dynamics involved in transcription, cytosine deamination is more pronounced among genes that are being expressed.[69] As a consequence, a specified set of mutated amino acids is being thrown at every transcribed gene. It is as if the proteins commonly used by living things are continually being coaxed to evolve. If such transcriptionally-activated evolution has played a significant role in the history of life, it would also be consistent with the hypothesis that the genetic code, protein synthesis, and DNA-based transcription all arose concomitantly, a view that cannot be entertained from a non-teleological perspective.

Third, cytosine deamination has a similar effect on RNA. Since RNA uses uracil (U) instead of thymine, the resulting mutation would be a C-to-U substitution. Stephen Holbrook, a chemist who works with RNA, has referred to uracil as the "universal partner in RNA structure" after finding that U can bind with any of the other bases in RNA.[70] Just as the hydrophobic amino acids play a crucial role in protein structure, thus function, uracil appears to play such a role in RNA structure and function. There is an apparent *conceptual* tie between the effects of cytosine deamination on protein and RNA structure/function. In both cases, the most common base substitution appears to have significant functional potential, as both hydrophobic amino acids and uracil seem to make the greatest impact on protein and RNA structure, respectively. It looks like an engineer is trying to extract a lot of evolution from using a simple nitrogenous base poised for change.[71]

Return of the Rabbit

Throughout this chapter, one might get the impression that I am trying to establish the reality of evolution as a front-loaded phenomenon. Yet all I am doing is giving the Rabbit his say. Many people have strange notions about design and evolution. If evolution was designed, it should not be so messy. It should not be characterized by so much contingency. There should not be so many extinctions and there should be a clear and distinct trend that leads specifically to humans. Yet what I have tried to show in this chapter is another way to view design in relation to evolution, where none of these objections succeed. And while we have spoken of human genomes and mammal-like animals, those examples were purely heuristic, helping the reader to visualize potential ways to design the future through the present. The perspective of the Design Matrix simply allows us to begin asking certain questions, start seeing things in new ways, and start developing ways to test our suspicions. Design can now come in two forms—the direct intervention comparable to human engineers in action and the indirect expression of such design through the medium of evolution.

While I have been trying to better illustrate the overall perspective of evolution's design, there are certain vantage points that allow us to consider it a serious contender in explaining life. When we compare the hypothesis of front-loaded evolution to the more conventional non-teleological perspective of Darwinian evolution, the former appears to have an explanatory edge. Consider the fact that evolution so thoroughly borrows from earlier functions. After noting that most of the proteins involved in gene regulation are multi-functional, and many of the mechanisms of development are deeply shared in very different organisms, biologists Denis Duboule and Adam Wilkins speculate as follows:

> Yet just how similar or how different the regulatory molecules and mechanisms might be between butterflies and bats was anyone's

guess. Most biologists, however, would probably have bet that the diversity and difference in the underlying molecular systems was the general rule.[72]

Such deep functional borrowing was indeed surprising to scientists. Yet from the perspective of front-loaded evolution, we would have indeed bet against molecular diversity and difference, as the more diversity and difference in the present, the more the present is cut off from the originally designed initial state. If design is to be propagated, and used to constrain and bait the evolution that follows, the signal of design cannot be swamped out by the evolutionary noise of too much diversity and difference. It must persist.

The explanatory edge that comes with the teleological view provides the ability to ask questions such as: Why does life reproduce? Why does life proofread? Why does evolution so thoroughly borrow from past functions? Why do proteins have multiple functions? Why is gene duplication the main means of generating new genes? Why, as the *New York Times* reporter noted, does the human genome seem to "have *almost too much in common* with many other kinds of animal genomes?"[8] The design of life such that it front-loads evolution answers all of these questions and ties them together. Life reproduces to perpetuate the designs, which give form and constraint to evolution. Such constraint is not a form of determinism or predestination, but is instead an outflow of the manner in which the cards were stacked.

When it comes to Darwinian evolution, there are important points to remember. Darwinian evolution does not necessarily entail that cooption, gene duplication, or multi-functionality must exist. Neither does it dictate that preadaptation must take place. This is because Darwinian evolution can exist without cooption, gene duplication, or preadaptation. Consider a mutation in a ribosomal gene that confers antibiotic resistance, the kind of thing that is selected and preserved. This is a classic example of Darwinian evolution. But it does not involve cooption. It does not involve gene duplication. It does not involve multi-functionality. And if we explain this as preadaptation, then we would essentially drain that concept of all its meaning. In other words, cooption and preadaptation do not necessarily follow from random variability culled by maximizing fitness. Cooption and preadap-

DESIGNING EVOLUTION

tation are phenomena that follow from the architecture of life itself. This architecture provides the potential for such phenomena and Darwinian evolution simply exploits this inherent potential as one way to maximize fitness. But Darwinian evolution would still exist without them. In contrast, it is very difficult to imagine front-loaded evolution without multi-functionality, gene duplication, cooption, and preadaptation, as these are just the type of mechanisms one would use to unmask secondary designs buried in primary designs. In fact, the hypothesis of front-loaded evolution predicts the existence of such mechanisms of evolution. Life itself, and its stem parts, was designed such that cooption and preadaptation would be made available to Darwinian evolution.

Many, still relying on the Traditional Template, are probably tempted to argue that front-loaded evolution should entail mechanisms other than those used by Darwinian evolution. This would be an attempt to isolate the Duck from the Rabbit. Yet front-loaded evolution is not necessarily an attempt to erase the Duck. It is a Gestalt shift that allows us to see the Duck in terms of the Rabbit. Front-loaded evolution is about how a designer might employ and exploit Darwinian evolution to carry out a design objective. In the end, scientists all agree on three basic facts: random mutations occur and generate variability; natural selection culls this variability in terms of fitness; and natural selection is myopic (so myopic that Dawkins labels this watchmaker "blind"). From here, the teleologist asks a question—how can one use these facts to carry out a design objective? How does one design X such that Darwinian evolution will eventually extract Y as a function of X? When you begin to ask such questions, you will begin to see the Rabbit.

References

1. It is important to highlight this as many might think the decision to focus on the origin of life is a decision to "hide" in the current ignorance of science in order to engage in a "god of the gaps" type of argument. The five reasons outlined above help us to appreciate that the origin of

life would be a very natural place to look for fingerprints of Intelligent Design.

2. Harold, F.M., 2001. *The Way of the Cell: Molecules, Organisms and the Order of Life*. Oxford University Press, Oxford, p. 11.

3. Watson, J.D. and Crick, F.H.C., 1953. "A Structure for Deoxyribose Nucleic Acid." *Nature*, 171:737-738.

4. Miller, K., 1999. *Finding Darwin's God: A Scientist's Search for Common Ground Between God and Evolution*. Cliff Street Books, New York, p. 207.

5. Ibid, p. 206.

6. Breaker, R.R. and Joyce, G.F., 1994. "Inventing and Improving Ribozyme Function: Rational Design versus Iterative Selection Methods." *Trends in Biotechnology*, 12:268-275.

7. Smith, G.P. and Petrenko, V.A., 1997. "Phage Display." *Chemical Reviews*, 97:391-410.

8. Wade, N. "Scientists Announce First Interpretations of Human Genome." http://cmbi.bjmu.edu.cn/news/0102/90.htm; last accessed 07/03/05.

9. Cited in "Rivalry and Wonder." 2001. *Nature Reviews Genetics*, 2:158-159.

10. Press release material, written by *Nature*'s science writing team; http://www.nature.com/genomics/human/overview/press-releases.html; last accessed 07/26/04.

11. Baltimore, D., 2001. "Our Genome Unveiled." *Nature*, 409:814-816.

12. "Of Mouse and Man." *ScienCentralNews*, December 04, 2002. http://www.sciencentral.com/articles/view.php3?language=english&type=241 19&article_id=218391841&cat=1_2; last accessed 07/26/04.

13. "Trees and Flowers More Akin than Dissimilar: Homology of Expressed Genes in Loblolly Pine and Arabidopsis Thaliana." *Science Daily*, May 29, 2003. http://www.sciencedaily.com/releases/2003/05/030529081013.htm; last accessed 07/26/04.

14. "Yeast Genome Should Provide Insights to Human Disease." *The Scientist*, February 21, 2002. http://www.biomedcentral.com/news/20020221/03; last accessed 07/27/04.

15. For example, see Mondesert O., Ducommun B. and Bugler B., 2002.

"Human CDC25B and CDC25C Differ by Their Ability to Restore a Functional Checkpoint Response after Gene Replacement in Fission Yeast." *Biochemical and Biophysical Research Communications*, 295:673-677 and Dotan, I., Ziv, E., Dafni, N., Beckman, J.S., McCann, R.O., Glover, C.V. and Canaani D., 2001. "Functional Conservation Between the Human, Nematode, and Yeast CK2 Cell Cycle Genes." *Biochemical and Biophysical Research Communications*, 288:603-609. Also see Plon, S.E., Leppig, K.A., Do, H.N. and Groudine, M., 1993. "Cloning of the Human Homolog of the CDC34 Cell Cycle Gene by Complementation in Yeast." *Proceedings of the National Academy of Sciences of the United States of America*, 90:10484-10488.

16. For example, see Beinhauer, J.D., Hagan, I.M., Hegemann, J.H. and Fleig, U., 1997. "Mal3, the Fission Yeast Homologue of the Human APC-Interacting Protein EB-1 Is Required for Microtubule Integrity and the Maintenance of Cell Form." *Journal of Cellular Biology*, 139:717-728 and Chen, C.R., Li, Y.C., Chen, J., Hou, M.C., Papadaki, P. and Chang, E.C., 1999. "Moe1, a Conserved Protein in *Schizosaccharomyces pombe*, Interacts with a Ras Effector, Scd1, to Affect Proper Spindle Formation." *Proceedings of the National Academy of Sciences of the United States of America*, 96:517-522.

17. Figueroa, J.D. and Hayman, M.J., 2004. "The Human Ski-Interacting Protein Functionally Substitutes for the Yeast PRP45 Gene." *Biochemical and Biophysical Research Communications*, 319:1105-1109.

18. Lu, B., Liu, T., Crosby, J.A., Thomas-Wohlever, J., Lee, I. and Suzuki, C.K., 2003. "The ATP-Dependent Lon Protease of Mus Musculus Is a DNA-Binding Protein That Is Functionally Conserved Between Yeast and Mammals." *Gene*, 306:45-55.

19. Le Goff, C., Zemlyanko, O., Moskalenko, S., Berkova, N., Inge-Vechtomov, S., Philippe, M. and Zhouravleva, G., 2002. "Mouse GSPT2, but Not GSPT1, Can Substitute for Yeast eRF3 *In Vivo*." *Genes Cells*, 7:1043-1057.

20. Cavallini, B., Faus, I., Matthes, H., Chipoulet, J.M., Winsor, B., Egly, J.M. and Chambon, P., 1989. "Cloning of the Gene Encoding the Yeast Protein BTF1Y, Which Can Substitute for the Human TATA

Box-Binding Factor." *Proceedings of the National Academy of Sciences of the United States of America*, 86:9803-9807 and Sherman, J.M., Stone, E.M., Freeman-Cook, L.L., Brachmann, C.B., Boeke, J.D. and Pillus, L., 1999. "The Conserved Core of a Human SIR2 Homologue Functions in Yeast Silencing." *Molecular Biology of the Cell*, 10:3045-3059.

21. McKune, K., Moore, P.A., Hull, M.W. and Woychik, N.A., 1995. "Six Human RNA Polymerase Subunits Functionally Substitute for Their Yeast Counterparts." *Molecular Biology of the Cell*, 15:6895-6900.

22. Keefe, A.D. and Szostak, J.W., 2001. "Functional Proteins from a Random-Sequence Library." *Nature*, 410:715-718.

23. Tenenbaum, D., 1998. "Microbial Population Explosion." http://whyfiles.org/shorties/count_bact.html; last accessed 07/29/04.

24. I am referring to *Escherichia coli* strain K12-MG1655. See The Institute for Genomic Research (TIGR) at http://www.tigr.org/tigr-scripts/CMR2/GenomeTabs.spl?database=ntec01#1; last accessed 07/29/04.

25. I used the "Genome versus Genome Protein Hits" analysis available at The Institute for Genomic Research's (TIGR) web page: http://cmr.tigr.org/tigrscripts/CMR/shared/MakeFrontPages.cgi?page=circular_display. This analysis also provided the remaining graphs in Figure 7-1.

26. The genome from *E. coli* was used as a reference to search the genome from *S. typhimurium* where minimal sequence similarity was set at 40, 50, 60, 70, 80, and then 90 percent.

27. Ochman, H. and Wilson, A.C., 1987. "Evolution in Bacteria: Evidence for a Universal Substitution Rate in Cellular Genomes." *Journal of Molecular Evolution*, 26:74-86.

28. The genome of *E. coli* was used as the reference to separately search the genomes of *Caulobacter crescentus*, *Nitrosomonas europaea*, *Bdellovibrio bacteriovorus*, and *Helicobacter pylori J9* as in reference 26. The average values for each increment (for example, 40-50 percent sequence similarity) were calculated. The average genome size among these four bacteria was also much smaller, containing 2867 genes.

29. The genome of *E. coli* was used as the reference to separately search the genomes of *Aquifex aeolicus*, *Bacillus subtilis*, *Chlorobium tepidum*, *Deinococcus radiodurans*, *Synechocystis sp.*, *Treponema pallidum*, and *Thermotoga*

maritima and average values were calculated. The average genome size for these seven bacteria was 2520.

30. The genome of *E. coli* was used as the reference to separately search the genomes of *Thermoplasma acidophilum*, *Pyrococcus abyssi*, *Halobacterium sp.*, and *Methanosarcina acetivorans* and average values were calculated for each increment. The average genome size for these seven bacteria was 2597.

31. For those unfamiliar with bacteria and their diversity, the above analysis would be analogous to first comparing human proteins with ape proteins, then comparing human proteins with those from other mammals, then comparing human proteins with all animal proteins, and finally comparing human proteins with bacterial proteins.

32. Ullman, D.G., 1992. *The Mechanical Design Process*. McGraw-Hill, New York, p. 20.

33. Human Protein Reference Database. http://www.hprd.org/; last accessed 08/02/04.

34. Moghaddam, A. and Bicknell, R., 1992. "Expression of Platelet-Derived Endothelial Cell Growth Factor in *Escherichia coli* and Confirmation of Its Thymidine Phosphorylase Activity." *Biochemistry*, 31:12141-12146 and Miyadera, K., Sumizawa, T., Haraguchi, M., Yoshida, H., Konstanty, W., Yamada, Y. and Akiyama, S., 1995. "Role of Thymidine Phosphorylase Activity in the Angiogenic Effect of Platelet Derived Endothelial Cell Growth Factor/Thymidine Phosphorylase." *Cancer Research*, 55:1687-1690.

35. Jeffery, C.J., 1999. "Moonlighting Proteins." *Trends in Biochemical Sciences*, 24:8-11.

36. Ramasarma, T. "Is It Fair to Describe a Protein Recruited for Many Cellular Chores as 'Moonlighting' and 'Promiscuous'?" http://www.ias. ac.in/currsci/dec101999/articles2.htm; last accessed 08/02/04.

37. Copley, S.D., 2003. "Enzymes with Extra Talents: Moonlighting Functions and Catalytic Promiscuity." *Current Opinion in Chemical Biology*, 7:265-272.

38. Atlas of Genetics and Cytogenetics in Oncology and Haematology; http:// web.archive.org/web/20040603072600/http://www.infobiogen.fr/serv-

ices/chromcancer/Genes/GPHNID317.html; last accessed 08/02/04.

39. Stallmeyer, B., Schwarz, G., Schulze, J., Nerlich, A., Reiss, J., Kirsch, J. and Mendel, R.R., 1999. "The Neurotransmitter Receptor-Anchoring Protein Gephyrin Reconstitutes Molybdenum Cofactor Biosynthesis in Bacteria, Plants, and Mammalian Cells." *Proceedings of the National Academy of Sciences of the United States of America*, 96:1333-1338.

40. Jeffery, C.J., 2003. "Moonlighting Proteins: Old Proteins Learning New Tricks." *Trends in Genetics*, 19:415-417.

41. Jeffery, C.J., 2003. "Multi-Functional Proteins: Example of Gene Sharing." *Annals of Medicine*, 35:28-35.

42. Davis, P.J. and Davis, F.B., 1996. "Nongenomic Actions of Thyroid Hormone." *Thyroid*, 6:497-504.

43. Bernstein, J.A., Lin, P.H., Cohen, S.N. and Lin-Chao, S., 2004. "Global Analysis of *Escherichia coli* RNA Degradosome Function Using DNA Microarrays." *Proceedings of the National Academy of Sciences of the United States of America*, 101:2758-2763. I have also used the hypothesis of design to predict the enolase functions to plug the degradosome machine into the energy circuitry of the cell. See "A Teleological Hypothesis about a Machine." http://www.idthink.net/biot/degrad/index.html.

44. For example, the bacterial protein, PutA, functions as an enzyme when inserted into the membrane and functions as regulator of transcription when released into the cytoplasm of the cell. See Muro-Pastor, A.M., Ostrovsky, P. and Maloy, S., 1997. "Regulation of Gene Expression by Repressor Localization: Biochemical Evidence That Membrane and DNA Binding by the PutA Protein Are Mutually Exclusive." *Journal of Bacteriology*, 179:2788-2791.

45. Moore, R.C. and Purugganan, M.D., 2003. "The Early Stages of Duplicate Gene Evolution." *Proceedings of the National Academy of Sciences of the United States of America*, 100:15682-15687 and Hennig, W., 2004. "The Revolution of the Biology of the Genome." *Cell Research*, 14:1-7.

46. Moore, J.D. and Endow, S.A., 1996. "Kinesin Proteins: A Phylum of Motors for Microtubule-Based Motility." *Bioessays*, 18:207-219.

47. Piatigorsky, J. and Wistow, G., 1991. "The Recruitment of Crystallins:

New Functions Precede Gene Duplication." *Science,* 252:1078-1079.

48. The exact original sequence does not need to be retained. A designer simply designs the sequence such that the important residues for primary function also poise it for unpacking a secondary function. Thus, the blind watchmaker can toy with the original sequence, but not erase what the intelligent watchmaker needed.

49. Force, A., Lynch, M., Pickett, F.B., Amores, A., Yan, Y.-L. and Postlethwait, J., 1999. "The Preservation of Duplicate Genes by Complementary Degenerative Mutations." *Genetics,* 151:1531-1545.

50. "COTS—Why Modular Solutions?" http://www.hunteng.co.uk/corporate/modular.htm; last accessed 08/09/04.

51. Hansen, T.F., 2003. "Is Modularity Necessary for Evolvability? Remarks on the Relationship Between Pleiotropy and Evolvability." *Biosystems,* 2189:1-12.

52. For example, see Rainey, P.B. and Cooper, T.F., 2004. "Evolution of Bacterial Diversity and the Origins of Modularity." *Research in Microbiology,* 155:370-375.

53. Orr, H.A., 2000. "Adaptation and the Cost of Complexity." *Evolution,* 54:13-20.

54. Buckling, A., Wills, M.A. and Colegrave, N., 2003. "Adaptation Limits Diversification of Experimental Bacterial Populations." *Science,* 302:2074-2075.

55. Mayr, E., 1976. "The Emergence of Evolutionary Novelties." *Evolution and the Diversity of Life: Selected Essays.* Harvard University Press, Cambridge, Massachusetts, pp. 96-98.

56. Gould, S.J. and Vibra, E.S., 1982. "Exaptation—A Missing Term in the Science of Form." *Paleobiology,* 8:4-15.

57. Ganfornia, M.D. and Sanchez, D., 1999. "Generation of Evolutionary Novelty by Functional Shift." *BioEssays,* 21:432-439.

58. Conway-Morris, S., 2000. "Evolution: Bringing Molecules into the Fold." *Cell,* 100:1-11.

59. True, J.R. and Carroll, S.B., 2002. "Gene Co-Option in Physiological and Morphological Evolution." *Annual Review of Cell and Developmental Biology,* 18:53-80.

60. Cited in Nei, M., 1987. *Molecular Evolutionary Genetics*. Columbia University Press, New York, p. 28.

61. Florian, V. and Klein, A., 1996. "A Nascent Micronuclear Pseudogene in the Ciliate *Euplotes crassus*." *Nucleic Acids Research*, 24:3195-3200 and Yokoyama, S., Meany, A.,Wilkens, H. and Yokoyama, R., 1995. "Initial Mutational Steps toward Loss of Opsin Gene Function in Cavefish." *Molecular Biology and Evolution*, 12:527-532. Also see Zhao, Z. and Boerwinkle, E., 2002. "Neighboring-Nucleotide Effects on Single Nucleotide Polymorphisms: A Study of 2.6 Million Polymorphisms across the Human Genome." *Genome Research*, 12:1679-1686 and Yatagai, F. and Glickman, B.W., 1990. "Specificity of Spontaneous Mutation in the lacI Gene Cloned into Bacteriophage M13." *Mutation Research/DNA Repair*, 243:21-28.

62. Kreutzer, D.A. and Essigmann, J.M., 1998. "Oxidized, Deaminated Cytosines Are a Source of C->T Transitions *In Vivo*." *Proceedings of the National Academy of Sciences of the United States of America*, 95:3578-3582.

63. Trinquier, G. and Sanejouand, Y-H., 1998. "Which Effective Property of Amino Acids Is Best Preserved by the Genetic Code?" *Protein Engineering*, 11:153-169.

64. Kamtekar, S., Schiffer, J.M., Xiong, H., Babik, J.M. and Hecht, M.H., 1993. "Protein Design by Binary Patterning of Polar and Nonpolar Amino Acids." *Science*, 262:1680-1685.

65. I explore this in more detail at http://www.idthink.net/biot/deam/index.html.

66. For example, see Doucet, A., Williams, M., Gagnon, M.C., Sasseville, M. and Beauregard, M., 2002. "Engineering Nutritious Proteins: Improvement of Stability in the Designer Protein MB-1 via Introduction of Disulfide Bridges." *Journal of Agricultural and Food Chemistry*, 50:92-98.

67. Chothia, C. and Janin, J., 1975. "Principles of Protein-Protein Recognition." *Nature*, 256:705-708 and Jones, S. and Thornton, J.M., 1996. "Principles of Protein-Protein Interactions." *Proceedings of the National Academy of Sciences of the United States of America*, 93:13-20.

68. Honjo, T., Muramatsu, M. and Fagarasan, S., 2004. "AID: How Does It Aid Antibody Diversity?" *Immunity*, 20:659-668.

69. Beletskii, A. and Bhagwat, A.S., 1996. "Transcription-Induced Mutations: Increase in C to T Mutations in the Nontranscribed Strand during Transcription in *Escherichia coli*." *Proceedings of the National Academy of Sciences of the United States of America*, 93:13919-13924.

70. "Researchers Unlock Secret of RNA's Versatility." http://www.lbl.gov/Science-Articles/Archive/rna-uracil-research.html; last accessed 01/07/03.

71. For more teleological perspectives on this, see http://www.idthink.net/biot/ihe/index.html and http://www.idthink.net/biot/deam2/index.html.

72. Duboul, D. and Wilkins, A.S., 1998. "The Evolution of 'Bricolage.'" *Trends in Genetics*, 14: 54-58.

PART IV — THE MATRIX

CHAPTER 8

ANALOGIES AND DISCONTINUITIES

Two simple questions must guide any attempt to reliably detect design. The first question stems from the fact that we live in a reality populated by things we have designed and things we have not designed. Do these designed things carry some fingerprint that reflects the fact they were designed? Mathematician and design theorist William Dembski puts it another way: "Can objects, even if nothing is known about how they arose, exhibit features that reliably signal the action of an intelligent cause?"[1] Some would answer no, and explain that we need to have information about the designer in order to detect his or her products. Without knowing what motivates the designer, and what design methods and resources were available to the designer, how could we ever detect the features of the product that supposedly reflect the expression of the designer? We can call this the designer-centric approach, since it would have us revolve our analysis around independent information about the designer. The argument is appealing because our science of archaeology and forensics rely heavily on our independent knowledge about human beings and the things we create and design.

The designer-centric approach entails an unsupported assumption which creates a problematic flow in its logic. It assumes that if something was designed, then it should always be possible to clearly and independently detect its designer. Yet the truth of any design inference does *not* entail that we should be able to uncover independent evidence of the designer. For example, what if the original living cells on earth were designed by some form of extra-terrestrial intelligence some three billion years ago? If these original cells were indeed designed, does this mean we should be able to find these extra-terrestrial designers present and lurking somewhere on Earth in 2008

A.D.? If a design inference is held hostage to the necessity of having independent evidence about its designer, then there is a high risk of failing to perceive the reality of what exists.

Because the detection of design does not depend on the prior and independent detection of designers, not all scientists subscribe to the designer-centric approach. Luc Arnold, of the Observatory of Haute-Provence in France, is an example. He published an article in *The Astrophysical Journal* entitled, "Transit Lightcurve Signatures of Artificial Objects."[2] Arnold suggests a novel approach for detecting the presence of extraterrestrial intelligence—look for artificial structures in space. He explains his reasoning as follows:

> We propose here an alternative approach for a new SETI: considering that artificial planet-size bodies may exist around other stars, and that such objects always transit in front of their parent star for a given remote observer, we may thus have an opportunity to detect and even characterize them by the transit method, assuming these transits are distinguishable from a simple planetary transit. These objects could be planet-size structures built by advanced civilizations, like very lightweight solar sails or giant very low density structures may be specially built for the purpose of interstellar communication by transit.

He then examines whether the artificial nature of a planet-sized body can be detected:

> Although the sphere is the equilibrium shape preferred for massive and planet-size bodies to adapt to their own gravity, one can consider non-spherical bodies, especially if they are small and lightweight, and transiting in front of a dwarf star to produce a detectable signal. Non-spherical artificial objects—like triangles or more exotic shapes—have each a specific transit lightcurve, as we show in this paper.

Arnold is saying that we will soon have the ability to detect such things as triangles in space. Yet how would such examples of design be detected?

Arnold does assume a motive—the alien life form would be motivated to generate an "attention-getting signal." But is there any evidence of such life forms with such motivations? To construct a planet-sized triangle simply to signal your existence across space would be assuming a great deal about the designers. Arnold does not address the question of resources and knowledge. Is there independent evidence that another race of beings have the resources and knowledge to construct a planet-sized triangle? Of course not. We are still looking for evidence that microbes exist on other planets. In other words, there is no description in Arnold's article about how such a design would possibly be implemented. Arnold's only justification for detecting design is to find transits that are distinguishable from a simple planetary transit; to find shapes *not explainable by currently-understood natural law.*

Even though Arnold proposes a way to detect design without relying on the designer-centric approach, his article has been published. Does this mean the peer-review process has broken down? Is there a conspiracy among those who believe in aliens to mold science to fulfill their own desires?[3] Or is it simply because the designer-centric approach has always been only one way to detect design?

If we wake up one day and read about a giant triangle that has been detected in space, should we all dismiss it as evidence for design (and extraterrestrial intelligence) until someone can scientifically explain how it got there and who put it there? Of course not. The designer-centric approach is more a matter of convenience than necessity. If we have information about the designers, by all means, use it and exploit it. But we should not hold a design inference hostage to demands for this type of information. So let us answer Dembski's question affirmatively. That is, we will suppose that designed things can indeed come with some type of fingerprint signaling their origin as something that was designed. This would then take us to the second and equally crucial question: What are the fingerprints that signal design?

HELP FROM THE SKEPTICS

Before exploring what the fingerprints of design might look like, it would be helpful to reach some type of consensus between skeptics and design proponents about the type of data needed to proceed through the Explanatory Continuum. If agreement can be reached, then all parties can participate in the investigation regardless of their level of skepticism. However, if the parties disagree on what type of data is required, such disagreement must be highlighted in order to interpret the meaning of the skepticism. For example, does the skeptic need us to effectively "prove" Intelligent Design? Does the skeptic require Epistemological Evidence, when it is Ontological Evidence that will fuel the investigation?

Throughout the years I have asked skeptics about the type of data that would cause *them* to suspect Intelligent Design. What data would *they* count as evidence for Intelligent Design? All of the replies[4] fell into four categories: 1) provide independent evidence of the designer; 2) identify something that evolution cannot explain; 3) demonstrate a strong analogy with things that are known to be designed and; 4) a confession of ignorance. What is striking is how little things have changed, since these are very similar to the answers Charles Darwin supplied to Asa Gray when asked what would convince him of design (see Chapter 2). When Darwin needed to see an angel, we can liken this to independent evidence of the designer (in Darwin's case, the designer would be God). When Darwin raised the possibility that life was a function of an imponderable force, this is close to admitting we can never really answer the question. When Darwin proposed the discovery of brass or iron men disconnected from all other organisms, this is essentially proposing something that evolution could not explain. Darwin may even have been hinting at analogy, as humans had long constructed artifacts from brass or iron. If Darwin were alive today, he might simply substitute "robot" for brass men.

It is interesting that the most common skeptical response revolved around the ability to find something that evolution cannot yet explain. Often cited was the presence of some trait that would be useless to the organism that possessed the trait, yet useful to another organism that did not possess the trait. While such a feature could not be reconciled with Darwinian evolution, neither is it a good design. A trait that posed no benefit to the bearer of the trait is at the mercy of mutational decay. Acquired mutations that effectively eliminate the trait are not pruned away with selection. As a result, such a trait could only be maintained through continual intelligent intervention, where the designer must continually supervise and erase any mutations that occur. Yet the truth of a design event does not entail that the designer is constantly monitoring and fixing the design. Nevertheless, it may be possible to use and build on the second and third criteria offered by the skeptics of design.

In the process of characterizing the fingerprints that signal design, the context I have provided in the previous chapters becomes more important than ever. In Chapter 2, we decided to steer away from the traditional approach of looking for some extraordinary marker that would unequivocally "prove" design. We are not looking for data that scream "Design!" Instead, we adopt an incremental approach and systematically gather clues to determine if they converge on a signal of design. We surveyed some of those clues in Chapters 3-5. But then, in the following chapters, we encountered obstacles. Our attempt to infer design was clouded by the existence of natural selection acting as a designer-mimic (Chapter 6), and further by the possibility that an intelligent designer may indeed make use of the designer-mimic (Chapter 7). If we assume designed things carry with them some residual trace of their history of being designed, can it ever be strong enough to break through all the noise?

Perhaps the Face on Mars, discussed in Chapter 1, will again provide an example to help us find fingerprints of design. If the Mars Orbiter Camera had returned high-resolution photographs of a detailed Face on Mars, the strongest explanation for its origin would be design. We would infer design because two criteria were satisfied: 1) the Face looked like something that was designed and 2) the Face did not look like something non-teleological processes commonly form. We could formulate our reasoning to make it sound more sophisticated than a case of "looking like this and not looking like that." But as ocular-centric beings, that is really what it boils down to in the end. The key to this method of inferring design is the synergistic relationship between the two criteria. It is not simply that the Face looks designed. It is *also* the fact that it does not look like something non-teleological processes spawn. In one swoop, the features of the Face satisfy *both* criteria.

Or consider the example of a message in the DNA from Chapter 6.

The discovery of written text in the DNA might trigger a design inference even among the most extreme of skeptics because it would simultaneously satisfy both criteria. The text itself would be strongly analogous to things human beings produce and such text would unlikely have been spawned by non-teleological processes. What about Darwin's brass men that could not be connected to any other living thing? Again, this is something that looks man-made and does not look evolved. The key is that an *analogy* to designed things is coupled to a *discontinuity* with non-teleological processes. They are two sides of the same coin.

Returning to the PCP degradation example from Chapter 6, we can see how a design inference fails to take root when the two criteria of analogy and discontinuity are not connected. At first glance, this biochemical pathway may look designed, as some complex chemistry is carried out in an orderly fashion, allowing bacteria the uncanny ability to survive in a toxic environment. Yet there does not appear to be any discontinuity between the bacteria's biochemistry and the ability to evolve such a system. In fact, since the pesticide PCP is man-made and was introduced into the environment only a few decades ago, it certainly appears the pathway evolved into existence quite recently. Furthermore, as with the Face on Mars, the design inference for the PCP pathway disappears under higher resolution. Shelley D. Copley noted that the pathway was "far from ideal,"[5] as there are many design problems with the system. For example, the first enzyme in the system is rather sloppy and could be vastly improved in terms of efficiency. And the regulation of the pathway is "rather primitive," as only two of the three enzymes are under regulatory control in response to the presence of PCP, which looks like something the blind watchmaker would patch together to solve an immediate problem. It does not look like something a sophisticated engineer would design. Just as the Face on Mars turned out to fit within the planet's geological landscape, the PCP degradation pathway seems to fit comfortably within the surrounding context of non-teleological evolution.

The examples of the Face on Mars, a message in the DNA, Darwin's brass men, and the PCP degradation pathway all converge to highlight the power of a demonstrated analogy with designed things coupled to a demonstrated discontinuity when concluding design. Join the two and there is a strong design inference. Fail to join the two and there are serious problems trying to infer design. Let us now deepen and extend this insight as we prepare a methodology that will help us traverse the Explanatory Continuum in an effort to better assess our suspicions of design.

THE POWER OF ANALOGY

The argument from analogy is a common form of inductive reasoning. It basically works by finding similarities between two things and using these similarities to argue that two things have even more similarities. Analogous reasoning is both common and quite useful in science. For example, a scientist might discover that protein X shares biochemical properties with another protein, Y. If there is much knowledge about Y, this knowledge, coupled with the argument from analogy, can then be used to go back and make predictions about X, where X is expected to share other features with Y. If the predictions hold true, the similarities between the two proteins grow and the analogy is strengthened. Actual examples of such reasoning in science are easy to find. In one study on kidney transplants, researchers appeal to analogy using information about heart transplants: "In analogy with similar reactions described recently in heart allografts, we suggest. . . ."[6] In another study that focuses on the machinery inside the cell, the researchers invoke analogy between two different pathways: "Hence, these data further extend the analogy between the ubiquitin and SUMO pathway."[7] The list would be endless. In fact, a PubMed search with the keyword "analogous" retrieves no less than 23,478 hits.[8]

While the argument from analogy is a useful tool in science, its association with the concept of design has a troubled past. Anyone attempting to use analogy to infer design will be perceived as following in William Paley's misguided footsteps. But remember Paley set out to use analogy to prove the existence of God. It is quite an ambitious endeavor to set out to convince all rational people that they must accept the existence of God because an eye is somewhat similar to a watch! There is no need to be so ambitious. Rather than trying to prove anything, an analogy may simply function as a signpost, pointing us in a particular direction. And instead of trying to uncover the identity of the designer, and insisting it is God, we pay tribute to the philosophers who have criticized such effort and simply settle for an intelligent being. Rather than use analogy to prove a particular metaphysical position, the investigator can use it to explore the plausibility that something was intelligently designed. In his *Philosophy Pages*, philosopher Garth Kemerling explains the significance of this approach: "In general, arguments by analogy are improved when their conclusions are modest with respect to their premises."[9]

The clues outlined in Chapters 3-5 all appeal to analogy. Unlike other areas of science, biology is deeply dependent on teleological concepts and thinking. Life looks like carbon-based nanotechnology. The cell exists because of its sophisticated molecular machines. The machine parts are built using a genetic code. Such features demonstrate a deep similarity between life and things we have designed. So we suspect Intelligent Design. But we suspect rather that conclude design because analogy by itself is not strong enough to get us further. By agreeing to restrict our inference to this level, the analogy is actually strengthened and more difficult to ignore or dismiss.

Nevertheless, the analogy between things that are designed and biological features can be further strengthened, which, in turn, would strengthen our conviction of the plausibility of life's design. Kemerling's discussion provides useful criteria in this regard. First, he notes that the more instances behind the analogy, the stronger the analogy. If we were to return to the discussion of molecular machines in Chapter 5, we would see dozens of instances of such machines performing just about every sort of task needed by the cell. The examples are so numerous that the cell can be safely scored as a machine-dependent entity. If, on the other hand, only one or two examples of a molecular machine existed, the analogy between life and artifact would not be as strong.

The second criterion suggested by Kemerling centers around variety: "the more variety there is among the instances, the stronger the analogical argument becomes." Thus, the arguments from Chapters 3, 4 and 5 all converge to strengthen the analogy as a function of bringing more variety to the table: the dependence on engineering concepts, the machines, the code, the optimality of the code, DNA as a parity code, and the essential proofreading. If we could only cite one, the analogy would be weaker.

The third criterion is the number of similarities contained in any one instance. The more similarities, the stronger the argument. Here we could recount the multiple similarities between engineering and the study of biology. Or the multiple similarities between the genetic code and Morse code. Or the multiple similarities between a molecular machine and a man-made machine.

Thus far, the multiple instances, the variety, and the multiple similarities involved in the analogies from Chapters 3-5 all converge to make the argument of design stronger. But I can now add a fourth criterion, one of my own: The analogy becomes stronger as it stands the test of time. If the analogy *persists and deepens* as we uncover more relevant information, our conviction concerning the validity of the analogy increases. If research, over time, adds to the list of similarities, we have reason to think we are on the right track. Let us illustrate this approach by turning to three examples from these previous chapters and considering them this time from the perspective of this fourth criterion: 1) the analogy between biology and engineering; 2) the analogy between DNA and computers and; 3) the analogy between man-made and molecular machines.

Deepening the Analogy

In 1870, French physiologist Claude Bernard introduced a new philosophy during a series of lectures. Bernard had noticed that the functioning of highly developed animals was not significantly effected by their environmental surroundings, but nevertheless they had to interact with these surroundings. He proposed an idea that would become the core of modern physiology:

> The constancy of the internal environment is the condition that life should be free and independent . . . . So far from the higher animal being indifferent to the external world, it is on the contrary in a precise and informed relation with it, in such a way that its equilibrium results from a continuous and delicate compensation, established as by the most sensitive of balances.[10]

By the 1930s, American physiologist Walter Cannon popularized this new view in his book, *The Wisdom of the Body*.[11] Cannon would call this ability homeostasis. Paul Agutter and other scientists would comment:

> To maintain a constant internal environment requires control mechanisms: sensors, effectors, information processing and feedback systems. *These terms were imported into the language of twentieth century physiology from control engineering in the 1940s*—but they do not belong to the language of physics (or, indeed, of nineteenth century physiology).[12] (emphasis added)

Thus, it was the analogy with engineering concepts that transformed Bernard's new philosophy into a very fruitful scientific program. The imported concepts from control engineering[13] have withstood the test of time and extended into the deepest reaches of the cell where everything, from the concentration of amino acids and ATP to the expression of genes, is under complex feedback control. In fact, in March 2002, John Doyle, an engineer from the California Institute of Technology published an article entitled "Reverse Engineering of Biological Complexity" in the journal *Science*.[14] Biologists have recently begun to appreciate a "systems-level" of analysis[15] as they have accumulated such massive amounts of molecular information about the cell. Doyle notes that "systems-level design has been at the core of modern engineering, motivating its most sophisticated theories in controls, information, and computation." He then highlights many of the insights from modern engineering and how they would apply to biology, ending his article by noting, "Biologists and engineers now have enough examples of complex systems that they can close the loop and eliminate specious theories. We should compare notes."[14] Just as the engineering concepts from the 1940s greatly advanced biology at the physiological and then molecular levels, sixty years later, more modern and sophisticated concepts surrounding the systems we design promise to shed even more light on the workings of the cell. This principle even extends to our understanding of how the humble cell membrane works:

We commonly describe membrane function using concepts (conductivity, insulation, capacitance and so on) established previously in electrical engineering.[16]

The similarities between engineering and biology have deepened with time and knowledge and promise to continue this trend.

If we turn our attention from the design principles to the designed artifacts, another instance of similarity between biology and engineering deepens as a function of time. Engineer David Ullman has noted that over the last 200 years, the complexity of our mechanical devices has grown quite rapidly.[17] For example, if this book was written in 1950, I would be using a rather simple typewriter. But with fifty years of advances in engineering principles and technology, I use a complex computer and complex word processing program. The theme of increasing complexity is seen in many of our artifacts, ranging from automobiles to airplanes.

Complexity is not the only feature of our own devices that has changed over time. Things have also gotten smaller. The computer is again a good example. In their article on nanotechnology, chemist Vincenzo Balzini and colleagues note:

> The outstanding development of information technology has been strictly related to the progressive miniaturization of the components employed for the construction of such devices and machines. The first electronic computer was made of 1800 valves, weighed 30 tons, occupied an entire room, and lasted an average of 5.6 hours between repairs. A state-of-the-art microprocessor today has more than 40 million transistors, a number that is destined to increase in the future.[18]

Computers, with their ability to control events, have not only allowed us to design more complex artifacts, but the ability to compute has relied on smaller components.

Yet another theme we see in engineered devices as a function of time is increased autonomy. More and more, we design things that are "user-friendly," needing less input from an intelligent agent in order to run them. Simply consider the auto-focus abilities of your digital camera or the voice activated dialing on your cell phone. What is most striking is that all three trends of miniaturization, increased complexity, and increased autonomy in our own designs converge on the cell, the ultimate expression of small scale, autonomous complexity. If we were to extrapolate from the trends in engineered devices over the last few centuries, all trends would fuse and terminate with what we find in biology. Looking at a cell is like looking into the future of our own designs.

The second example of a deepening analogy concerns the way our computer technology is used to better describe the cell. For a long time, it was known that the genomes of most organisms contained huge amounts of DNA that did not code for proteins. Most of this DNA is repetitive in nature, where certain sequences of nucleotides can be repeated thousands to millions of times. These sequences were labeled "junk DNA." Such junk is easily absorbed into the perspective of non-teleological evolution. While science itself does not seriously weigh the question of teleological versus non-teleological evolution, individual scientists writing Internet articles have been quite clear about what this junk DNA means to Intelligent Design:

> One argument against an intelligent designer is the amazing amount of flotsam and jetsam in genomes. The human genome is 90-95% apparent junk, useless sequences, many of which resemble functional genes, but are clearly beaten up beyond working order (pseudogenes).[19]

And:

> Although the high content of "junk DNA" was initially surprising when it was discovered, our current understanding of the mechanisms of genome expansion (duplication and insertion) and the apparent lack of significant selective pressure to minimize genome size combine to make the accumulation of useless sequences in our DNA seem inevitable.[20]

Yet biologists James Shapiro and Richard von Sternberg have proposed a very interesting function for junk DNA.[21] They draw upon a very strong

ANALOGIES AND DISCONTINUITIES

analogy with computer storage information systems and argue the "junk DNA" actually formats coding information:

> The view of the genome advocated here as a hierarchically organised data storage system formatted by repetitive DNA sequence elements implies that each organism has a genome system architecture, in the same way that each computer data storage system has a characteristic architecture. In the computer example, architecture depends upon the operating system and hardware that are used, not upon the content of each data file. Macintosh®, Windows® and Unix® machines can all display the same images and text files, even though the data retrieval paths are operationally quite distinct. Similarly, many protein and RNA sequences (data files) are conserved through evolution, but different taxa organise and format their genomes in quite different ways for replication, transmission and expression. An overall system architecture is required since these processes must be coordinated so that they operate without mutual interference. DNA segments must be in the right place at the right time for function.[21]

In a review packed with supporting examples, they argue that as "we increasingly apply computational metaphors to cellular function, we expect that a deeper understanding of repetitive elements, the integrative fraction of cellular DNA, will reveal novel aspects of the logical architecture inherent to genome organisation." Shapiro and von Sternberg's hypothesis would not have to confer function to all "junk DNA" in order for a suspicion of design to be strengthened. The key lies in the ability of this design metaphor to truly explain the function of much of this repetitive DNA. If the hypothesis is even partly correct, the analogy between life and artifact is further deepened and the suspicion is strengthened, as the design architecture of our own advanced technology provides the needed light to understand what is happening inside the cell.

The third example of a deepening analogy takes us back to our previous discussion of the molecular machines. The December 2003 issue of the journal *BioEssays* published a series of review articles about some of life's molecular machines. Adam Wilkins, the editor of the journal, offered some introductory comments, including a short discussion explaining why the machine "metaphor" so nicely applies to life several years after Bruce Alberts originally introduced the concept:

> In closing, it is worth considering for a moment the question of how well the "machine" metaphor when applied to molecular complexes actually holds up. . . the articles included in this issue demonstrate some striking parallels between artifactual and biological/molecular machines. In the first place, molecular machines, like man-made machines, perform highly specific functions. Second, the macromolecular machine complexes feature multiple parts that interact in distinct and precise ways, with defined inputs and outputs. Third, many of these machines have parts that can be used in other molecular machines (at least, with slight modification), comparable to the interchangeable parts of artificial machines. Finally, and not least, they have the cardinal attribute of machines: they all convert energy into some form of "work."[22]

Wilkins then cites the authors from one of the articles, who note that thinking about man-made and molecular machines "in parallel" is not only instructive, but "continues to be useful in guiding our thinking about biological processes." In fact, as two German researchers noted in 2004, "the currently fashionable interpretation of biological macromolecules as molecular machines. . . seems more than metaphorical, hinting at an amalgamation of concepts derived from engineering and molecular biological sciences."[16] The analogy also deepens from the other side of the coin. In their article on human nanotechnology, Balzini and colleagues define a molecular machine. Note how closely their definition maps to the molecular machines previously described in Chapter 5:

> A device is something invented and constructed for a special purpose and a machine is any combination of mechanisms for utilizing, modifying, applying, or transmitting energy, whether simple or complex. In everyday life we make extensive use of macroscopic devices and machines. Generally speaking, devices and machines

are assemblies of components designed to achieve a specific function. Each component of the assembly performs a simple act, while the entire assembly performs a more complex, useful function, characteristic of that particular device or machine. For example, the function performed by a hairdryer (production of hot wind) is the result of acts performed by a switch, a heater, and a fan, suitably connected by electric wires and assembled in an appropriate framework. The macroscopic concepts of a device and a machine can be straightforwardly extended to the molecular level. A molecular-level device can be defined as an assembly of a discrete number of molecular components designed to achieve a specific function. Each molecular component performs a single act, while the entire supramolecular assembly performs a more complex function, which results from the cooperation of the various components. A molecular-level machine is a particular type of molecular-level device in which the component parts can display changes in their relative positions as a result of some external stimulus. Molecular-level devices and machines operate through electronic and/or nuclear rearrangements and, like macroscopic devices and machines, they need energy to operate and signals to communicate with the operator.[18]

Thus, scientists working on the development of nanotechnology define a molecular machine as an extension of macroscopic machines and outline several features that just happen to perfectly map to the biological machines.

The whole concept of analogy can thus be used in an investigative sense to strengthen our suspicion of Intelligent Design. The investigator tests for multiple instances of analogy, a variety of instances, and an increasing number of similarities in any given instance of analogy. It also entails a rather simple prediction: the design principles underlying our own machines and devices will continue to illuminate the workings of the cell, as one form of technology is being used to make sense of another technology. The analogies will therefore deepen and continue to bear fruit by illuminating biology. Furthermore, continued advances in our own designs can be expected to shed even more light on the workings of the cell, thus further strengthening the analogy.

WEAKENING THE ANALOGY

The use of analogy does not simply entail a search for similarities. What makes analogy a productive investigative tool is its ability to move us away from the suspicion of Intelligent Design. This takes us to the last criterion outlined by Kemerling—the number of dissimilarities. As Kemerling notes, "In general, the fewer dissimilarities between instances and conclusion, the better an analogical argument is."[9] The flip side is that the greater the dissimilarities, the weaker the analogical argument. We should not ignore any significant differences. If they begin to accumulate and deepen, our design suspicion becomes shaky. So let's turn back to the molecular machines.

In the Wilkins article quoted earlier, he also notes two differences between the molecular machines and man-made machines. First, he notes that molecular machines are the products of evolution and not "designed" by engineers. Secondly, he notes that man-made machines (existing on the macroscopic level) and molecular machines are controlled by different forces. Man-made machines, existing on a large scale, are affected by things such as gravity and inertia. Molecular machines deal in the realm of diffusional processes and conformational change.[22] Yet the first difference simply begs the question, unless there is compelling evidence that non-teleological evolution did indeed spawn a particular machine. The second difference simply reflects scale, where we are comparing macroscopic technology to nanotechnology.

But there are more significant differences to note. Molecular machines tend to exist in a state of constant flux or turnover, where they are continuously being synthesized and eliminated. And unlike the components of man-made machines, which are firmly attached together with screws and bolts at discrete points, molecular machine components are typically held together by multiple weak interactions smeared out across their interfaces. Furthermore, in many cases, the molecular machines function as a population to serve the needs of the cell, not as a single unit. Thus, if we were to compare a ribosome, for example, with an automobile, and imagine the car taking on the properties of the ribosome, we would end up with a rather strange entity. Our car would easily fall apart and thus be under a continual state of construction and reconstruction. In fact, the analogy seems to break down completely when you consider it does not take a fleet of cars to get you to work; it takes only one. What do these differences really mean?

We must remember that an analogy need not deliver an identity. Human beings, at the time of this writing, did not design life's molecular machines. Thus do not expect the molecular machines to be *identical* to human artifacts. Nevertheless, how are the differences significant to the proposed analogy between molecular machines and man-made machines?

When faced with such dissimilarities, there are two possible explanations. First, the dissimilarities signal that we are not looking at truly analogous phenomena. The unstable, dynamic molecular machines differ from the things we design for the simple reason that molecular machines are not the products of design. Yet there is another explanation that accounts for the differences. It is safe to assume that if life, and its molecular machines, were designed, they were designed by an intelligence and/or technology that is vastly superior to ours. We can assume this for the simple reason that we are currently incapable of designing something as small, complex, and integrated as a bacterial cell. We have come a long way in describing and understanding cells, but we are far away from creating cells. Thus, the differences between our machines and the molecular machines may not reflect design versus non-design, but instead may reflect primitive design versus advanced design.

One way to distinguish between the two possible explanations is to consult our cutting-edge technologies. The most natural place to look would be the developing field of nanotechnology, not only because it is on the cutting-edge, but because life, if designed, would represent a real-world example. Recall that nanotechnology is expected to be different from macro-technology for the simple reason that the machines must deal with different forces. When we begin to think about machines at the nano-level, two problems quickly emerge. First, how do you build such tiny, microscopic machines? Secondly, since all machines break down, how would you repair such tiny machines?

To solve the assembly problem Drexler originally envisioned a nanorobot called the assembler.[23] The basic idea is to have a nanodevice that could be programmed to pick up atoms and assemble molecular structures atom-by-atom. Most scientists, however, do not think this approach is workable. Balzini et al. explain the fundamental problems:

> 1) the fingers of a hypothetical manipulator arm should themselves be made out of atoms, which implies that they would be too fat to have control of the chemistry in the nanometer region; 2) such fingers would also be too sticky: the atoms of the manipulator hands will adhere to the atom that is being moved, so that it will be impossible to place it in the desired position. In more general terms, the idea of the "atom-by-atom" bottom-up approach to nanotechnology, which seems so appealing to physicists, does not convince chemists who are well aware of the high reactivity of most atomic species and of the subtle aspects of chemical bond. Chemists know that atoms are not simple balls that can be moved from a place to another place at will. Atoms do not stay isolated; they bond strongly to their neighbors, and it is difficult to imagine that the atoms constituting the nanomanipulator fingers could take an atom from a starting material and transfer it to another material. Thinking that such assemblers can really work is tantamount to ignoring the complexity and subtlety of bond-breaking and bond-making processes.[18]

If the assembler is unworkable, perhaps there is a better solution. In their book on nanotechnology, Mark and Daniel Ratner outline several methods of constructing nanostructures, including the nanoscale versions of bulldozing, rubber-stamping, and writing with an old fashioned dip pen.[24] It is not clear if these methods could conceivably build something like a molecular machine, but even if they could, the authors note that these techniques involve a lot of work. In fact, they point out it would be much better if we could just mix the molecules and let them sort themselves out:

> One approach to nanofabrication attempts to do exactly this. It is called self-assembly. The idea behind self-assembly is that molecules will always seek the lowest energy level available to them. . . . Self-

assembly techniques are based on the idea of making components that. . . naturally organize themselves the way we want them to.[24]

The authors further note that self-assembly is "the most important nanoscale fabrication technique" because it can be applied in many areas and because of its ability to produce different structures.

The design solution of self-assembly would explain many of the differences between man-made machines and molecular machines. Inherent in the process of self-assembly is the reliance on weak chemical forces, which gently guide the components in their effort to "sort themselves out." Thus, the dynamic and relatively fragile state of the molecular machines (when compared to man-made machines) may simply reflect their existence as self-assembled entities. Furthermore, this feature also solves the repair problems. If a machine breaks, there is no need to reach inside the cell and fix it. Instead, if we have a population of machines that are constantly being made and eliminated, any broken machine will be "washed away" in the constant stream where new replaces old. It is this constant flux which essentially means there is no need to repair the machines.

What we can see from this example is how differences must be probed more deeply to determine whether they are signaling us away from a design inference or helping us appreciate the true depth of the design. While there are other ways to account for the differences from the perspective of design,[25] what is striking about this example is that the differences, upon closer inspection, actually add to the similarities to enhance the analogy with design. The hypothesis of life as carbon-based nanotechnology accounts for *both* the similarities and dissimilarities. This need not be the case, as the differences could just as well have widened the gap between life and things known to be designed. In weighing the differences, the investigator should consider them in light of the similarities[26] and to determine if they better reflect non-design versus advanced design.

THE BLIND WATCHMAKER RETURNS

Analogy can both provide the clues for Intelligent Design and a means to further test that suspicion. Yet we must come to terms with natural selection acting as the designer-mimic. Since natural selection results in changes with an apparent purpose, it can be expected to produce things analogous to human artifacts. Thus, any argument for design that relies solely on analogy cannot proceed very far along the Explanatory Continuum.

But consider what happens if we shift our analogical comparison from the designed to the designers and compare random mutation and natural selection (the designer-mimic) to a human-like designer. The list of dissimilarities has already been spelled out for us by mainstream scientists. For example, Richard Dawkins sets out to show us why the evidence for evolution reveals a universe without design and helps us to understand the gulf between the designers:

> All appearances to the contrary, the only watchmaker in nature is the blind forces of physics, albeit deployed in a very special way. A true watchmaker has foresight: he designs his cogs and springs, and plans their interconnections, with a future purpose in his mind's eye. Natural selection, the blind, unconscious, automatic process which Darwin discovered, and which we now know is the explanation for the existence and apparently purposeful form of all life, has no purpose in mind. It has no mind and no mind's eye. It does not plan for the future. It has no vision, no foresight, no sight at all. If it can be said to play the role of watchmaker in nature, it is the *blind* watchmaker.[2]

A true watchmaker has foresight while natural selection is blind. Yet not only is natural selection blind, it "has no mind and no mind's eye," meaning it is both blind and ignorant. So how does a blind, ignorant process actually work to mimic a designer?

The French molecular biologist and Nobel laureate François Jacob proposed that evolution designed as a tinkerer, not an engineer. Jacob's views have taken root in mainstream evolutionary thinking[28] and are nicely encapsulated by Uri Alon from the Weizmann Institute of Science:

> Engineers and tinkerers arrive at their solutions by very different routes. Rather than planning structures in advance and drawing up

blueprints (as an engineer would), evolution as a tinkerer works with odds and ends, assembling interactions until they are good enough to work.[29]

The tinkerer must make use of whatever available bits and pieces might already be lying around. The tinkerer then randomly cobbles them together in various combinations and if something just happens to benefit the bearer of the new device, it will be propagated. For the tinkerer, "success" occurs when something simply "works" to do anything to enhance reproductive output. Tinkering is exactly the type of design that a blind, ignorant watchmaker can handle. Such a watchmaker is not trying to design anything in light of any objective, it merely stumbles upon workable outcomes as a function of it messing with the machinery of life.

Evolution as tinkerer helps us further distinguish the designer-mimic from human-like intelligence. Because a tinkerer cannot invent, and instead must work with what is already laying around, the blind watchmaker leaves its fingerprints behind as "the opportunistic modification of a pre-existing structure rather than the clean elegance of design." After noting that both the blind watchmaker and Paley's watchmaker can account for something like the human eye, Miller wonders if there is a way to tell them apart:

In fact, there is a way to tell. Evolution, unlike design, works by the modification of pre-existing structures. Intelligent design, by definition, works fresh, on a clean sheet of paper, and should produce organisms that have been explicitly (and perfectly) designed for the tasks they perform.[30]

He also adds:

Evolution, on the other hand, does not produce perfection. The fact that every intermediate stage in the development of an organ must confer a selective advantage means that the simplest and most elegant design for an organ cannot always be produced by evolution. In fact, the hallmark of evolution is the modification of pre-existing structures. An evolved organism, in short, should show the tell-tale signs of this modification. A designed organism should not . . . . A true designer could begin with a clean sheet of paper, and produce a design that did not depend, as evolution must, on re-using old mechanisms, old parts, and even old patterns of development.[30]

So the hallmark of evolution is the modification of pre-existing parts. What if we find structures that lack this hallmark? What if we find something that does not appear as a modification of a pre-existing structure? This would hint of that "clean sheet of paper" and count against borrowing. With this criterion, we may not only have something that helps us better assess our design suspicion, but we may actually have a clue to help distinguish between front-loading and intelligent intervention. Since front-loading likewise relies on the modification of pre-existing structures, such missing evidence tips the balance toward intelligent intervention.

As an aside, it is worth noting that evolution as a blind, ignorant, tinkerer also happens to further enhance the plausibility of front-loading. If evolution is blind, it can be led. If evolution is ignorant, it can be instructed. If evolution is a tinkerer, it depends on what you give it. The blind, ignorant tinkerer can be more easily enlisted as a servant of the intelligent watchmaker. You do not have to worry about the blind, ignorant tinkerer seeing some unintended goal and reaching for it. You do not have to worry about the blind, ignorant tinkerer figuring out how to invent its own way through deep time. You do not have to worry about the blind, ignorant tinkerer rebelling against the plan you have for it. Thus, Intelligent Design and blind, ignorant tinkering can indeed co-exist in our biotic reality. They simply have a defined relationship as a function of their differences. It is the relationship of master designer and servant designer. The servant may meander, may make mistakes, and even be incredibly slow, but the servant remains in his place. He serves the master.

IRREDUCIBLE COMPLEXITY

As we have seen, an analogy to something that is designed is stronger when the analogy is coupled to a discontinuity with non-teleological processes. In this case, the discontinuity is a "clean sheet" somewhere within natural history, where the tinkerer needs pre-existing material and the engineer does not. Thus, if we find machines that have no precursors, the hallmark of evolution is missing. In that sense, we may hypothesize that evolution did not spawn that particular feature. And this takes us very close to the type of data many skeptics would count as evidence for Intelligent Design, namely, something not explained by evolution.[4] So how might we determine whether a discontinuity is in play?

Enter biochemist Michael Behe. In his book, *Darwin's Black Box*,[31] Behe explains the challenge originally provided by Charles Darwin: "If it could be demonstrated that any complex organ existed which could not possibly have been formed by numerous, successive, slight modifications, my theory would absolutely break down." Behe attempts to meet this challenge by offering things that are irreducibly complex. He defines Irreducible Complexity as follows:

> A single system composed of several well-matched, interacting parts that contribute to the basic function, wherein the removal of any one of the parts causes the system to effectively cease functioning.

Behe argues that irreducibly complex structures challenge Darwinian evolution because they entail the non-existence of precursor states. To illustrate this point, Behe uses the common mousetrap as an example. The trap is made up of five parts: the hammer, the spring, the holding bar, the catch, and the platform. If you were to buy a trap from the local hardware store that was missing just one of these parts, you would probably kick yourself if you threw away the receipt. The trap works only when all five parts are present. This means that a trap with only four out of five parts does not work. Likewise a trap with only three out of five parts does not work. The same holds true for a trap with only two out of five parts and one out of five parts. Since this device will only catch mice when all five parts are present, the incomplete "precursor" states are completely useless. If something like a mousetrap exists in the living world, how would Darwinian evolution possibly explain it? An irreducibly complex structure would only provide benefit to the organism when all parts are simultaneously present. Thus, an irreducibly complex structure lacking parts, as would be entailed by the gradual, step-by-step, Darwinian evolution of such a structure, would provide no selective benefit. Without selective benefit, the incomplete structure would accumulate all sorts of destructive mutations. It could not evolve toward the needed level of complexity to achieve its function.

Before we begin to assess this argument, we should note that in his attempt to meet Darwin's challenge, Behe inadvertently captures crucial aspects of a machine. When Wilkins speaks of molecular machines, he notes they perform highly specific functions and feature multiple parts that interact in distinct and precise ways. This is essentially the same as Irreducible Complexity, where the function is dependent on these multiple, precise interactions. And when Balzini and colleagues define a molecular level device, as mentioned earlier, they echo the theme of Irreducible Complexity: "an *assembly* of a *discrete number of molecular components* designed to achieve a *specific function*. Each molecular component performs a single act, *while the entire supramolecular assembly performs a more complex function*, which results from the cooperation of the various components."[18] They then define a molecular machine as a special class of molecular level devices, one in which the components alter their relative positions in response to an external stimulus (like setting off the mousetrap). Thus, while all irreducibly complex phenomena are not machines, it certainly appears all machines are irreducibly complex. Rather than use Irreducible Complexity in a generic sense, let us therefore restrict its use to the machines. Since the concept is embedded in the concept of a machine, it can be used to help determine whether or not the machines did indeed come into existence through Darwinian evolution.

Let us now consider the force of Behe's argument. Irreducible Complexity describes a system whose function is dependent on the interaction of multiple components, such that the removal of even one component results in the complete loss of function. It can thus be represented as follows:

$$A + B + C + D \longrightarrow F$$

where A, B, C, and D represent specific components (gene products) and F represents the function that is elicited by the interaction of these four parts.

From this observation, it is argued that F could not evolve, as F requires the presence of all four components. In other words, there would be no selective advantage of having parts A, B, and D compared to an organism having only parts A and B. Why? Because both combinations fail to elicit the function.

The basic problem with this argument is as follows: while it is true that function F requires components A, B, C, and D to exist, it does not follow therefore that parts A, B, C, and D require function F to exist. It is this problem that has been exploited by the critics of Behe.

In 2000, biologists David Ussery and Richard Thornhill considered Behe's argument and published a response in the scientific literature.[32] They outlined four possible routes of Darwinian evolution to determine if Irreducible Complexity really posed an obstacle. It is not all bad news for Behe's thesis. In their article, Ussery and Thornhill acknowledge that Irreducible Complexity does indeed pose an obstacle for two of the four Darwinian pathways. The first pathway they describe is "serial direct Darwinian evolution." This simply means change along a single axis. A classic example of this would be the evolution of the giraffe's neck, in that giraffes with longer necks would be able to out-compete others with shorter necks by reaching for leaves in tall trees. The longer the neck, the better the food supply, and thus the greater the reproductive success. Over time, subsequent populations would be enriched with giraffes having increasingly longer necks over time.

Another example of serial direct Darwinian evolution is provided by Richard Dawkins, as he explains the evolution of the photoreceptors in the eye. The photoreceptors have an array of stacked membranes that capture photons. Speaking about the number of membrane layers, Dawkins writes:

> The point is that ninety-one membranes are more effective in stopping photons than ninety are more effective than eighty-nine, and so on back to one membrane, which is more effective than zero. This is the kind of thing I mean when I say that there is a smooth gradient up Mount Improbable. We would be dealing with an abrupt precipice if, say, any number of membranes above forty-five was very effective while any number below forty-five was totally ineffective.

Neither common sense nor the evidence leads us to suspect any such sudden discontinuity.[3]

Unfortunately for Dawkins, the very year he made this argument was the same year Behe identified such an "abrupt precipice." The sudden discontinuity is entailed in an irreducibly complex machine, where a lack of just one crucial component renders the machine totally ineffective with regard to the proposed function. The examples of giraffe necks and photoreceptor membranes can be accounted for by Darwinian evolution because they involve only the modification and enhancement of function that is there from the start. This is serial direct Darwinian evolution. But as Thornhill and Ussery note, while this evolutionary route can generate complicated structures, "it cannot generate irreducibly complex structures."[32]

The second mechanism is "parallel direct Darwinian evolution." This means approximately synchronous changes in more than one component, so that modification to other components always occurs before the total modification to any one component has become significant. Thornhill and Ussery cite some examples:

> Most complex supramolecular biological structures have primarily this type of accessibility by Darwinian evolution, with examples being bat echolocation, spiders' web construction, honeybee waggle dances, and insect mimicry by orchids. Some complex (but not irreducibly complex) molecular systems, such as the globin proteins, could also have evolved in this manner.

But they also add:

> Parallel direct Darwinian evolution can generate irreducibly complex structures, but not irreducibly complex structures of functionally indivisible components, and this is the valid conclusion to draw from Behe's thesis.

When we are dealing with molecular machines (which are composed of functionally indivisible parts), many of the most well documented examples of Darwinian evolution become irrelevant. None of these data amount to evidence that irreducibly complex machines likewise evolved through Darwinian mechanisms. This is a significant point. We evolutionists rely heavily on extrapolation, where knowledge about the evolution of one lineage or structure is often applied to other lineages and structures. But if irreducibly complex structures cannot be explained by these two routes of Darwinian evolution, then evolutionary evidence for structures created by these two routes cannot be extrapolated as evidence for the evolution of the irreducibly complex structures. Ironically, most of the examples of evolution described in Richard Dawkins's books involve serial or parallel direct Darwinian evolution. This means that most of his evidence fails as a promissory note for the Darwinian evolution of the machines.

The two remaining routes for the Darwinian evolution of irreducibly complex structures are the "Elimination of Functional Redundancy" and "Adoption from a Different Function." Thornhill and Ussery use the analogy of an arch to illustrate how these mechanisms might work:

> The arch is irreducibly complex, and, assuming that cement does not set instantaneously, any arch one sees must therefore either have been built using scaffolding, analogously to redundancy elimination, or have been built elsewhere, perhaps horizontally, and moved into position when the cement had set, analogously to adoption.

We will thus consider both these routes and add another possible one below. While these three pathways exploit the inability to prove it is impossible for irreducibly complex systems to evolve, whether they succeed as valid explanations for the evolutionary origin of any particular system remains in question. To see this, return to the original Irreducible Complexity formula, where parts A through D elicit function F, and make one modification. Consider systems in which F, the function, can only exist if multiple gene products interact with each other.

Possible Ways to Evolve Irreducible Complexity

Original Helping Activity Becomes Essential. In this scenario, one envisions a component fortuitously associating with a protein complex that initially serves a non-essential, but helpful activity. But as the organism containing this modified system itself evolves, the originally helpful activity now becomes essential in this new context.

Original Helping Activity may be a plausible explanation for the modification of an irreducibly complex system, but it fails to explain the *origin* of that system. For example, we can imagine the following modification:

$$A + B + C \sim D \longrightarrow F$$

where A, B, and C are essential for function F and ~D helps to make a more efficient F. D is thus not part of the irreducibly complex system as F can exist without it. Then, as the organism evolves, this increased efficiency becomes essential to maintain the newly evolved state, giving:

$$A + B + C + D \longrightarrow F$$

The problem is that this scenario begins with a system needing A, B, and C. Thus, for Original Helping Activity to explain the origin of Irreducible Complexity, we would need to see the following. First, $A \longrightarrow F$. Then, $A \sim B \longrightarrow F$. Then $A + B \longrightarrow F$, and so on. But this explanation violates the assumption that F is dependent on the interaction of multiple gene products. For example, consider Table 8-I, which contains a small sample of molecular machines and their functions (long recognized by molecular biologists). The functions carried out by these machines could no more be carried out by a single gene product than an internal combustion engine could work being built from only one part. This is obvious from our study of the functions carried out by these machines, as several subsystems divide up the labor and then integrate to generate the function. It is no surprise that the living world does not provide any examples of these functions being carried out by single gene products. Original Helping Activity therefore fails as an explanation for the *origin* of irreducibly complex systems. However, it may be a useful scenario for explaining how a core system can be modified and become more complex over time.

Table 8-I. Representative Sample of Molecular Machines

MOLECULAR MACHINE	FUNCTION
Ribosome	Translate mRNA to synthesize proteins
Flagellum	Propel bacterial cells
F-ATP Synthase	Convert proton/ion gradient into ATP
Replisome	Replicate pre-existing DNA

Elimination of Functional Redundancy. In this scenario, one envisions the original functional state as being complex (involving many gene products) and thus bypasses the fatal flaw of the Original Helping Activity scenario. However, the complex state originally envisioned is redundantly complex:

$$A + B + C + D + E + G \longrightarrow F$$

where B/E and C/G share the same subfunction. In other words, a loss of B or C or E or G alone still allows for function F to be elicited. Thus, such a system fails the classic definition of Irreducible Complexity as provided by Behe. Since B/E and C/G share redundant subfunctions, one member of each two-member family can be lost by mutation. For example, the system could then evolve through the loss of components E and G, yielding:

$$A + B + C + D \longrightarrow F.$$

This explanation, however, involves some sleight of hand. While the originally proposed six-part system does not need all six parts, it still contains an essential core that is irreducibly complex. That is, this system still requires a four-part interaction involving A, B/E, C/G, and D to elicit F; Irreducible Complexity is simply embedded in the redundant complexity. Since this explanation starts by assuming an irreducibly complex core, Elimination of Functional Redundancy also fails to account for the *origin* of such systems.

Like the Original Helping Activity scenario, however, the Elimination of Functional Redundancy may explain how some systems have been modified since their origin. For example, in using the above scenario, it might

THE DESIGN MATRIX   221 explain why one organism carries out function F using components A, B, G, and D and another uses A, E, C, and D, etc. After all, it is not unreasonable to suppose that some originally designed complex systems were redundantly complex. This would buffer these systems against failure and also provide an avenue to front-load evolution. Therefore, if Irreducible Complexity harkens back to an originally redundant complexity, this, by itself, does not necessarily damage the design inference.

Cooption of Alternative Function. This explanation best exploits the logical flaw in the "Irreducible Complexity = evolution is impossible" argument. Since the existence of A, B, C, and D need not be F-dependent, Cooption of Alternative Function simply proposes that A, B, C, and D did indeed exist prior to F, whereby these components performed some alternative, original function. As such, this is really the only evolutionary explanation that has the potential to explain the origin of an irreducibly complex system. So let's take a closer look at it. Figure 8-1 will help us better envision a simplified version of this explanation.

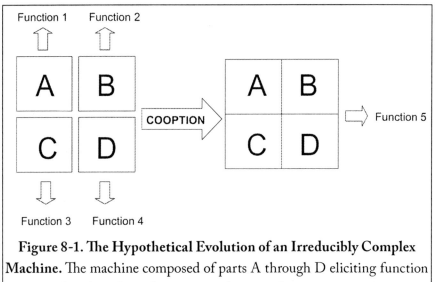

Figure 8-1. The Hypothetical Evolution of an Irreducibly Complex Machine. The machine composed of parts A through D eliciting function 5 evolves through cooption of previously existing parts.

Imagine a four-part machine that carries out function 5. In order for function 5 to occur, all four parts (A—D) must be present. How could this evolve? Simply imagine that parts A through D previously carried out different functions (1-4). If a mutation were to occur that allowed these four parts to interact, a new function might emerge as a consequence of this interaction. A, B, C, and D could be directly donated into the newly formed irreducibly complex system if functions 1-4 become dispensable. Or a series of gene duplications may occur for each of the gene products, allowing the duplicates to be recruited into the newly formed irreducibly complex system. Or gene products A—D could be multi-functional and now carry out dual roles in the cell.

This explanation becomes even more plausible if we accept the working hypothesis of front-loaded evolution. Recall that front-loading involves the ability to bury secondary designs in original states. One strategy was to design multi-functional proteins whose secondary designs could be unmasked when the appropriate context appeared later. Another strategy was to place secondary designs nearby in sequence space to the original design, where gene duplication followed by mutational divergence would have a decent shot of unmasking it. Both of these strategies are likely to involve cooption, where the buried design, once unmasked, can be coopted into a new context and function. Since cooption remains an effective vehicle for expressing front-loaded design, the evolution of irreducibly complex structures fits well within the perceptual Design Matrix. The viability of the front-loading explanation would depend on whether the original state was stacked such that a random search was likely to stumble upon a new irreducibly complex state. We would have a situation where evolution was designed to spawn certain of these systems when the conditions were right.

Nevertheless, the Cooption of Alternative Function should be invoked with caution. The most basic problem with the conventional use of this explanation is its complete reliance on chance. If we return to the originally proposed pathway above, we are asked to believe that while A, B, C, and D have long been shaped by selection to carry out their original alternative functions (1, 2, 3, and 4 respectively), a fortuitous interaction among them all would spawn a brand new function. Selection might be invoked to fine tune and improve the new function but, according to the non-teleological perspective, raw chance must still be credited for creating the novel function. It does not matter if we envision the irreducibly complex system, and all its parts, coming into existence gradually, piece by piece over time, as fortuitous interactions are still being invoked to bring the new component into the fold.

The problem of invoking chance to explain the origin of a new function is quite serious when dealing with molecular machines. For these machines to work, their components are usually fitted into a whole through the multiple interactions of their complementary conformations. It would seem unlikely that four various proteins, pruned by selection to carry out their original unrelated functions, just happen to have sufficient conformational complementarity to assemble into a novel machine with a novel function.

We can appreciate the problems that machine-like Irreducible Complexity poses to Darwinian evolution by comparing it to the evolution of a metabolic pathway. The PCP degradation pathway involved three different enzymes, where each one was needed to degrade PCP (see Chapter 6). As such, the pathway would seem to qualify as an irreducibly complex system, yet it apparently evolved rather easily.

The irreducibly complex nature of molecular machines and metabolic pathways differ in a significant manner. Machines depend on direct, specific contacts between components while such dependence is lacking in metabolic pathways. A molecular machine functions when energy (usually in the form of ATP binding and hydrolysis) enters the complex through a specific input portal. This energy input then triggers a cascade of uni-directional, conformational changes among the parts. Using the symbolic conventions in Figure 8-1, think of A changing shape to induce a shape change in B, which induces a shape change in C, which induces a shape change in D, which then elicits the functional output. The parts require a series of direct contacts to convey the energy/information/mechanical flow that brings about the function. Removing any part interrupts this flow and renders the entire complex functionless.

A metabolic pathway functions differently. In this case, protein A reacts with an original substrate to produce product 1. Product 1 is then converted into product 2 by protein B. Protein C then converts product 2 into product 3. And finally, protein D converts product 3 into product 4. We then define the appearance of product 4 from the original substrate as the function (F).

One could reasonably interpret this as example of Irreducible Complexity as proteins A, B, C, and D are needed to convert the original substrate into product 4. Yet such a pathway could evolve because various metabolic pathways are typically interlocked indirectly, through their substrates/products. That is, product 2 may bind to protein C (for conversion into product 3), but product 2 may also react with several other proteins and thus be useful elsewhere. Since the products of metabolic pathways can exist apart from any particular pathway, it is easier for the proteins in a pathway to exist apart from any particular function.

To appreciate just how different this is from a machine, consider the bacterial flagellum. You can isolate each individual component on the flagellum and fill test tubes with those individual parts. Most of the flagellar parts will not do anything and they would certainly not elicit flagellar function. This is analogous to taking your toaster apart and putting some or all the pieces in a box. If you add a piece of bread to that box, it certainly will not be toasted. In contrast, you can take any protein from a metabolic pathway and fill a test tube with it and it will do something significant—catalyze the specific chemical reaction that is part of the pathway. The components of a pathway are not F-dependent; they will perform their subfunction apart from F. In contrast, most parts of a molecular machine are F-dependent and will not perform their subfunction apart from F. This was the reason Original Helping Activity failed to account for the origin of the machines.

This means that a metabolic pathway may be poised to evolve (as we might expect from front-loading). Using nothing more than simple chemical rules and selection pressures, various components of metabolic pathways may realign themselves to carry out new functions. Since the proteins of any pathway interact through the intermediaries of their substrates and products, and these can exist independently of the proteins, readjustments are plausible, especially when aided by gene duplication. The parts of a molecular machine, however, are not interacting through independent intermediaries, but through direct physical contact. It is the *assembly-dependent* nature of the machine's function that makes it different from metabolic pathways. And this places much more stringent constraints on the system.

THE DESIGN MATRIX

Irreducible Complexity in the Matrix

Since there is a viable evolutionary pathway for the appearance of Irreducible Complexity, how can we use this concept in the context of the Design Matrix? First, we need to distinguish between indirect design through front-loading and direct design through intelligent intervention. The former interpretation of design allows us to see how Irreducible Complexity fits within the design of evolution, while the latter interpretation involves something other than evolution explaining features of our biological reality.

Let us begin with front-loading and Irreducible Complexity. I have already raised the possibility that some machines may have been front-loaded to exist. Recall Wilkins noted that molecular machines often have parts that can be used in other molecular machines comparable to the interchangeable parts of artificial machines. The evolution of a molecular machine may pose a problem for coincidental cooption, relying entirely on chance, but front-loaded cooption events are plausible. How could we hope to detect this? Say we find machine X and it is composed of subsystems A, B, and C. If we also find these same basic subsystems[34] in some other machines, or existing as independent modules, and these subsystems all predate machine X, we have a decent candidate for front-loading. That is, the pre-existence of these subsystems may have front-loaded the eventual appearance of machine X. This would be especially true if the three subsystems provided some generic function for the cell that would be expected to be propagated and could later coalesce into a more specialized role.

There are other ways to couple front-loading with Irreducible Complexity. Instead of viewing it as something that is a product of front-loading, it can likewise be seen as a means to facilitate front-loading. Because irreducibly complex machines function only when all parts are present, it is a mechanism of propagating entire sets of gene products. Lose one gene and the blind watchmaker steps in and prunes away the rest. But if the function is central to the cell, then all genes will be carried forward across deep time. This creates a vehicle to transport multi-functional genes, which can at some point escape from the machine state through gene duplication and divergence and actualize their new functions. Thus, homologs of irreducibly complex components that post-date the machine in question may reflect a reach toward such an intended state. Finally, while Irreducible Complexity may not make it impossible for evolution to produce something, it can be likened to a rate-limiting step in a metabolic pathway. Biochemists often focus on rate-limiting steps, as these steps are the "logjams" of pathways that not only serve to dictate the ultimate speed of the pathway, but can also serve as effective points of regulation. If machines are merely difficult to evolve, rather than impossible to evolve, a designer that endowed cells with a variety of these machines has the foreknowledge that they are likely to be propagated much as is, by being simply tweaked rather than replaced or completely redesigned. They can thus be used to channel evolution. If this is true, we would predict that many irreducibly complex machines are ancient and have thus played important roles in shaping subsequent evolution.

Yet let us focus primarily on using the concept of Irreducible Complexity much in the spirit that Behe intended it to be used. Let us consider it as a phenomenon that poses a serious obstacle to Darwinian evolution, thus opening the door to some form of design through intelligent intervention. Because we are dealing with machines that depend on specific interactions made possible through the assembly of their parts, and the non-teleologic view of cooption ultimately relies on chance to cobble these interactions together, there is no obligation to treat Cooption of Alternative Function as a default explanation. Instead, independent evidence is needed to support such a hypothesis of cooption cobbling a machine together. This does not mean we need something that amounts to a proof. Nor does it mean that an exhaustive Darwinian explanation is needed. On the contrary, the evidence we need is extremely modest and lacking in detail.

The first step is to define the irreducibly complex machine such that it is sensitive to evolution. This means doing a comparative analysis where the same basic machine from various distantly related organisms is considered. A "least common denominator" approach is adopted to score the number of parts shared by all these distantly related machines. This will make it possible to converge on the core set of parts that have been retained independently and many times over across vast expanses of evolution. Once this core has been defined, the evidence for cooption can be considered.

First, if an irreducibly complex machine did evolve into existence through cooption, then the parts must have predated the machine. They must have been doing something else prior to being recruited into the machine. Thus, some evidence of this pre-machine activity is needed. Since we cannot travel back in time, we will have to settle for traditional evidence of common descent. Do the various parts of the machine have homologs that are in turn part of a system that is more ancient than the machine?

Second, what is the "information content" of the machine components? When distantly related components are compared, do they demonstrate a "low-information" state as reflected by tolerance for huge changes in amino acid sequence? Or do they demonstrate significant sequence conservation, suggestive of a higher information state? Since low-information proteins are likely to be more easily coopted into a new role by chance, a machine composed of primarily such proteins is more plausibly explained by cooption. However, such a consideration must also pay tribute to the reality of Irreducible Complexity. By definition, we must account for *all* core components of the machine since all are required for function.

Since an origin through cooption requires that the machine parts have functioned previously in different contexts, this explanation fails if the parts of the machine are system-dependent. *A system-dependent part would be something that does not exist or function apart from the context of the machine.* It thus depends on the machine system for its existence and continued propagation through time. System-dependence actually sheds light from two different perspectives. If a part is system-dependent such that there are no viable homologs that predate the machine, then there is no evidence that evolution had something to coopt in order to stumble in the direction of the machine.[35] If there are no viable homologs that postdate the machine, then evolution (through gene duplication) has not extracted any further alternative function from the protein and this raises the specter of a part that is not very cooptable in a general sense. As for the low-information components, if they nevertheless demonstrate system-dependence, then the set of all such components must be considered together when dealing with an irreducibly complex machine.

The significance of system-dependence can also be appreciated from another angle. The cooption event as represented in Figure 8-1 is unlikely to happen. In this representation, all four parts simultaneously interact to elicit the new function. As such, we can think of this as *quantum cooption*, where a multi-part system leaps into existence and functions. If we were to postulate this type of evolution, this would be like the infamous tornado putting together a Boeing 747 as it moved through the junkyard. As evolutionary biologist H. Allen Orr noted:

> . . . we might think that some of the parts of an irreducibly complex system evolved step by step for some other purpose and were then recruited wholesale to a new function. But this is also unlikely. You may as well hope that half your car's transmission will suddenly help out in the airbag department. Such things might happen very, very rarely, but they surely do not offer a general solution to irreducible complexity.[36]

Darwinian evolution is going to have to construct such an irreducibly complex machine through gradual cooption. Figure 8-2 therefore shows a more

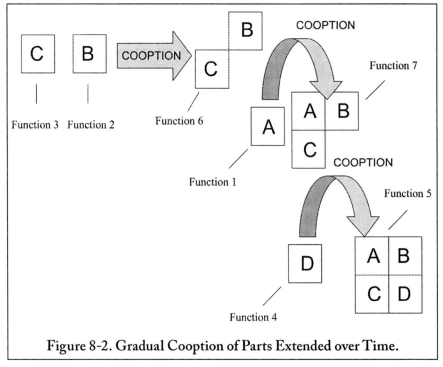

Figure 8-2. Gradual Cooption of Parts Extended over Time.

accurate representation of such evolution. We begin with part C and part B each participating in a different function (3 and 2, respectively). Then, these two parts (or their duplicates) interact in a fortuitous manner such that a new function (6) emerges that just happens to occur in an environmental context such that the function imparts a selective advantage. Some time later, we can imagine that part A, which is responsible for function 1, is duplicated and the duplicate, through another fortuitous interaction, is recruited to BC yielding yet another new function, 7. Again, some time later, the story repeats itself, but this time part D is added to finally elicit function 5. Since the cooption events have been smeared across time, and can occur step-by-step, this looks more like Darwinian evolution than a tornado in a junkyard.

If parts A through D are system-dependent, there is a problem. Gradual cooption predicts that remnants of such an evolutionary history should be found. For example, imagine this type of evolution occurring in bacteria. When parts B and C initially interact to elicit function 6, this will occur in a single species of bacteria. That this species has a new function that imparts some advantage means only that it will out-compete other members in the population of the same species. Other species in other environments carrying only functions 2 and 3 are not necessarily impacted by the appearance of function 6 someplace else on the Earth. Furthermore, there is no reason to think the appearance of function 6 will displace functions 2 and 3 in the same species, as the new emergent function 6 may be unrelated to the previous functions, meaning the species will now have all three functions.

The bottom line is that the appearance of a BC complex yielding function 6 will not necessarily erase B and C and their ability to produce functions 2 and 3. And the same point holds true for each advance in complexity through cooption. Thus, if gradual cooption has brought ABCD into existence, we should expect to find simpler versions that are descended from the various precursor states. We might even expect such a pathway to provide a phylogenetic signal, where the more closely related the bacteria, the more "complete" the irreducibly complex structure. In the case of Figure 8-2, bacteria closely related to the species with function 5 might be expected to possess function 7 while species much more distantly related may have only functions 2 and 3.

Evolution can, however, lose functions and parts along the way. Nevertheless, if the irreducibly complex system is loaded with system-dependent parts, the cooption explanation looks awfully *ad hoc*. With our ABCD system that produced function 5, we would be asked to believe that while functions 1, 2, 3, 4, 6, and 7 once existed and were likely spread throughout the evolutionary tree, they all effectively vanished once function 5 came onto the scene. And the problem gets much worse as the irreducibly complex system gets more complex. For example, a twenty-part system built through step-by-step gradual cooption might entail as many as thirty-nine functions to bridge all the gaps.[37] Would thirty-nine functions, which must have been useful in many contexts for extended periods of time, so readily vanish from the living world leaving nothing but the irreducibly complex system behind?

THE SYSTEM-DEPENDENT CORE

The explanation of gradual cooption requires the previous existence of simpler precursors and multiplied functions, many of which should have been carried along with the irreducibly complex structure somewhere in the tree of life. Yet the focus provided by Irreducible Complexity provides a deeper insight. Recall we began the analysis by comparing distantly related machines and looking for a set of shared parts—its core. Yet the more complex the core, and the more system-dependent parts it contains, the greater the problem for the explanation of gradual cooption.

Mitosis will help us appreciate this problem for gradual cooption. Mitosis is the complex and orderly process of dividing up the newly replicated chromosomes just prior to cell division. It consists of four stages that every biology student must learn: prophase, metaphase, anaphase, and telophase. Each stage comes with its own well-defined characteristics, making it possible for students to break a complex phenomenon down into four tidy blocks of facts to learn. However, such a tidy set of events is best seen in "advanced" organisms such as plants and animals. In the world of single-celled eukaryotes mitosis often looks messy. Lynn Margulis, an esteemed biologist from the University of Massachusetts, noted the significance of these permutations on the mitotic theme:

Mitotic cell division was the crucial genetic step toward further evolutionary advance. *One would not expect it to have developed in a straight-line manner, starting with no mitosis and concluding with perfect mitosis. There must have been numerous dead ends, variations, and byways.* Evidence of just such uncertain gradualism is found today among the lower eukaryotes, for example, the slime molds, the yellow-green and golden-yellow algae, the euglenoids, the slime-net amoebas and others. Many of their mitotic arrangements are unconventional. The perfection of mitosis may have occupied as much as a billion years of Precambrian times.[38] (emphasis added)

A complex process or structure would take a long time to gradually appear. It is this very gradualism, stretched out over time, coupled with the blind watchmaker's meandering and myopic groping, that generates many permutations along the way. As Margulis notes, you will not have a case where there is no complex structure followed by a "perfect" structure (unless, of course, engineering is involved); you will have your "perfect" structure amid a whole series of different flavors, all reflecting the products of the byways

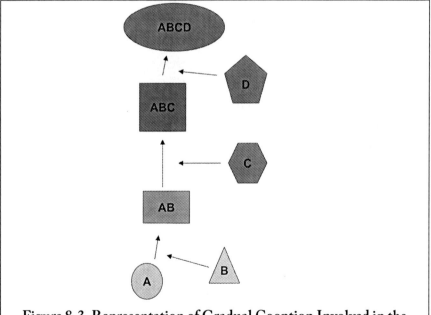

Figure 8-3. Representation of Gradual Cooption Involved in the Evolution of Irreducibly Complex Structure, ABCD.

232   ANALOGIES AND DISCONTINUITIES

and detours explored by the blind watchmaker giving some organisms something that enhances fitness is some fashion.

To further illustrate this point, consider the standard cooption explanation as shown in Figure 8-3. Here we have the standard story of each part (A through D) being coopted over time, step-by-step. Smearing the cooption events sequentially across time allows us to invoke the full power of cumulative selection.[27] While Figure 8-3 paints a convincing picture of the evolution of an irreducibly complex structure, we have just seen that it neglects an important context. Such evolutionary scenarios involve simpler precursor states and alternatively functioning parts and there is no reason to think they would all disappear. But there is more missing context. If cooption is a purely random process, and likely to occur over evolutionary time, there is no reason to think evolution would leap from A to the specific target of ABCD. The potential for byways and detours exist at *every node* along the way.

Figure 8-4 corrects this problem by adding more context. For example, if A can fortuitously interact with B to form AB in one lineage, what is to keep

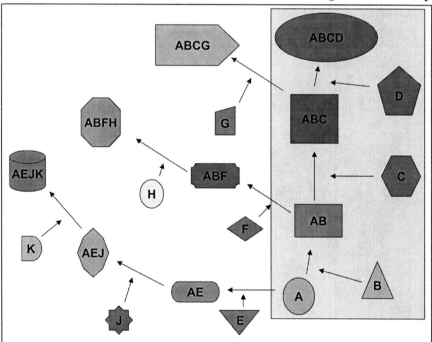

Figure 8-4. The Gradual Cooption of ABCD along with Some Possible Byways. The scenario from Figure 8-3 is highlighted in the box.

A from fortuitously interacting with E in another lineage? Once AE forms, it might fortuitously interact with J, and then K, and ultimately form AEJK. AB, in addition to interacting with C, might interact with F, ultimately leading to the formation of complex ABFH. And ABC might interact with D in one lineage, but G in another lineage, forming ABCG. There are byways all along the road to ABCD that allow the blind watchmaker to stumble upon all kinds of variations. Of course, even this is overly simplistic.

In addition to A interacting with B and E at the base of the evolution pathways, it might be able to interact with a hundred other partners to carve out thousands of byways. If interactions were all fortuitous, how can we rule these others out? Also, since this evolution was occurring over great time spans, we might also then expect another phylogenetic signal: the more distantly related the organism, the more significant the variation on the ABCD theme. Furthermore, as we add more and more distantly related organisms to the hopper, and as we begin to compare their irreducibly complex machines, the number of permutations should increase. But even here, the picture is again too simple.

Why assume parts B, C, and D are exclusively channeled into the

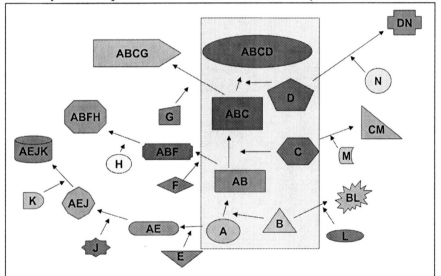

Figure 8-5. Gradual Cooption Scenario Where All Parts (ABCD) Can Be Coopted into Different Structures. The scenario from Figure 8-3 is again highlighted in the box.

ABCD structure? Figure 8-5 expands on this point and illustrates how the complexity of the evolutionary pathways further explode. In this example, not only does part A interact with E and B to carve out two pathways toward increased complexity, but part B can interact with L to carve out a route toward a permutation.

The complexity illustrated in Figure 8-5 helps us appreciate the significance of system-dependence. If we hypothesize that system ABCD arose through gradual cooption as a consequence of a series of fortuitous interactions, it would be most surprising if ABCD is the only remnant of this evolution. In addition to finding ABCD, why wouldn't we also be able to find AE, AEJ, AEJK, ABFH, ABF, BL, CM, DN, ABCG, and so on? Such permutations and variations are the expected byproducts of evolving ABCD through gradual cooption. In fact, the more complex the system, the more variations and permutations should exist. Yet system-dependence, by definition, means that we don't find A, B, C, or D apart from the system ABCD. This is not a pattern that is expected from the hypothesis of gradual cooption, but it is expected from a hypothesis that views design as being expressed through intelligent intervention.

Summing Up

The suspicion of Intelligent Design can be strengthened in two ways. First, the proposed analogy between a biological feature and something known to be designed can be explored. If, for example, designed biological features are compared with advanced versions of our own technology, we would expect the analogy between them to deepen over time. If a biological feature is designed, yet there are differences between the feature and our own products of design, we would predict that the biological feature, when properly understood, exhibits aspects of superior design. Successful attempts to strengthen the analogy can serve two purposes. First, any attempt to strengthen an analogy can generate testable hypotheses about the biological feature and thus serve as a vehicle for guiding scientific research in the light of design. Second, any such success in this regard would constitute positive evidence for design. A design hypothesis, drawing upon analogy, would thus be supported by experiment and data.

The second way to strengthen our Intelligent Design suspicion is to use Irreducible Complexity to evaluate the applicability of non-teleological causation. This is especially true when dealing with molecular machines, which already imply design based in part on a credible analogy to man-made machines. However, the criterion of Irreducible Complexity is not used to prove the machines could not have evolved. It is used to bring a higher resolution focus, where it becomes clear that coincidental cooption is really the only plausible non-teleological explanation for the origin of the machine. If the machine evolved through cooption, we would then expect to find remnants of this evolution in the form of simpler precursors, a myriad of permutations, and functions existing apart from the irreducibly complex system. If, however, the machine did not come into existence through cooption, we would expect to find the system to be composed largely of system-dependent parts, with little or no evidence of any precursor states that predate the machine in question.

When the Irreducible Complexity analysis is coupled to the positive approach generated by a focus on analogy, we find our biotic equivalent of Mount Rushmore—something that not only looks designed, but also does not look like it was spawned by a non-teleological mechanism.

References

1. Dembski, W., 2003. "Intelligent Design." http://www.designinference.com/documents/2003.08.Encyc_of_Relig.htm; last accessed 08/23/04.
2. Arnold, L., 2005. "Transit Lightcurve Signatures of Artificial Objects." *Astrophyical Journal*, 627:534-539.
3. After all, isn't France the home of the Raelians?
4. "Evidence for Intelligent Design: From the Perspective of the ID Critic." http://www.idthink.net/back/evidID/index.html.
5. Copley, S.D., 2000. "Evolution of a Metabolic Pathway for Degradation of a Toxic Xenobiotic: The Patchwork Approach." *Trends in Biochemical Sciences*, 25:261-265.
6. Eggertsen, G., Nyberg, G., Nilsson, B., Nilsson, U. and Svalander,

C.T., 2001. "Complement Deposition in Renal Allografts with Early Malfunction." *Acta Pathologica, Microbiologica et Immunologica Scandinavica*, 109:825-834.

7. Schmidt, D. and Muller, S., 2002. "Members of the PIAS Family Act as SUMO Ligases for c-Jun and p53 and Repress p53 Activity." *Proceedings of the National Academy of Sciences of the United States of America*, 99:2872-2877.

8. Search conducted on 09/21/04.

9. Kemerling, G., "Analogy." http://www.philosophypages.com/lg/e13. htm; last accessed 09/21/04.

10. Quoted by Mellerio, J. http://users.wmin.ac.uk/~mellerj/bernard.htm; last accessed 01/21/07.

11. Cannon, W.B., 1932. *The Wisdom of the Body*. W.W. Norton & Company, New York.

12. Agutter, P.S., Malone, P.C. and Wheatley, D.N., 2000. "Diffusion Theory in Biology: A Relic of Mechanistic Materialism." *Journal of the History of Biology*, 33:71-111.

13. Cybernetics is the science of control and information. For example, see http://www.biologie.uni-hamburg.de/b-online/e15/15.htm; last accessed 09/24/01.

14. Csete, M.E. and Doyle, J.C., 2002. "Reverse Engineering of Biological Complexity." *Science*, 295:1664-1669.

15. In systems analysis, the scientist looks at the whole as an integrated, dynamic population of molecules (for example) rather than focusing on parts isolated from the whole.

16. Knoblauch, M. and Peters, W.S., 2004. "Biomimetic Actuators: Where Technology and Cell Biology Merge." *Cellular and Molecular Life Sciences*, 61:2497-2509.

17. Ullman, D.G., 1992. *The Mechanical Design Process*. McGraw-Hill, New York, pp. 50-51.

18. Balzini, V., Credi, A. and Venturi, M., 2002. "The Bottom-Up Approach to Molecular-Level Devices and Machines." *Chemistry - A European Journal*, 8:5525-5532.

19. Robison, K., 1996-1997. "Darwin's Black Box: Irreducible Complexity

or Irreproducible Irreducibility?" http://www.talkorigins.org/faqs/behe/review.html; last accessed 09/24/04.

20. Max, E.E., 1986-2003. "Plagiarized Errors and Molecular Genetics: Another Argument in the Evolution-Creation Controversy." http://www.talkorigins.org/faqs/molgen/; last accessed 09/24/04.

21. Shapiro, J.A. and von Sternberg, R., 2005. "Why Repetitive DNA Is Essential to Genome Function." *Biological Reviews*, 80:1-24.

22. Wilkins, A.S., 2003. "A Special Issue on Molecular Machines." *BioEssays*, 25:1145-1146.

23. Drexler, K.E., 1986. *Engines of Creation: The Coming Age of Nanotechnology*. Anchor Press, New York.

24. Ratner, M. and Ratner, D., 2003. *Nanotechnology: A Gentle Introduction to the Next Big Idea*. Prentice Hall PTR, New Jersey.

25. We must also remember that even if the design hypothesis is correct, the molecular machines did not come off the designer's table yesterday. What we study are the descendants of design, thus they may have accumulated differences as a function of acquired evolutionary noise. Furthermore, from the perspective of front-loaded evolution, we are dealing with machines intended to propagate across deep time without the intervening help of the designer. Thus, differences that actually facilitate the ability to front-load evolution may also fit under the category of design.

26. If we have a situation where the similarities far outweigh the differences, the nature of the difference(s) must be profoundly fundamental to counter the current of similarity.

27. Dawkins, R., 1986. *The Blind Watchmaker: Why the Evidence of Evolution Reveals a Universe without Design*. W. W. Norton & Company, New York.

28. A Google search string "evolution as tinkerer" will turn up dozens of articles and university lectures that embrace this metaphor.

29. Alon, U., 2003. "Biological Networks: The Tinkerer as an Engineer." *Science*, 301:1866-1867.

30. Miller, K., 1994. "Life's Grand Design." *Technology Review*, 97:24-32.

31. Behe, M., 1996. *Darwin's Black Box: The Biochemical Challenge to Evolu-*

tion. The Free Press, New York.

32. Thornhill, R. and Ussery. D.W., 2000. "A Classification of Possible Routes in Darwinian Evolution." *Journal of Theoretical Biology*, 202:111-116.

33. Dawkins, R., 1996. *Climbing Mount Improbable*. W.W. Norton & Company, New York, pp. 144-145.

34. The subsystems may be differently modified by evolution, but would nevertheless reflect a core homology.

35. Such an analysis, however, does not guarantee the elimination of fuzz. The possibility of common design remains, such that similar parts are mistakenly viewed as homologs. Since the concept of common design is easily misused in *ad hoc* arguments, its consideration must be carefully weighed.

36. Orr, H.A., 1996. "Darwin v. Intelligent Design (Again) The Latest Attack on Evolution Is Cleverly Argued, Biologically Informed—and Wrong." http://web.archive.org/web/20040101144302/http://boston review.net/br21.6/orr.html; last accessed 10/14/04.

37. The number of functions needed for cooption alone to evolve IC is $n + (n-1)$, where n = number of parts of the IC system.

38. Margulis, L., 1971. "Symbiosis and Evolution." *Scientific American*, 225:49-57.

Chapter 9

Rationality and Foresight

William Paley introduced the vertebrate eye as an example of a design so wondrous that he considered it sufficient to establish the existence of design. Paley compared the eye to a telescope, noting their many similarities. But he went beyond an attempt to find similarities between the two:

> As far as the examination of the instrument goes, there is precisely the same proof that the eye was made for vision as there is that the telescope was made for assisting it. They are made upon the same principles, both being adjusted to the laws by which the transmission and refraction of rays of light are regulated. I speak not of the origin of the laws themselves; but such laws being fixed, the construction in both cases is adapted to them. For instance, these laws require, in order to produce the same effect, that rays of light in passing from water into the eye should be refracted by a more convex surface than when it passes out of air into the eye. Accordingly, we find that the eye of a fish, in that part of it called the crystalline lens, is much rounder than the eye of terrestrial animals. What plainer manifestation of design can there be than this difference? What could a mathematical instrument maker have done more to show his knowledge of his principle, his application of that knowledge, his suiting of his means to his end—I will not say to display the compass or excellence of his skill and art, for in these all comparison is indecorous, but to testify counsel, choice, consideration, purpose?[1]

When Paley asks what more could a "mathematical instrument maker" have done "to show his knowledge of his principle," he is appealing to an *intelligent* watchmaker. The eye not only looks like an artifact, but an understanding of its principles demonstrates a designer working in light of knowledge and purpose. Unfortunately for Paley, we now know that the blind watchmaker is quite capable of altering the shape of the lens to alter the degree of refraction. We do not need to appeal to a mathematical instrument maker.

Paley's infamous eye argument has actually been turned back on those who use it to "prove design." Yes, we can think of the human eye as an organic camera. Light enters a hole in the eye called the pupil, is focused by the lens, and impacts on light receptor cells at the back the eyeball that are then triggered to send electrical signals through cellular wiring to the brain. However, many people have noted the arrangement of the parts is not rational[2], as the wiring that carries the electrical signals to the brain actually lies between the light and the receptor cells. The wiring gets in the way! A truly rational design, it is claimed, would place the wiring behind the receptors so that there would be no interference. This, of course, makes sense. Someone who thinks the vertebrate eye was designed by a rational and intelligent agent must then explain why this "poor design" is not in fact poor, and come up with a rational reason for putting the wiring in front of the light receptors.[3] Unless we find such a rational reason, we are left with something that looks hodgepodge—which is exactly what we expect from natural selection.

Regardless of whoever is right about the eye, this debate provides an excellent illustration of the difference between Intelligent Design and evolution by natural selection. The former invokes a rational watchmaker who uses sound design principles to construct things, where things do not have to be perfect, only well made in light of the intended objectives. The latter invokes the blind watchmaker, who, without any foresight, haphazardly cobbles things from various parts in order to come up with something that simply works. Let us return to François Jacob as he unequivocally highlights this difference:

> Natural selection has no analogy with any aspect of human behavior.
> However, if one wanted to play with a comparison, one would have
> to say that natural selection does not work as an engineer works. It
> works like a tinkerer—a tinkerer who does not know exactly what

he is going to produce but uses whatever he finds around him. . . in short it works like a tinkerer who uses everything at his disposal to produce some kind of workable object.[4]

In the last chapter, we explored how the tinkerer was dependent upon pre-existing states, and this aspect was helpful in developing a criterion to infer design (discontinuity). Now we can focus on the fact that the tinkerer "does not know." It has no mind's eye. It is dumb. In contrast, the engineer does know things, has a mind's eye, and is smart.

Dr. Howard Van Till is Professor Emeritus of Physics and Astronomy at Calvin College. In his criticism of Intelligent Design, Van Till provides us with a distinction that is very useful when inferring design:

> We speak often today of things that have been designed. Cars are designed; clothing is designed; buildings are designed. Suppose, then, we were to walk into the headquarters of a major automobile manufacturer and ask to observe the process of cars being designed. What kind of activity would we be shown? Would we be taken to the assembly line to see cars being put together by human hands and mechanical robots? No, we would be taken to the "design center" where we would see people working with their minds (augmented, of course, by computers and various means of modeling what their minds conceive) to conceptualize new cars of various styles to achieve the intentions of the manufacturer in the marketplace. In other words, to say that a car was designed is to say that a car was thoughtfully conceptualized to accomplish some well-defined purpose. In contemporary parlance, *the action of design is performed by a mind, intentionally conceptualizing something for the accomplishment of a purpose.*

> This *mind-like* action of *designing* is clearly distinguishable from the *hand-like* action of *actualizing* (assembling, arranging, constructing) what had first been designed. On a tour of an automobile manufacturing facility, for instance, we would have no difficulty in distinguishing the mental work done at the design center from the manual work done on the assembly line.[5] (emphasis not added)

If a biological feature was designed, the residual trace of its design is not going to be found in the hands that put it together, but in the mind that conceptualized the design. When someone argues the backward wiring of the retina is evidence against the eye's design, they are not taking issue with the method by which the eye is constructed. They are focused on the "design center," where people working with their minds would not have designed the eye in this fashion.

Van Till's distinction also helps us to realize that we should not expect a teleological cause to be treated as if it is a non-teleological cause. When focused on a non-teleological cause, we need only concern ourselves with how things happen. This mechanistic viewpoint would ask how things are assembled or constructed. We can get up close and ask how the eye is constructed during embryological development or we could step back and ask how this process of construction itself was constructed by evolution. But if we were to apply this approach to a teleological cause, it would be akin to focusing on the assembly line and not the "design center." We would thus miss the design completely. You are not going to approach the "design center" by asking *how* the eye is constructed or *how* the eye-construction process itself was constructed. Mechanism is secondary. You have to ask *why* the eye is constructed as it is. And this is the very question that leads many people to reject the eye as something that was designed. Why are those photoreceptors behind the wiring?

Yes indeed, the action of design *is* performed by a mind. You are unlikely to find it by looking for hands and trying to describe what type of hands assembled the product. You are going to find design as an echo of a mind. Now, it does not seem unreasonable to suppose that a mind, guided by understanding, might come up with something that is detectably different from a blind, ignorant, tinkerer. So let us now draw out some differences we might expect from the two.

Rational Engineer versus the Tinkerer

Biologist Massimo Pigliucci, from the University of Tennessee, spells out the implications of Jacob's tinkerer. Pigliucci argues that organisms are "made of several parts that have no unique and irreplaceable function." He adds:

> As biologist François Jacob put it, this is exactly what you would expect if natural selection worked like a bricoleur rather than a cunning engineer. A bricoleur is somebody who assembles new things out of old parts that are easily available. The result is bound to be complex, redundant, suboptimal, and not too pretty. Exactly like living organisms, and precisely what you would expect from a natural phenomenon.[6]

Thus, the blind watchmaker gives us a messy, redundant complexity.

Ken Miller captures the essence of this form of design as he describes the genome as a product of the blind watchmaker: "In fact, the genome resembles nothing so much as a hodgepodge of borrowed, copied, mutated, and discarded sequences and commands that has been cobbled together by millions of years of trial and error against the relentless test of survival."[2]

Like Pigliucci says, it is not too pretty. You would think such design should stand out against the blind, ignorant tinkerer's haphazard cobbling. But then again, some contradict such claims and argue instead that the blind, ignorant tinkerer actually mimics the best of engineers.

Richard Dawkins recognizes that many factors may be at work in evolution, yet he insists on one thing: "Wherever in nature there is a sufficiently powerful illusion of good design for some purpose, natural selection is the only known mechanism that can account for it."[7] He further pushes this point by noting that if "an engineer looks at an animal or organ and sees that it is well designed to perform some task, then I will stand up and assert that natural selection is responsible for the goodness of apparent design."[7] Apparently, while natural selection does not work as an engineer would, engineers would not know this.

Does natural selection work like an engineer or not? I suppose we could argue both. Biologist George Williams does. As he explores the backward wiring of the eye's retina, he asks:

> What might Paley's reaction have been to the claim. . . that mun-

dane processes taking place throughout living nature can produce contrivances without contrivers, and that these processes produce not only functionally elegant features but also, as a kind of cumulative historical burden, the arbitrary and dysfunctional features of organisms?[8]

Here the blind watchmaker both crafts functionally elegant, arbitrary, and dysfunctional features. It is both brilliant and stupid. That all the bases are covered allows an apologist to explain any biological feature in light of the blind watchmaker. However, this *ad hoc* explanatory power is purchased with the loss of predictive power, as the blind watchmaker mechanism cannot predict if a feature should be elegant or a hodgepodge. It predicts both and will always be verified.

Perhaps we can tease apart the significance of an elegant feature from a jury-rigged feature with the help of Behe's concept. We saw that Irreducible Complexity steers us toward cooption as the non-teleological explanation for origins. And it is here that we no longer have any reason to think the blind watchmaker would make a good impersonation of an engineer. Why? The cooption events that are needed to bring together distinct components and crystallize a new machine-like function are ultimately rooted in blind chance. That parts A, B, and C come together to provide an immediate benefit to the bearer of the complex means simply that ABC work better than having no ABC. It does not necessarily mean that ABC can then be fine tuned into something that looks like it was the product of a mathematical instrument maker. There is no reason to think ABC can necessarily be tweaked into something that would cause Dawkins's engineer friends to declare it a good design. As H. Allen Orr points out:

> Organisms aren't trying to match any "independently given pattern": evolution has no goal, and the history of life isn't trying to get anywhere. If building a sophisticated structure like an eye increases the number of children produced, evolution may well build an eye. But if destroying a sophisticated structure like the eye increases the number of children produced, evolution will just as happily destroy the eye. Species of fish and crustaceans that have moved into the

total darkness of caves, where eyes are both unnecessary and costly, often have degenerate eyes, or eyes that begin to form only to be covered by skin—crazy contraptions that no intelligent agent would design. Despite all the loose talk about design and machines, organisms aren't striving to realize some engineer's blueprint; they're striving (if they can be said to strive at all) only to have more offspring than the next fellow.[9]

Non-teleological evolution is only about finding a way, any way, "to have more offspring than the next fellow." It is not about generating elegance.

The blind watchmaker mechanism not only implies nothing more than "it works," but also implies that if it could generate rational designs, these would be strikingly rare. Consider the following example as an illustration: "I won't be home in time for supper since I will be working late." The specificity inherent in the sequence of letters arranged in a particular fashion is important in conveying this message. We know there are vastly more ways to arrange letters so that this message is not conveyed. In fact, one can use the letters of the alphabet to generate far more lines of gibberish than any coherent sentence. But there is one more added dimension that is often overlooked. *There are other ways to arrange letters so that the same basic message is conveyed.* Consider just a few possible arrangements:

- Supper no. Late work.
- Me not home food job busy.
- I don't he home in dime for supper since I dill be workeeng laight.
- I won't be home in time for supper, supper will thus be missed, but I have to work late tonight, at a job that I almost always work late at, so don't expect me home for supper.

All these sentences convey the same basic message (the function), but they all lack the same degree of rationality inherent in the original. How do we tell? Our understanding of the rules of grammar and the rules of spelling allow us to detect irrational elements in these four sentences, while the same rules allow us to detect the original as one that conforms to these rules. *There*

Rationality and Foresight

are more ways of making things that work than there are of making them work in a rational fashion. And since natural selection only cares if things work, and things that work are more common than things that work rationally (but still far less common than things that do not work), it is unlikely natural selection will consistently generate inherently rational specified complexity. In fact, the more examples of rational specified complexity we find, the more unlikely it is that the blind watchmaker masterminded them.

It is important to point out that our investigation is open to the action of both the rational watchmaker and the blind watchmaker over the entire span of natural history. If we take our sentences as an example, we would tentatively attribute the first to the rational watchmaker and the others to a blind watchmaker. What is more, we might then be interested in determining if the original sentence is the ancestor of the other four, which were subsequently handled by the blind watchmaker. If a good argument could be made for this hypothesis, then all the activity of the blind watchmaker would not constitute any evidence that it also stumbled upon the first sentence. In this case, the blind watchmaker would have done what it did only because it was handed something by the rational watchmaker. Thus, the whole concept of Intelligent Design may go beyond the mere detection of design, and also imply things about how the patterns associated with life have developed and evolved since the initially designed state.

To determine if the essence of a biological feature reflects Rational Design, we need something analogous to the spelling and grammar rules used to distinguish the sentences above. To find the rules of Rational Design, it seems only reasonable to once again look to engineering, but this time for assistance in outlining these specific rules.

STRUCTURAL AND FUNCTIONAL DECOMPOSITION

Many people who design and build things for a living will tell you they started as young children by taking things apart and then putting them back together. The process of disassembly is related to that of assembly. A methodical and organized process of disassembly, coupled with an appreciation for each part disassembled, makes it easier to reassemble. The design process employed in mechanical engineering involves the concept of *decomposi-*

tion, where complex things are literally and/or conceptually broken down into less complex things. By decomposing something into simpler parts, the process of composing them into something that is ultimately more complex becomes much easier. For example, if a novel piece of technology was stolen by a spy, the engineers in the spy's country would start their analysis of this new technology by taking it apart, one piece at a time. By taking the technology apart, carefully cataloging the process of disassembly, and monitoring the effects of this disassembly, the engineers could begin to understand what the parts do and how they interact. This information would then be used to design copies or perhaps even engage in redesign.

In mechanical engineering, there are two types of decomposition.[10] *Structural decomposition* is concerned with the actual assembly and the form of the physical components. The assemblage known as a car can be decomposed into sub-assemblies such as the engine, the chassis, the body, etc. Each of these can be decomposed into further sub-assemblies. For example, the engine can be decomposed into sub-assemblies such as the carburetor, the block assembly, and the valve assembly. These in turn can be further decomposed until, ultimately, the level of individual parts or components is reached.

The second type of decomposition is concerned with systems and their functions. It is called *functional decomposition*. Looking at the same car that was structurally decomposed, David Ullman redefines it as a transportation system whose function is to move goods and people.[10] We can then begin decomposing along these lines; the engine would be the power subsystem and its function is to convert potential energy stored in the fuel to kinetic energy. The engine can be further decomposed into subsystems, like the ignition system that functions to start the energy conversion.

Although the viewpoints are related, given that form and function go hand-in-hand, when mechanical engineers design something, generally, functional decomposition is considered first. And once the functions have been decomposed to their finest level possible, assemblies and components can be developed to provide these functions. Intended function guides the selection of form.

Ullman further notes that function is something that a system does and it is the task of the engineer to come up with components that have the proper structure/form to conduct the function. He offers a crucial insight in noting that function can be viewed in terms of "the logical flow of energy, material, or information." Energetic flow is concerned with the type of energy and its action in the system. It can be described using the functions listed in Chapter 3. For example, energy can be transformed, stored, transferred, and dissipated. Information flow is concerned with not only the software output, but mechanical and electrical signals that specify and direct processes. Finally, mechanical flow can be divided into three types. First, there is through flow, where material is manipulated to change its position or shape. Typical terms used to describe through flow are hold, support, move, translate, rotate, guide. Second, there is diverging flow, where material is divided into more than one part. Typical terms used here are disassemble and separate. Last, there is converging flow, where two or more parts come together. Typical terms used here are join and assemble. By coupling these types of logical flow to form, function can be designed within the overall context of decomposition.

Ullman's description of these logical flows maps nicely to the processes of the molecular world, perhaps echoing life's origin through design. Consider a widespread, generic example where two proteins, A and B, exist in the nucleus of a cell. Say that protein A interacts with another protein, C, so that a phosphate group is attached to A which, in turn, changes its shape so it becomes "activated." As a consequence, the activated A protein now interacts with B to change its shape so it too becomes activated to join yet another protein, D, resulting in the formation of a BD complex that now binds to the DNA to help express a gene. This process can be interpreted through the filters of the three different forms of logical flow. From the perspective of energy flow, energy that is stored in ATP can be transferred to protein A (via protein C) resulting in the cascade of conformational changes. From the perspective of material flow, we have examples of through flow in the form of conformational changes (in A and B) and perhaps positional changes along with converging flow where proteins B and D join. The material and energetic flow merge into the function of DNA binding. Information flow can be appreciated when we inquire why, when, and where this event happens. When and how did the proteins get in to the nucleus; why did protein C interact with protein B? Of course, to understand informational flow, we would have to invoke mechanical and energetic flow to explain the origin of proteins A, B, C, and D. And this mechanical and energetic flow, in turn, would require us to invoke informational flow in the form of the DNA sequence. This is not surprising, as Ullman notes that the "three flows—energetic, mechanical, and information—are rarely distinguishable."

There is one more important insight that can be gained from Ullman's outline of structural and functional decomposition—the concept of interfaces. Ullman notes that a basic assumption among mechanical engineers is that function occurs at the interface between the components. Consider the simple example of scissors, something that is comprised of three components: the two shears and the pin that joins them at one side. The function of scissors is to cut, and the process of cutting occurs at the interface of the two shears as a consequence of their interface with the pin. Biological functions are no different. Proteins will bind to DNA because of interactions that take place at the interface between the protein and the DNA. Even an individual protein functions because of interface interactions. For example, enzymes function to speed up chemical reactions because when they bind to their substrate, they do so through multiple interfaces created by the molecule and several different amino acids that are in close proximity.

The exciting thing about interfaces is that they help to flesh out the details behind Michael Behe's concept of Irreducible Complexity. An understanding of the interface interactions that occur, for example, with the scissors explains why all three parts are needed to perform the function of cutting (as scissors represent a very simple example of Behe's irreducibly complex systems). Likewise, when we understand the individual components of a machine and how they interact to perform a function, we begin to understand why all the various components are needed. As we begin to seriously think about biology from the perspective of engineering, we begin to realize how it is that Irreducible Complexity is indeed tied to design. The function depends on the interfaces presented by the conformation and sequence of any given protein and that both the conformation and the actual interfaces depend on multiple, independent parts that all need to be present.

If structural and functional decomposition characterize designed things, this criterion can be used to help gauge the strength of a suspicion of Intelligent Design. First of all, if we hypothesize that some process of life reflects design, we would predict that this process would be further susceptible to structural and functional decomposition (depending on our state of knowledge). Second, if something is rationally designed, the process of functional decomposition should eventually map to the logical flow of material, energy, and information. We would thus be able to appreciate the design in a conceptual and abstract form such that it conforms nicely to the rules of reason. If this happens, we would come as close as possible to the conceptions of the intelligent designer that always precede the implementation of any design. The blind watchmaker, in contrast, simply cobbles a protein complex together through random cooption and there is no good reason to think the system should be decomposed in a way that reflects a *logical flow*.

However, the significance of structural and functional decomposition may primarily be tied up in its ability to weaken or falsify a design inference. Consider two examples. First, contained within the genome of many cells are the pseudogenes. I would not consider a pseudogene the product of design (which means they can serve as good markers of common descent) simply because they have no function. They cannot be structurally and functionally decomposed, since there is nothing to decompose. However, if it turns out a particular pseudogene does have a function, the status of its origin might have to be re-evaluated since the criterion of structural and functional decomposition would no longer discard it as a candidate for design.

Second, consider the degradosome from *E. coli*. It can be viewed as a modular system composed of four parts: an exoribonuclease (PNPase), an endoribonuclease, an RNA helicase, and enolase. The apparent function of the degradosome is to serve as a universal RNA degradation machine (capable of digesting any RNA in the cell). Three of the four parts have interacting activities—endonuclease, exonuclease, and helicase. These three functions may act in concert to degrade any RNA and are probably required to give the machine its globalized role in the economy of the cell. But what about the enolase? It is a metabolic enzyme that helps break down the sugar molecules, a process that does not seem to have any connection to RNA degradation. What is it doing, glommed on to three enzymes that transact with RNA? From the perspective of structural and functional decomposition, the enolase seems out of place and thus argues against the design of the degradosome. However, this anomaly can be turned around to serve as a springboard for a teleological hypothesis.[11]

ATTRIBUTES OF RATIONAL DESIGN

Rational Design is revealed when a logical form of structural and functional decomposition is present. Yet François Jacob offers another way to distinguish between Rational Design and design at the hands of a tinkerer: "the objects produced by the engineer. . . approach the level of perfection made possible by the technology of the time. In contrast, evolution is far from perfect." Since we have no access to the technology used by life's putative designer and no mechanism to measure perfection, Jacob's distinction cannot be used literally. Nevertheless, the essence of the distinction can be applied to argue that a rational design would have certain attributes that reflect engineering.

Efficiency. Rational Design is often reflected in terms of efficiency, which can be understood in two ways. First, how well does a system carry out its objective? Is it needlessly wasteful and/or in constant need of help? Second, efficiency can be understood as using the minimum number of parts to carry out an objective. Ullman suggests that one way of evaluating whether something is a good design is to determine if the actual number of parts in a system greatly exceeds the theoretical minimal number needed to carry out that objective. If a system appears to contain needless complexity, it looks less efficient and more like the hodgepodge product of a jury-rigged design.

Specificity. Rational Design is also reflected in precisely specified interactions. Such specified interactions work to maximize the fidelity of the flow of information, energy, and/or material. If something works in a messy and error-prone fashion, not only is it inefficient, but its lack of specificity does not conform to our experience with things that humans typically design.

Robustness. Rational Design should reflect itself in a certain degree of robustness, where the designer would endow his system with properties that resist decay and/or repair its effects, such that constant supervision and intervention are not required. If something is constantly breaking down or requires constant intervention to work, it does not possess Rational Design. We can include the ability to self-monitor and self-repair in this category.

Elegance. This is a subjective measure, but Rational Design often looks sophisticated, elegant or beautiful once the design objective and obstacles are appreciated. Something that employs impressive amounts of specificity and efficiency to surmount such obstacles can be considered as elegant. In contrast, something that surmounts these obstacles sloppily would lack this elegance and not speak to an intelligent origin.

Flexibility. Flexibility is an overlooked design principle, but it is essential if the designed thing must interact with a changing and often stingy environment. Flexibility is also important to keep in mind when considering efficiency, as there is usually a trade-off between the two. That is, the more efficient something is, the less flexible it becomes and visa versa. Mechanical engineer Daniel Whitney writes:

> Unfortunately there is a symmetry in the flexibility-efficiency issue. Not only can too much efficiency stifle flexibility, but too much flexibility can stifle efficiency. . . . Flexibility and efficiency are thus deeply in conflict, and the conflict seems fundamental rather than a consequence of incomplete understanding.[12]

Flexibility is thus a caveat to inefficiency. An inefficient state may exist for a good design reason, namely, to endow the bearer of that state with a degree of flexibility in which to cope with the changing environment (or even to provide a substrate for evolution). Thus, we will keep this fundamental conflict in mind as we search for evidence of Rational Design, and perhaps seek to determine if the two dynamics are balanced in a logical fashion.

Coherence. A logical balance of efficiency, specificity, robustness, elegance, and flexibility would reflect a Rational Design. In addition, the hypothesis that something was designed for a particular purpose may actually serve as the fulcrum for bringing various facts about the system into a coherent whole.

These factors will not prove if something is rationally designed or "perfect," but they do help to determine which way the inferential wind is blowing; showing just how much something looks rationally designed as opposed to looking like it evolved. For example, if we find something with intrinsic robustness, where efficiency is high or balanced by flexibility, and where specificity is high, with elegance and coherence, this is a candidate for intelligent origins. At the other extreme, something that breaks down often, is messy and inefficient in a way that does not serve flexibility, speaks to the jury-rigged design of the blind watchmaker. Anything between these two extremes will be more difficult to judge. Is it something that started out sloppy and has been improved through evolution? Or would it be something that started out in a sophisticated state and has decayed over time?

Our investigation is thus clearly interested in the *quality of the design* and seeks to measure these factors and relate them to each other. As an understanding of the system improves, these data can be fed into something like a matrix or algorithm which spits out a "rationality score" that allows investigators to compare the subject to things known to be intelligently designed and to those known to be products of natural selection. These types of data would not completely resolve the ambiguity behind origins. After all, what we study are not the originals, but the descendants of the originals. Nevertheless, by determining the quality of the design, we may justify an inference as part of a larger case.

The Plan

Jacob cites a final difference between engineering and natural selection that also proves quite helpful. He notes that an engineer is different from evolution in that the engineer "works according to a preconceived plan" guided by the fact that "he foresees the product of his efforts." Natural selection employs no plan, has no goals, has no foresight, and simply makes due with what works (where what works simply survives). Thus, detecting evidence of a preconceived plan would be very good evidence for Intelligent Design. But how does one go about detecting a plan given that plans exist only in the mind? Since our investigation does not depend on our ability to identify and communicate with an intelligent designer, how can it make use of this difference?

Clearly, any plan would have to be detected indirectly. And in this way, our investigation can simply use the same basic logic employed by science in studying origins, which itself necessarily involves an indirect approach. In their booklet on creationism and science, the National Academy of Sciences notes:

> Science is practiced in many ways besides direct observation and experimentation. Much scientific discovery is done through indirect experimentation and observation in which inferences are made, and hypotheses generated from those inferences are tested. . . we can learn about the natural world even if we cannot directly observe a phenomenon.[13]

The basic logic is to simply argue that if X is true, Y should be true. And since thoughts and plans cannot be directly observed, though they may exist, such thoughts and plans might be indirectly detected using this very same logic.

A plan may be detected by one of two indirect paths. First, let us imagine we are studying X. This component could be part of a larger plan, such that we can detect design from the hypothesis of *large scale planning*. For example, if there is a preconceived plan to design a city, the existence of X should make sense in light of this larger city-wide plan. X might be a police station and since a city needs law enforcement, X's existence makes sense in light of the overall plan. An understanding of a plan to make a city would explain X and even cause us to expect X to exist.

Second, X can be the product of a plan to actualize an otherwise general abstract role or function. We can detect such design from the hypothesis of *small scale planning*. Here X is not necessarily viewed as part of a larger plan, but instead viewed as something planned to bring about a function. Again, we could design a police station in a city that already has police stations. In this case, designing the police station is not part of designing a larger system like a city, but instead simply represents the actualization of a general theme, one that implements law enforcement. This means that if something was planned to be a police station, we would expect to find things that fulfill this plan. If we found a building without a jail and without a parking lot to handle all the police cars, we would surmise that it was not planned as a police station. But if we found such a jail and parking lot, we could detect that the building was designed with the intention to make a police station.

The difference between the hypotheses of large scale and small scale planning can be further illustrated with Dawkins's light switch examples.[7] Light switches are flipped up in America to turn on a light, while flipped down in England to turn on lights. From a large scale perspective, when light switches were invented, was there a single plan to implement light switches in both countries? It does not seem so given that the arbitrary way in which they work does not reflect a rational mind. Yet from a small scale perspective, where we understand the role of a light switch and find various components hooked up in specific ways to carry out this role, we can detect a plan. Thus, light switches themselves are part of a plan to carry out a function, but there does not seem to have been a larger plan where some intelligent agent took it upon himself to endow all houses in America and England with light switches.

The crucial point is that if a plan was employed, and we correctly decipher that plan, along with having sufficient information to understand it and its implementation, we will acquire much understanding about the object that actualizes the plan. A specific example can further illustrate this point.

Consider your average automobile. We know that it is engineered and we know why it is engineered. But let us pretend the Apocalypse has happened and, never having seen a car, we do not have this knowledge anymore. Then one day, a research expedition happens upon a group of people who live in a junkyard. Many of these people live in the cars but do not drive them, as there is no more gasoline. The research team initially thinks the people designed the cars as shelters, but soon learns from the people that they did not design them; they simply moved into what already existed. Nevertheless, they still think the cars were designed because many complex parts come together to make a functional shelter. They point to the doors and the roof as providing good protection from the rain, the comfortable seats for sitting and sleeping, a compartment to store personal items, windows to survey the outside world from within the safety of the shelter, and even a mirror to help with grooming. But after several months of research, some begin to suggest the car was not designed by an intelligent agent, but was instead the product of a non-teleological mechanism. Why? What intelligent agent would design a shelter in which you cannot stand? Why is it that the seats do not face each other? Why is the big compartment in the front loaded with useless metal, rubber, and plastic? And the plastic wheel in the front seat does not seem to play any role, suggesting it is some vestigial remnant from a precursor shelter-car. This idea begins to take hold until one day another researcher comes up with a novel hypothesis—this shelter was originally designed to be a transportation device. This researcher proposes something about the intention behind the design and this proposal is explanatory and helpful. You cannot stand in the car because transportation devices are normally planned and designed so that the driver and passengers sit. The mirror is not for grooming, but is used by the driver for surveying the world in relation to the vehicle's boundaries. After all, this explains why the mirror is where it is (something the grooming hypothesis could not do). The metal, plastic, and rubber actually compose a motor. The wheel in the front seat was used to steer the car, and with further study, it is found to be connected, through a series of parts, with the front wheels of the machine. We can thus see from this example that once a hypothesis correctly identifies the intended function, or plan, for any designed artifact, just about everything begins to make sense in light of this purpose.

This type of insight is helpful to our investigation. If we suspect something is designed, then the next step should propose that the functions stem from an intended purpose of an intelligent mind. If the object was designed, and the function-purpose equation is valid, we can expect further understanding to follow. Like the car, various attributes would begin to fall into place. The more success our investigation has in making sense of the object in question by using this hypothetical purpose, the more our confidence increases with regard to our initial design inference.

This is especially true when we consider that tinkering does not require this type of dynamic. The blind watchmaker has no plan in mind because it has no mind. Instead, it coopts things, recycles things, and tinkers in such a way that jury-rigged features are the likely outcome. Functional relativism, where functions are purely relative to the immediate benefits they confer upon the organism, is at the heart of tinkering. Such functions can change simply because of a mutation and the quirky advantage it grants that organism. Original functions are lost and replaced by secondary functions, yet the machinery carrying out the secondary function was originally "designed" to carry out another function. The hypothesis of any type of plan would not be likely to generate any insight when working with a slippery, quirky, jury-rigged system built up over time for a variety of selective reasons. Unlike the hypothesis of Darwinian evolution, Rational Design allows us to propose and utilize the concept of purpose to its fullest extent. Thus, its success would be best attributed to the validity of our original design inference.

Looking Ahead

Good planning not only requires the use of reason and knowledge, but it also involves an element of foresight. Foresight, which is essentially rationality applied to prediction, is something the blind watchmaker cannot possibly have. Jacob notes that the tinkerer "does not know exactly what he is going to produce," which fits nicely with Dawkins's characterization: "It does not plan for the future. It has no vision, no foresight, no sight at all." Any hint of foresight would therefore count strongly toward a design inference. Yet how in the world could we ever hope to detect examples of foresight—planning—amid the complexities of biotic reality?

I propose that two phenomena speak to foresight. The first example can be extracted from engineering and is something I will call Original Mature Design. Ullman[10] describes *mature design* as a type of design that has "remained virtually unchanged over many years." He cites several examples we might find on any office desk: pencil sharpeners, staplers, and hole punches. He then adds, "For these products, knowledge about the design problem is complete. There is nothing more to learn." Mature design shows little change because there is little to change in order to improve the design.

Ullman defines *original design* as "the development of a process, component, or assembly not previously in existence." He notes that if we had never seen a wheel before, and invented one, this would be an example of original design. So let us combine these two types of design. If something

258   RATIONALITY AND FORESIGHT

rather novel appeared three billion years ago, it can be viewed as original design. And if three billion subsequent years of evolutionary tinkering does not significantly redesign and improve it, the original design can likewise be viewed as mature design. In simple terms, whatever put that feature on the Earth got it right the first time.

Original Mature Design can be viewed as an echo of foresight because there is no reason to think the blind watchmaker would have a decent chance of getting things right from the beginning. After all, when the blind watchmaker cobbles something together through cooption, it does not know what it is producing. A rational mind, on the other hand, can see beyond the immediate state and contemplate how something might need to be constructed in light of future contingencies. The blind watchmaker is likely to put something together that will need extensive change and improvement at a later time, but a rational mind has the ability to create something that will not require further significant modifications.

Original Mature Design becomes most significant when the design is reused and built upon by many different life forms. Again consider the implications of the universal genetic code. There is no evidence of any simpler, precursor genetic code. One might speculate about how the code could have evolved, but all such speculations remain on the chalkboard or in the computer. As such, the biological data are consistent with the genetic code as an original design. The data are also consistent with the appearance of the code coinciding with the appearance of the first life forms on this planet. From any perspective, you end up with the code originating in a simple organism.

From the conventional scientific perspective, the genetic code was strung together to serve some primitive cell-like organism as it interacted with an environment unlike anything that exists today. That a few billion years of extensive, subsequent evolution and environmental changes have not significantly changed the original code clearly indicate the code is also an example of mature design. So how does Original Mature Design speak to foresight? Apparently, whoever or whatever invented the code got it right the first time. The code that was selected to serve some primitive cell-like organism in the primordial environment also just happens to nicely serve a myriad of modern day organisms, including bacteria, alligators, roses, mold, and human beings. The blind watchmaker did not have to subsequently redesign or tinker with the code to serve these newly evolved organisms, existing at different levels and within very different environments, while experiencing different selection pressures. A very ancient code just happens to serve very modern organisms quite well, thank you. How did that happen?

Yet we are back to the Duck and Rabbit. There is a non-teleological way of viewing Original Mature Design. It is called the frozen accident, a concept originally developed by Francis Crick. One group of researchers explains the frozen accident as follows:

> A feature on which other features are built becomes so central to the working of the "machine" that it cannot be replaced in evolution, even if there is a conceivably better alternative. All those features that are built on the central feature would also have to be changed, so the central feature is effectively "frozen." *Frozen accidents are therefore a consequence of evolution through tinkering.* (emphasis added).[14]

Any irrational hodgepodge of parts could effectively appear as mature design simply because too many other things are dependent on that hodgepodge. If evolution begins to tinker with or try to replace the hodgepodge, all the other things built upon it would collapse to the ground. A frozen accident is indeed a prediction of the blind watchmaker, as its extreme myopia is likely to cause it to paint itself into the corner again and again.

A nice way to illustrate the frozen accident is to consider something else Francis Crick gave to biology—the concept of the central dogma. The central dogma is taught to all biology students who are introduced to DNA and molecular biology. It is essentially a one-way information flowchart that tells us the information from DNA is used to make RNA and the information from RNA is used to make proteins. While the central dogma has been significantly modified, what is more interesting is the fact that biology teachers are teaching something called "dogma," which is typically an authoritative tenet, usually associated with some aspect of religious faith. As such, dogma does not belong in science, as it violates its provisional essence. Yet because of Crick's choice of words, science teachers around the world are put in the position of introducing dogma after first teaching their students that science does not revolve around authoritative tenets. How did this happen?

Crick himself sheds light on this incident. He explains why he chose the term:

> I called this idea the central dogma for two reasons, I suspect. I had already used the obvious word hypothesis in the sequence hypothesis, and in addition I wanted to suggest that this new assumption was more central and more powerful. I did remark that their speculative nature was emphasized by their names.[15]

And added:

> As it turned out, the use of the word dogma caused almost more trouble than it was worth. Many years later Jacques Monod pointed out to me that I did not appear to understand the correct use of the word dogma, which is a belief that cannot be doubted. I did apprehend this in a vague sort of way but since I thought that all religious beliefs were without any serious foundation, I used the word in the way I myself thought about it, not as most of the rest of the world does, and simply applied it to a grand hypothesis that, however plausible, had little direct experimental support.[15]

That Crick chose a term that the rest of the world would so easily misinterpret shows that no foresight was involved in the choice. Had he suspected this term would turn out to be widely inscribed in introductory biology textbooks years later, he would likely have been more careful and chosen a better term. However, since the term has become so widely taught and used, it is now too difficult to change it, as it would probably cause confusion. Crick's term "dogma" is, in itself, a frozen accident.

How can Original Mature Design be distinguished from a frozen accident? We dip into the criterion of rationality. There is no reason to think that whatever falls into place and becomes frozen should also be inherently rational. Crick originally described the genetic code as a frozen accident.

This is because any other code would have worked; the one we have just happened to win the lottery. But as we saw in Chapter 4, the code has too many attributes that make it appear designed. It is unlikely that such an optimal code would have fallen into place in one swoop and then be frozen into place. Since frozen accidents are inherently the product of an excessively myopic tinkerer, why think such products would be so well-suited for new features that appear millions, if not billions, of years later? A frozen accident does not lead us to think that evolution got it right the first time. On the contrary, it is a phenomenon that is often used to argue evolution has no foresight.

The second phenomenon that speaks to foresight involves a shift in the way we look at history. Normally, to understand the present, we explore what happened in the past, trying to uncover all the relevant past events that led to the present state. This is the standard historical approach. For example, if a historian wants to understand how America became involved in World War II, he will explore the history prior to America's entry into war and consider all the relevant events associated with America's relationships with Asia and Europe. But if we are, in fact, dealing with foresight in action, we can reverse this approach and attempt to use *the present to understand the past*. I will call this new perspective PREPA (the present explains the past). How does PREPA work? Consider a mundane example. Your friend becomes concerned because his wife has been acting strangely lately. On Monday, she stayed away from home for an uncharacteristically long time. "She said she was shopping, but she rarely shops on Monday," he explains. On Tuesday, he says he entered the bedroom and she quickly hung up the phone. He asked her who she was talking to, and she fumbled about with words and eventually said it was one of her friends. On Wednesday, she gave the house a good cleaning, "Which is odd," he says, "because she normally does that on Saturday." On Thursday evening, she tells him that he should go bowling with his friends Friday evening. "Now, she normally complains when I go bowling," he explains. So you take your friend bowling. After one game, you take him home early to check on his wife. He enters the door and it is dark. He then flips on the light and people everywhere jump out and shout, "Surprise!" At that moment on Friday evening, suddenly the present

262   RATIONALITY AND FORESIGHT

explains the past (his wife's behavior Monday through Thursday). She was acting according to foresight, as she planned for the surprise party. What did not make sense in the past now all comes together.

A hypothetical biological example of PREPA might involve time travel back to the point when there were only single-celled organisms on the Earth. Suppose we captured various protozoa and took them back to the lab with us. We find something surprising—as a group, they all possess the complete set of proteins that are used by mammals to clot their blood. Yet these proteins do not seem to be doing anything very useful for the protozoa. Why then do these protozoa all happen to have mammalian clotting proteins? This would be a strong candidate for PREPA, as the crucial function these proteins play in mammalian life would give us an explanation for why they surprisingly existed in protozoa. One can think of biological examples of PREPA as classic preadaptation, an inherently teleological concept discussed in Chapter 7. Of course, if mammalian blood clotting proteins provided no service to protozoan life forms, they would be lost by mutation over time. Thus, as we saw in Chapter 7, some method for carrying such primordial designs into the future would be required. It is important to note whether a trait, as understood in the present, also sheds light on some anomaly or oddity from the past.

Since mammalian blood-clotting proteins in protozoa is an extreme, hypothetical example used merely to illustrate how PREPA works, consider something that is more modest and real. If the original single-celled life forms were front-loaded to evolve into multi-cellular organisms, we would predict that the uni-cellular creatures would be loaded with machinery needed for multi-cellular life. PREPA would help us detect such an event, as we might find that uni-cellular creatures contain information that better fit in a multi-cellular context. The following two examples will more clearly illustrate this.

Linker histone proteins (also known as H1) play an important role in packaging the large chromosomes of plants and animals. Although they are present in all eukaryotes, they are not essential for survival and reproduction in filamentous fungi, such as *Ascolobus* and *Aspergillus*. If H1 function is eliminated in these fungi, the cells are perfectly viable with no deleterious consequence on the sexual reproduction cycle. The same results were previously seen in the protozoan *Tetrahymena*. However, in the fungi mentioned, elimination of H1 does result in the cessation of growth within a week or two. So H1 does not affect viability or reproduction, but only the life-span of the individual organism (however, with *Aspergillus*, elimination of H1 does not even effect the life span of the organism and has no apparent effect). This all means that the linker histones may not be crucial for single-celled existence. Juan Ausio, from the Department of Biochemistry and Microbiology at University of Victoria, notes, "while linker histones may be dispensable for the relatively short life span of an individual cell, they are most likely indispensable for survival of higher eukaryote organisms."[16] Ausio argues that H1 may be essential for multi-cellular organisms because compaction of the genome is an important ingredient in the regulatory schemes used in generating and maintaining a multi-cellular body plan. If H1 was indeed designed, given its minimal role in protozoa, it might constitute a very good example of front-loading evolution such that the initial eukaryotic state was prepared to evolve a multi-cellular state. In other words, *the existence of H1 in protozoa may best be explained by the existence of H1 in metazoans.* That is one hypothesis that simply cannot be entertained, for the briefest of all moments, from a non-teleological perspective.

The second example involves the single-celled choanoflagellates. In 2001, Sean Carroll, a professor of genetics at the University of Wisconsin-Madison, and his colleague, Nicole King, searched for genes to help understand animal evolution. They found that these protozoa had a molecular sensor that is normally found in animals. According to the press release from the Howard Hughes Medical Institute:

> The search concentrated on molecules involved in cell adhesion and cell signaling, which single-cell organisms would not be expected to have, said Carroll. "Among several hundred common gene sequences we obtained, out popped this receptor tyrosine kinase, a molecule that has never before been found outside of metazoans," Carroll said.[17]

In 2003, the same researchers expanded on this finding and reported their results in a paper entitled, "Evolution of Key Cell Signaling and Adhesion Protein Families Predates Animal Origins."[18] They write:

> In marked contrast to their simple lifestyle, choanoflagellates express members of a wide variety of protein families involved in animal cell interactions, including cadherins, C-type lectins, tyrosine kinases, and a G protein—coupled receptor, as well as several multidomain polypeptides that contain protein-protein interaction domains involved in signaling and adhesion in animals [such as the epidermal growth factor motif, Src homology 2 domain, tumor necrosis factor receptor domain, and sushi or complement control protein domain]. We conclude that choanoflagellates and animals share, to the exclusion of other eukaryotes whose genomes have been analyzed, proteins that contain secretin-like GPCR, GPS, fibrinogen, somatomedin, and CCP domains, as well as members of the cadherin, C-type lectin, and TK protein families.

In other words, these single-celled organisms contained a whole toolkit of genes that allowed the researchers to conclude choanoflagellates have "key proteins required for animal development" that probably "evolved before the origin of animals." Since this animal development toolkit is unlikely to be essential for single-celled existence, its discovery speaks to PREPA, where such oddly endowed protozoa make sense if life was rigged to evolve multicellular organisms.

REFERENCES

1. Selections from William Paley's *Natural Theology*. http://web.archive.org/web/20040216171040/http://www-personal.umich.edu/~emcurley/paley.htm; last accessed 11/21/04
2. Miller, K., 1994. "Life's Grand Design." *Technology Review*, 97:24-32.
3. Lindsay, J., 2003. "The Lack of Design in Nature?" http://www.jefflindsay.com/DesignFlaws.shtml; last accessed 11/17/04.

4. Jacob, F., 1977. "Evolution and Tinkering." *Science,* 196:1161-1166.
5. Van Till, H. "What Does It Mean to Be 'Intelligently Designed'?" http://www.counterbalance.net/id-hvt/doesi-body.html; last accessed 11/14/04.
6. Pigliucci, M., 2000. "Rationally Speaking." http://www.darwin.ws/RationallySpeaking/RS%202000-12.htm; last accessed 11/01/04.
7. Dawkins, R., 1996. *Climbing Mount Improbable.* W.W. Norton & Company, New York.
8. Williams, G., 1998. *The Pony Fish's Glow: And Other Clues to Plan and Purpose in Nature.* Basic Books, New York.
9. Orr, H.A., 2005 "Why Intelligent Design Isn't." *The New Yorker,* May 30, 2005. http://www.newyorker.com/printables/fact/050530fa_fact; last accessed 07/14/05.
10. Ullman, D.G., 1992. *The Mechanical Design Process.* McGraw-Hill, New York.
11. "A Teleological Hypothesis about a Machine." http://www.idthink.net/biot/degrad/ and "Update on Degradosome Function: The Importance of Location." http://www.idthink.net/biot/degrad2/index.html.
12. Whitney, D.E., 1986. "Real Robots Don't Need Jigs." *IEEE International Conference on Robotics and Automation (ICRA),* 1:746-752; also see Whitney, D.E., 1993. "Nippondenso Co. Ltd: A Case Study of Strategic Product Design." *Research in Engineering Design,* 5:1-20 for more discussion of the conflict between flexibility and efficiency.
13. National Academy of Sciences, 1998. *Teaching about Evolution and the Nature of Science.* National Academies Press, Washington, D.C.
14. Poole, A., Penny, D. and Sjoberg, B.M., 2001. "Confounded Cytosine! Tinkering and the Evolution of DNA." Nature Reviews, *Molecular Cell Biology,* 2:147-151.
15. Crick, F., 1988. *What Mad Pursuit.* Basic Books, New York.
16. Ausio, J., 2000. "Are Linker Histones (Histone H1) Dispensable for Survival?" *BioEssays,* 22:873-877.
17. "Primitive Microbe Offers Glimpse of Animal Evolution." *Research News,* Howard Hughes Medical Institute, December 18, 2001. http://www.hhmi.org/news/carroll2.html; last accessed on 09/12/03.

18. King, N., Hittinger, C.T. and Carroll, S.B., 2003. "Evolution of Key Cell Signaling and Adhesion Protein Families Predates Animal Origins." *Science*, 301:361-363.

CHAPTER 10

THE DESIGN MATRIX
UNLEASHED

The Design Matrix is a method by which you can score a particular feature according to four different criteria to assess and quantify the strength of a design inference. Since detection of design may involve subtleties embedded in complexity and ambiguity, the Design Matrix taps into the most complex and sensitive "instrument" that we can work with to detect such subtleties—the human brain. Since we are by nature designers, we all have a certain awareness of design. The Design Matrix allows one brain's score to be thoroughly assessed by other brains, perhaps helping us to eventually reach consensus or to better understand why consensus has not been reached.

At first glance, this method may seem hopelessly subjective, as each score is ultimately a judgment call. Instead of building on concrete measurements and mathematical demonstrations, a circumstantial case for each criterion must be made. Yet the criteria need not be abandoned to the realm of pure subjectivity, as we can assign a numerical score to each criterion. There is plenty of precedent for such scoring. Olympic judges assign numerical scores to an athlete's performance. An emergency doctor might ask you to score your pain on a scale of 1-10. Medical researchers use interview data to come up with numerical scores to rate quality of life or the severity of a disease. Environmental scientists assign scores to rate the quality of a river or lake. And educators use rubrics to score the performance of their students. While the Design Matrix score might not be perfect, it is a significant step to scale the strength of the teleological signal. Furthermore, the Design Matrix score helps us move beyond the realm of suspicion, as the score itself can serve as both an impetus and a focal point for new research ideas that can in turn feed back into the score, either strengthening it or weakening it over time.

It is now time to grab the rabbit by its tail and pull him out of the hole. We have seen that there are four criteria that can be used to assess our original suspicions of design: *Analogy* with things known to be designed; *Discontinuity* with non-teleological processes; something that displays fingerprints of *Rationality*; and something that contains echoes of *Foresight*. The logic behind each of the four criteria is simple. The criteria of Analogy and Discontinuity are derived from our consideration of the vanishing Face. Had there been a real Face on Mars, its analogy with structures known to be designed (Mt. Rushmore, etc.) coupled with the inability of geological processes to craft such high-resolution structures, would indicate its designed origins. The other two criteria, Rationality and Foresight, derive from our attempt to differentiate between the products of non-teleological evolution and an intelligent designer. Rationality and Foresight are properties that only an intelligent designer can bring to bear on its designs.

Each of the four criteria not only can help us assess our design suspicions, but can also be used as a platform on which to generate testable hypotheses about biotic features (Table 10-I). For example, the criterion of Rationality has helped me generate testable hypotheses about transcriptional proofreading,[1] lagging strand synthesis,[2] and the use of cytosine as part of the DNA molecule.[3] The criterion of Discontinuity has been helpful when exploring the bacterial flagellum[4] and the eukaryotic flagellum.[5] I have used the criterion of Analogy to make predictions about the degradosome [6] and the use of nano-wheels in the cell.[7] And the criterion of Foresight was used to come up with the hypothesis of front-loading evolution (Chapter 7).

Research along the lines outlined in Table 10-I can provide further information and knowledge that can be used to modify a Design Matrix score. Thus, the Design Matrix can not only bring focus for research, but is also receptive to the findings of research.

To grasp the significance of these four criteria, Analogy, Rationality, Discontinuity and Foresight, consider two biological features, A and B. Let us say that feature A demonstrates a deep analogy with something that is known to be designed. It also is a multi-component irreducibly complex system where none of the highly conserved parts have any homologs participating in simpler, earlier systems. The system is neatly deconstructed along

Table 10-I. Research Questions from the Design Matrix

Analogy   Biotic feature X is similar to Y, something known to be designed

- What characteristic would strengthen the analogy between X and Y?
- What does Y predict about X?
- Are there other biological features that are analogous to Y?
- What are the differences between X and Y?
- Do the differences between X and Y plausibly reflect a superior design of X?

Discontinuity

- Is the system irreducibly complex?
- What is the irreducibly complex core? How many components predate this core?
- How many components of the irreducibly complex core demonstrate system dependence?

Rationality

- Does the system have a function?
- How neatly is the system functionally and structurally decomposed?
- Does the working hypothesis of a "purpose" explain the system?
- How well do engineering criteria for good design map to the system?

Foresight

- Does the system demonstrate Original Mature Design?
- Does the present state explain something about the past (PREPA)?

functional and structural lines, where a clear form-function relationship is exhibited. Criteria from engineering allow us to see this system as a very good design. The system effectively appeared in a fully functional form (as evidenced by a lack of any precursor state) and has remained essentially unchanged since its introduction. Finally, the system demonstrates a clear echo of foresight, as the system does not make much sense in its original protozoan context, but is essential and well-suited for a multi-cellular state.

On the other hand, consider biotic feature B. This feature shows no analogy with things that are known to be designed. On the contrary, it is analogous to something that would have been spawned by a non-teleological process. It shows clear homology with simpler, more ancient features and, in fact, nicely fits within a substantiated evolutionary continuum. Applying engineering criteria, the feature does not easily deconstruct along structural and functional lines and there are distinct aspects that make it appear clumsy and poorly designed. It not only appears to be a frozen accident, but there seem to be obvious choices an engineer would have made, yet were not made.

Although biotic features A and B are clearly different in many respects, we are still left with a choice: are these differences significant from the perspective of origins? For some people, the differences essentially evaporate, as all that matters is that we have no independent evidence of a designer at the time biotic feature A appeared and no one has proven that A could not have possibly evolved. For these people, a non-teleological cause is invoked to explain the origin of both features A and B, regardless of their differences. The Duck absorbs all data. For other people, the differences are meaningful, indicating A was designed while B was a product of some non-teleological cause. The Duck and the Rabbit co-exist.

If you, the reader, still find yourself wanting independent evidence of a designer and needing some part of evolution to be disproved, you will have been disappointed. We have no way of finding and interviewing life's designer. And proving the impossible has always been a very tricky endeavor. But if you find yourself intrigued by the differences between A and B, welcome to the Design Matrix. You understand the importance of the Explanatory Continuum (Chapter 2) and our need to think in terms of plausibility and probability, not just possibility and proof. You too may have been intrigued enough by the clues (Chapters 3-5) such that you likewise cannot help but suspect Intelligent Design. You too may perceive an ambiguous reality, where you can acknowledge the Duck, but with a slight perceptual nudge, you see that frisky Rabbit (Chapter 6). You too may realize that while clues that strengthen Analogy, Discontinuity, Rationality, and Foresight may not provide something as shocking and sensational to qualify as Epistemological Evidence (Chapter 6), these are indeed the features we might expect from design (Ontological Evidence). In fact, even the critics of design obliquely acknowledge this point, as lack of analogy, evidence of continuity, irrational design, and frozen accidents have all been used to argue against design. Why would anyone think the street could never run both ways? If you are fascinated by the possibilities granted by these four criteria, there is more to come.

First, in the spirit of the Explanatory Continuum, we should not treat each criterion as a binary choice. Instead, each criterion should exist along a continuum with each feature numerically scored. Consider Figure 10-1. Imagine we are trying to score an analogy between a biological feature and something that is known to be designed. It shows a range from -5 to 5. A score of 0 would represent a thoroughly ambiguous situation where we cannot decide if the two systems are analogous or not analogous. The same score might also occur if there is a lack of information that can be used to make the distinction. If the analogy between the biological and designed feature is deemed to be modest in strength, we give it a score of 1. The stronger the analogy, the higher the score, where 5 would represent the strongest possible analogy that we could realistically imagine. If the biological feature and designed object are deemed to be different in kind, but only to a modest degree, we give it a score of -1. The more the designed object and biological feature are deemed to be different in kind, the lower the score. The same basic scoring strategy can be applied with any of the Design Matrix criteria.

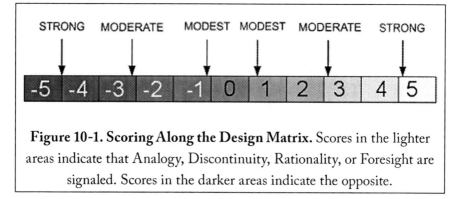

Figure 10-1. Scoring Along the Design Matrix. Scores in the lighter areas indicate that Analogy, Discontinuity, Rationality, or Foresight are signaled. Scores in the darker areas indicate the opposite.

Again, we must be clear that the scoring is not objective. The Design Matrix is not intended to be a scientific instrument, where we put a sample into a measuring chamber, push a button, and get a number. The Matrix works like a set of Olympic judges who score the performance of an ice skater or gymnast.[8] Of course each score is subjective, but since the judges have roughly the same experience with the sport, their scores are not completely subjective as they tend to be very similar. For example, if three judges score a performance as 9.7 and the fourth judge gives a 7.9, we would all wonder about the discrepancy and ask the fourth judge about his score. In the same spirit, imagine James using the Design Matrix to give a biological feature the score of 4. John gives the same feature a score of -3. We would want James and John to lay their reasoning on the table, explaining the basis for their scores. Upon hearing their arguments, we might decide to agree with James and score it 4, agree with John and score it -3, or disagree with both, giving it our own score of 1. What matters is that arguments are placed on the table such that everyone can evaluate the scoring. Once the score, and the basis for the scoring, has been made clear, it will be possible to conceive of research that can strengthen or weaken the score.

The Design Matrix then works by taking the scoring along each criterion and fusing them together as a whole (Figure 10-2). In this way, the four criteria are treated as independently as possible, yielding their own respec-

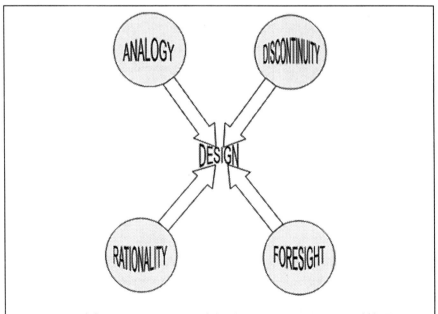

Figure 10-2. The Design Matrix. The four criteria, Analogy (A), Discontinuity (D), Rationality (R), and Foresight (F) all converge on a decision of "designed" or "not designed"—a Consilience of Clues.

tive score. Then, the scores are simply averaged to give a final score along the continuum. The reasoning for combining the scores into an average score again comes from the Face on Mars that could have been. We saw that by combining both the criteria of Analogy and Discontinuity, most people would have concluded design if a high-resolution Face did indeed exist on Mars. Then, by adding in the criteria of Rationality and Foresight, we can factor non-teleological evolution into the picture. In fact, these latter two criteria tilt things slightly in the favor of such evolution, as it will probably be difficult to come up with a high score for the criterion of Foresight and it will always be possible for someone to engage in *post hoc* argumentation that random mutation and natural selection can easily mimic a good engineer.

Combining the scores not only allows us to extract from four different realms of inquiry, but it also happens to eliminate one of the most popular arguments against design—"god of the gaps." A Discontinuity score, by itself, is quite vulnerable to this complaint. But if the Discontinuity score is combined with three lines of positive indicators of design, the "gaps" complaint no longer applies. Within the Matrix, design is not inferred simply because there is a lack of evidence that something evolved. Instead, such considerations are simply one piece of the puzzle, where Discontinuity, combined with Analogy, Foresight, and Rationality give us a broader perspective with which to reach a tentative conclusion.

Since the Design Matrix combines four different criteria to reach an average score, it is important that each criterion be treated as independently as possible. In fact, this is especially true of the three criteria of Analogy, Rationality, and Foresight due to the overlap that exists among them. Foresight represents a special case of Rationality and Rationality can be viewed as analogous feature. For example, if a system is deemed rational because it adheres to engineering principles, one can use this fact when scoring the Rationality criterion, but the same consideration should not then be used to score the Analogy criterion. Otherwise, the Matrix score will be artificially inflated. On the other hand, evidence of Continuity should not be used to weaken an Analogy, as again these are independent criteria. Such a move might cause us to overlook a potential example of teleological evolution.

Consider two extreme examples of scoring. First, let us assign a 0 value to Rationality and Foresight due to lack of information. But let us also assign a value of 5 for Analogy and -5 for Discontinuity. This would mean that something that shows very powerful evidence of having evolved, yet also demonstrates a very powerful analogy to something known to be designed, would have Design Matrix score of 0. This feature would thus remain ambiguous from a design perspective. While it would be clear that it evolved, the possibility remains that such evolution was teleological in some sense. On the other hand, consider a feature that has an Analogy score of -5 and a Discontinuity score of 5 (the Foresight and Rationality are 0). Again, the Design Matrix score is 0, preventing us from concluding design simply because it does not look like the feature evolved. The Design Matrix thus buffers against hasty conclusions in either directions. To eliminate design, you need something more than evidence of evolution. To conclude design, you need something more than evidence against evolution.

The Design Matrix may also help us differentiate between non-teleological evolution, design expressed through evolution, and design as intelligent intervention. The Matrix scores can be illustrated with histograms as seen in Figure 10-3. Figure 10-3a shows the best possible situation that would indicate design expressed through intelligent intervention. All the positive indicators are maximally scored in addition to a maximal score for Discontinuity. Figure 10-3b shows the opposite situation, indicating non-teleological evolution is at play. Finally, Figure 10-3c shows positive indicators of Intelligent Design, but because evolution is likewise indicated, represents a pattern that is consistent with some form of teleological evolution.

Lastly, the Design Matrix score is not intended to be a static figure. It merely represents a score that is dependent on the scorekeeper's knowledge

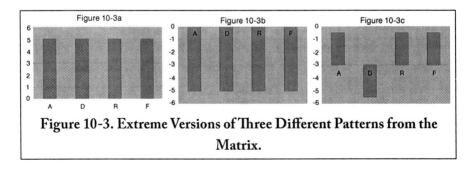

Figure 10-3. Extreme Versions of Three Different Patterns from the Matrix.

at the time. As such, a Design Matrix score can change, in either direction, in light of new information pertaining to any of the criteria. What would thus matter most is not a Design Matrix score at any point in time, but the persistence or trending of a score as new information is acquired.

TAKING THE MATRIX FOR A TEST DRIVE

Let us calibrate the Design Matrix by reconsidering various examples discussed in previous chapters. We will begin with things that are known to be designed, in order to evaluate how they are scored in the Matrix. A good candidate for design is this book itself. As the designer of this book, I have certain knowledge that it was, in fact, designed. So how would we score my book? First, consider the criterion of Analogy. Since this book is perfectly analogous with other books that are known to be designed, we can give it an Analogy score of 5. As for Discontinuity, I can safely say that there is no hurricane, volcano, beam of energy, or any other non-teleological force that can substitute for me as author. As such, the writings found within are fundamentally discontinuous with anything known to be caused by non-teleological processes found in nature. The book thus deserves a Discontinuity score of 5. When we turn to the criterion of Rationality, the rules of grammar and logic apply. I would like to think my sentences are perfect and every argument is perfectly logical, but I'll humble myself and take a mere score of 4. Finally, we turn to the criterion of Foresight. Here, as author, I can artificially inflate the score because I know that several of the points in this book were made with potential counter arguments in mind, while earlier chapters were written with later chapters in mind. Furthermore, the Design Matrix itself is a product of foresight. While I have laid out possible criteria for scoring Discontinuity, Rationality, and Foresight in biological features, I am also aware that others can come along later and modify these criteria. The criteria are not set in stone, but can be modified and adapted to new insights. Nevertheless, the four criteria would remain and function as presented in this book. As a result, I'll give the book a Foresight score of 3. Taken together, the average Design Matrix score for this book would be 4.25, near a "strong" indicator of design.

Consider another object that is known to be designed—the automobile. Imagine we know nothing about the origin of such a vehicle. Since the car is very strongly analogous to other transportation devices known to be designed by humans (trucks, tractors, etc.), we can score Analogy as 5. We would likewise give it a Discontinuity score of 5 for the simple fact that non-teleological forces are incapable of constructing a working car. As for the Rationality score, the car is easily susceptible to structural and functional decomposition. And it seems to excel when features of good design are considered. However, since I lack detailed knowledge of the car and how it works,[9] I'd give it a score of 4. Finally, foresight also comes into play. There are many aspects to the car that demonstrate Original Mature Design (four wheels and an axle coupled to the motor through a transmission). Furthermore, many features of the car show foresight–seat belts and air bags become important during a crash, a hood that becomes important when it is time to repair the motor, etc. As such, I would score the criterion of Foresight as 4. That then gives us a Design Matrix score of 4.5, quite similar to the book.

Finally, let us consider the Face on Mars that could have been. If high-resolution pictures had shown a Face every bit as detailed as something from Mt. Rushmore, the Analogy score would have to be 5. Furthermore, as Richard Dawkins explained, non-teleological forces simply cannot sculpt something as detailed as a face from Mt. Rushmore, thus the Face would get a Discontinuity score of 5. However, since there would be no further information that would help us determine a Rationality and Foresight score, these two criteria would each weigh in as 0. That would give us a Design Matrix score of 2.5, which is significant because most people would still conclude design even though the Matrix would position the Face as something that moderately indicates design.

Let us now turn our attention to features that most people would agree as having a non-teleological origin. We will begin with the pseudogene, a string of nucleotides that has no function. As a string of conventional symbols, the pseudogene could be said to be analogous with human text, but without a function, it is analogous to something like "y&gqo*4ggdt5o." As such, it looks like text that was corrupted by non-teleological noise. Unless someone discovers that pseudogenes are analogous to computer passwords, I would have to give them an Analogy score of -5. Furthermore, since there is good evidence that genes can duplicate and spawn pseudogenes (because of subsequent mutation in one of the copies) and there does not seem to be an obstacle in any form that would prevent non-teleological processes from spawning them, I would give them a Discontinuity score of -5. When it comes to the criterion of Rationality, pseudogenes cannot be decomposed in structural/functional terms; sets of nucleotides do not constitute subsystems with their own respective subfunction. In fact, their lack of function prevents us from even applying the rules of engineering, as there is nothing to assess. This gives them a Rationality score of -5. Finally, there is nothing to indicate that pseudogenes represent foresight, although they might represent the spin-offs of a gene elsewhere undergoing the process of unpacking a front-loaded state. Pseudogenes do, however, act as an energy sink, where energy is wasted replicating and maintaining them. Yet this negative feature is probably only significant in uni-cellular creatures, as the energy wasted in a multi-cellular creature is likely to be insignificant. I would thus give the pseudogene a Foresight score of -3, yielding an average Design Matrix score of -4.5.

In Chapter 6, we used the PCP degradation pathway to illustrate the blind watchmaker as a designer-mimic. How does it score? In terms of Analogy, given that we are dealing with a sequential pathway, it is vaguely analogous to an assembly line in a factory or a circuit. However, the three enzymes are not physically linked, directly handing off the product of one enzyme to the next one in line. Thus, I would say it is a very weak analogy and give it an Analogy score of 1. In terms of Discontinuity, given its recent appearance and rather obvious origin using pre-existing enzymes from other metabolic pathways, I would score this as a -5. We also saw that the PCP pathway displays several features that indicate a sloppy, jury-rigged approach to the problem of PCP degradation, giving it a Rationality score of -4. Finally, there doesn't seem to be anything that counts for or against Foresight, thus I would give this criterion a score of 0. The result is a Design Matrix score of -2.

Thus far, the designed features range from a score of 2.5 to 4.5 while features that I would consider as having originated from non-teleological causes range from -2 to -4.5. Again, the scoring is subjective and subject to change upon further reflection or the addition of new information. Nevertheless, the basic reasoning is presented here such that readers can get a sense for how the scoring is done and how to perceive the phenomena. So let us turn to two other more ambiguous cases.

We have seen that teleologists as far back as Socrates have traditionally used the human eye as an example of design, but that modern science supports the contention that it evolved. How does the eye fare in the Matrix? The eye can indeed be likened to a camera, complete with biological equivalents of the outer casing (the eyeball), shutter (eyelid), diaphragm (iris), lens, and even film (retina). In fact, the eye even has built in automatic focusing along with light intensity controls. Yet, unlike the camera, the eye is not an assembly of distinct parts, but is instead grown from interlaced tissues during embryological development. As such, it gets an Analogy score of 3. Scoring Discontinuity may be a little trickier than many assume. It is indeed true that Darwin and Dawkins have provided a continuum of eyes, showing us the existence of simpler precursors and different light gathering strategies, as there are over forty different types of eyes in the living world. However, the ancestor of most importance when considering human eyes are the amphioxus, small and "primitive" fish-like organisms showing characteristics intermediate between vertebrates and invertebrates. Since these creatures give us the best glimpse of the ancestral chordate state, a consideration of their eyes would seem prudent. Amphioxus have simple eye-spots, but once we get to the bony fish, we have essentially the same eye as we find in a human being. In other words, the continuum of different eyes is not found within the lineage that leads to the human eye. This does not really pose much of a problem for the thesis of eye evolution, but does raise the possibility that it did not take very long to evolve a simple cluster of cells that respond to light into the camera-like arrangement of the human eye. Nevertheless, since we do not have the precursors within the lineage leading to the human eye, I will give the eye a Discontinuity score of -3. When we turn to the Rationality score, we come up against the backward wired retina that not only leads to the blind spot, but makes the eye prone to such diseases as a detached retina. However, since teleologists have raised interesting speculations that justify such backward wiring,[10] I will give it a Rationality score of -2. Finally, there is the issue of Foresight. There may be a faint echo of front-loading involved. For decades, scientists assumed that the dozens of different eyes seen throughout the living world evolved independently as strategies to provide a selective advantage of using light. The morphological diversity exhibited by all these different types of eyes spoke of the blind watchmaker, choosing any strategy that just happened to work. Yet it has recently become clear that there is a deeply conserved molecular universality among eyes, where all are built from the same set of genes that get independently recruited to evolve new eyes.[11] For example, if we go back to amphioxus and its primitive eyespots, their formation is guided by the developmental gene Pax-6. The same also holds true for the much more complex human eye. If we compare the amino acid sequence coded for by the Pax-6 genes of vertebrates and amphioxus, they show striking similarity, where one domain shows 92% identity and another domain shows a 100% identity.[12]

Another interesting discovery pertains to the last common ancestor of vertebrates and invertebrates. Vertebrate and invertebrate eyes use different types of photoreceptor cells employing a different form of circuitry. Yet recent evidence has surfaced indicating their last common ancestor possessed *both* cell types,[13] raising the distinct possibility that Allan Force's front-loading-friendly hypothesis of gene duplication followed by subfunctionalization[14] may have played a role in teasing apart these different strategies already possessed by a complex ancestor. Even more friendly to the hypothesis of front-loading is "the finding of highly developed eyes with a lens, vitreous body, stacked membranes like a retina and shielding pigment in uni-cellular dinoflagellates" that "raises the possibility that the prototypic eyes might have been acquired from symbionts."[15] On the other hand, the eye itself may have been a vehicle of front-loading the nervous system and brain, as the eye may have helped channel the brain's evolution.[16] The newly emerging picture hints at front-loading, giving the eye a Foresight score of 2. Together, the Design Matrix score for the eye is 0, which is completely ambiguous. Again, this does not indicate the eye did not evolve (as it has a -3 score for Discontinuity), but that it remains a working hypothesis that its evolution was teleological in some form.

Finally, how does the genetic code fare when it is put through the Matrix? The fact that the code employs a string of symbols that conventionally connects one form of linear text to another, coupled with its strong similarities to Morse code, gives the genetic code a strong Analogy score of 4. When it comes to Discontinuity, we must pay tribute to the fact that there are dozens, perhaps hundreds, of papers where scientists have speculated about the evolutionary origin of the code and gathered circumstantial evidence to support their respective cases. Nevertheless, the various explanations remain largely in the realm of speculation and two simple facts remain. First, experience has shown us that codes typically are the products of mind, and non-teleological forces do not generate codes. In fact, if the genetic code is taken off the table, there is no evidence that a conventional code employing a linear array of symbols has ever been spawned by a non-teleological force. Second, the code is universal, lacking any trace of simpler precursors or permutations spawned from such ancient precursor states. Recall Lynn Margulis' lesson about mitosis from the last chapter: if the code was indeed spawned from non-teleological forces acting over great spans of time, we would predict the existence of such permutations someplace in the biological world. That they do not exist argues against such an origin. As a result of the above considerations, I give the code a Discontinuity score of 2.

Regarding Rationality, the recent discovery that the code has been apparently optimized to buffer against deleterious mutations[17] clearly reflects a rationality not appreciated when the code was originally viewed as a frozen accident. In addition, John Casti, in his book, *Five More Golden Rules*[18] observes:

> An optimal code is one that is both instantaneous and has the minimum average code-word length. It turns out that the genetic code does indeed make the most economical use of its nucleotide symbols.

Diego Gonzalez, from the St. George Foundation and National Research Council of Italy, also notes that the "digital nature of amino acid encoding allows for the development of computational models of DNA which in turn permit the application of information theory techniques for the analysis and interpretation of long genome sequences."[19] He develops a mathematical model that describes the degeneracy of the code and uncovers a new symmetry within. By assigning a binary string to each of the codons, he is able to classify them into "parity classes" (reminiscent of Dónall A. Mac Donaill's work with the nucleotide alphabet described in Chapter 4) and adds that this "is particularly appealing in connection with the fact that parity coding is the basis of the simplest strategies devised for error correction in man-made digital data transmission systems." Gonzalez ends his mathematical analysis with these final comments:

> It remains striking, however, that different fundamental properties of the genetic code, such as degeneracy distribution, and also unexpected hidden properties, such as the palindromic symmetry and the parity marking of triplets presented here, reflect a strong mathematical order which is accurately described by means of one of the most elementary operations at the root of mathematics: number representation.

Added to this is another highly sophisticated mathematical analysis from two Russian scientists that suggests the genetic code not only codes for amino acids, but also codes for the three-dimensional conformation of proteins.[20] When all these considerations are taken together, I would give the code a Rationality score of 4. That leaves us with Foresight.

The code clearly demonstrates Original Mature Design, as seen through its universal nature. Thus, whoever or whatever designed the code got it right from the start. What would make this even more significant from a front-loading perspective is whether this original code—that supposedly evolved in some primitive, proto-life form—also just happens to nicely serve intricately complex life forms that appeared billions of years later. In Chapter 4, we explored the fact that while error minimization may be crucial in an organism as complex as a human being, it is not clear it would also be just as critical in such proto-life forms. Yet why would a code, adapted to the needs of some primitive single-cell-like entity, newly birthed by the ancient planet Earth, also just happen to equally serve the adaptive needs of butterflies, corn, sharks, grasshoppers, kangaroos, and hawks? It is as if the design strategies used by primitive man to build his mud huts could be identically employed to build the Sears Tower in Chicago. Recall also that there *are* variants to the universal genetic code, largely restricted to the bacteria and mitochondria.[21] Thus, the code is not strictly frozen in place and can change. A recent study showed that even slight changes in the code can result in profound differences in patterns of nucleotide substitutions, raising the specter of the code actually filtering molecular evolution.[22] This is significant, as much of evolution is explained by random nucleotide changes, not pruned by selection (genetic drift). That most organisms have kept the code they were handed suggests that not only do they all adaptively approve of its error minimization qualities, but also of the way it filters their overall pattern of mutations throughout the ages. To this we can add my speculations about the way this "error-resistant" code also just happens to make maximal use of one of the most common forms of point mutation, cytosine deamination, to elicit the Increased Hydrophobicity Effect (Chapter 7). If it is determined that the Increased Hydrophobicity Effect has played a pivotal role in a significant evolutionary transition (i.e., uni-cellular to multi-cellular), this would add to the Foresight score. But as of now, I am content with scoring this criterion as a 2, as there are hints that allow us to perceive a code designed with the future in mind. Thus, I would give the genetic code an overall Design Matrix score of 3.

These various Design Matrix scores can be visually represented in one of three ways to help illustrate our thinking process. The first method is a loose representation, where the average scores are all arranged along a number line (Figure 10-4). When this is done, it becomes clear that the Matrix tends to lean toward design when the Design Matrix score is above 2, lean

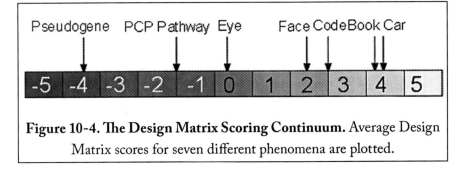

Figure 10-4. The Design Matrix Scoring Continuum. Average Design Matrix scores for seven different phenomena are plotted.

toward non-teleological evolution when the score is less than -2, and remain in limbo with scores in between. From here it becomes clear that the genetic code is in the neighborhood of things that are known to be designed (books, cars) and is also far removed from things that non-teleological evolution produced.

Second, each of the four categories can be visually represented by employing the metaphor of a traffic light that informs us whether or not to proceed with our design inference (Figure 10-5). Here, each category is represented by coding positive values as white ("go"), negative values as black ("stop") and zero as gray ("caution"). Then, by arraying them in tandem, we can visualize how each item being scored fares in the Matrix. I have scored something as having been designed (book, car, Face on Mars that could have been, and code) when there are no black lights and at least two white lights. On the other hand, when I score something as the product of non-teleological evolution (pseudogenes and PCP pathway), there are at least two black lights. I considered the origin of the eye as being ambiguous, as teleological evolution may be in play. Reflecting this perspective is a balance of two white lights and two black lights. But the most significant aspect of this analysis is that it demonstrates that our design inference for the genetic code is not rooted in a "god-of-the-gaps" argument. Such an argument would have a defining pattern of gray-white-gray-gray, where the only indicator of design would be an argument for discontinuity. Rather than showing us this pattern, the code exhibits white-white-white-white.

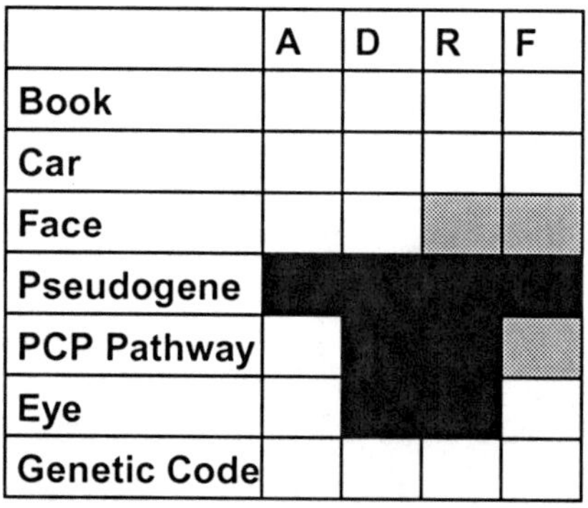

	A	D	R	F
Book				
Car				
Face			▒	▒
Pseudogene	■	■	■	■
PCP Pathway		■		▒
Eye		■	■	
Genetic Code				

Figure 10-5. The Matrix Design Inference Lights.

The final way to illustrate our analysis is to consider the four criteria in more detail with histograms (Figure 10-6). When this is done, the pattern exhibited by the book and car is the opposite of that seen with the pseudogenes. Also, the pattern exhibited by analysis of the Face on Mars that could have been is essentially the opposite of the PCP pathway. If we focus on the genetic code, it clearly shows a pattern reminiscent of the book and car. It is also easy to imagine how this situation could have been entirely different. For example, say there were many different codes that could be readily changed by natural selection, such that the code seen today would be just one among many. Further, imagine these codes could be arranged into a tree-like pattern, showing a nested hierarchy with a very simple code at the base. This would clearly move the Discontinuity score deep into the black realm. Or imagine that Francis Crick was right and the code is a frozen accident, and that none of the error minimization and mathematical features exist, but instead, the code appears to be irrational. This would move the Rationality and Foresight scores into the black realm. In other words, the design inference behind the code is in response to the pattern of data, not simply lack of a non-teleological demonstration. It is easy to envision data patterns that would be far more unfriendly to a design inference. They just do not exist.

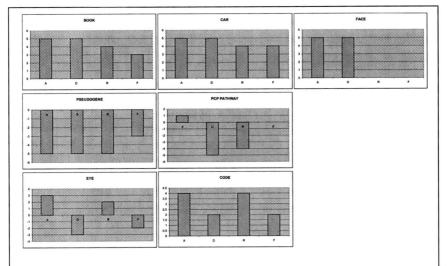

Figure 10-6. Histogram Representations of Design Matrix Scoring.

Getting Ready for the Quest

It is important to again stress that the Design Matrix is not an objective, physical measurement that detects design. The Matrix is a scoring system and, as such, is ultimately subjective. For example, when I give the genetic code a Design Matrix score of 3, this does not mean that all people everywhere are obligated to concur. Nor does it mean that the score cannot change as a consequence of new information or further consideration. Nevertheless, the Matrix focuses our thinking process and helps to clarify why people would and would not infer design in any particular instance. And while in the end the scoring is subjective, it is not whimsical. The Matrix allows us to examine a biological feature from four different perspectives and points of emphasis. In the spirit of the Explanatory Continuum (Chapter 2), it searches for the subtleties crucial to any investigation and helps to both gauge and illustrate our convictions. For those open-minded about various forms of design amid life, it allows such investigators the opportunity to compare notes and perhaps arrive at some kind of consensus. A comparison of Matrix scores between respective judges may even help to clarify if one scorer is thinking in terms of Ontological Evidence, while the other is looking for Epistemological Evidence (Chapter 6). The Matrix helps us to systematically clarify our mental picture of the Rabbit.

Despite its subjective nature, the Matrix helps assess our suspicion of Intelligent Design. It provides guidance for research, giving us direction for the formulation of testable hypotheses in accord with the four criteria. What is more, the four criteria can provide focus as we assess the mountain of mainstream scientific research that already exists, where data interpreted from the perspective of the Duck can be reinterpreted in light of the Rabbit.

Yet missing from all of this is a story. It is one thing to look around at isolated biological features and try to score them. It is another thing to use the Design Matrix as an integral part of storytelling. The Duck is obvious to so many because the Duck has a story about the past—our past. As such, the story has become more detailed, more tested, and more deeply intertwined with data over the years. Yet the Rabbit should have his own story to tell. A tentative historical narrative that factors in design as part of the plot might allow the Rabbit to become more obvious.

If we are to tell the Rabbit's story, it is important to understand something from the beginning. The Duck's story has been neatly groomed by decades of work involving thousands of brilliant scientists using billions of research dollars. We should not expect the Rabbit to jump out of his hole and be so neatly groomed. Forcing him out of the hole is a major accomplishment in and of itself; the grooming will take time. In other words, we should not expect a teleological story to be some perfect yin-yang equivalent to the non-teleological story relying heavily on neo-Darwinian evolution. Instead, since we are dealing with a thoroughly ambiguous topic, it would be better to compare the Rabbit's story to the stories currently being told to explain a non-teleological origin of life. And one such story helps us understand how to proceed.

There are many speculations about the origin of life and many contradict each other. This is so because the origin of life is biology's most ambiguous problem. One speculation suggests that the chemistry of the cell arose in a primordial mineral honeycomb, where the cell membrane was the last thing to evolve.[23] There is no need to explore the plausibility of this hypothesis, as the lessons are in the scientific community's reaction to the hypothesis, as reported by John Whitfield for the journal *Nature*.[24]

First, Whitfield reports the opinion of evolutionary biologist Ford Doolittle of Dalhousie University, who observes that we will never have much solid information about the origin of life. But Doolittle also notes, "just because we'll never know why the Roman Empire fell doesn't mean it isn't worth talking about."[24] Fair enough, but if life was designed, we would likewise probably be without much definite information. Just as standard origin-of-life accounts are still worth talking about, so too are notions of life's design. In fact, simply talking about life's design can lead to speculations of what this involves and this, in turn, can nurture a better understanding of life. Attempts to squelch discussions of design until we first extract a database of definite information (i.e., actual mechanisms, identity of designer, etc.) are seriously misguided and thwart the most useful way to brainstorm about an ambiguous topic.

THE DESIGN MATRIX

The second lesson comes from Thomas Cavalier-Smith, a leading expert in evolutionary biology. He reacted to the hypothesis by stating, "It's quite impossible that it could be right."[24] Yet the hypothesis was published in the peer-reviewed literature. Just because a leading authority may declare someone's speculation impossible does not mean we should not allow the speculation. All speculations, in their initial stages, are vulnerable to hyper-skepticism. To expect any speculation to somehow cause all the facts to suddenly fall into place is unrealistic.

Our third lesson comes from John Raven of the University of Dundee, UK. Whitfield quotes him as follows:

> It may be that no theory is going to fit all the evidence. The trick is to pick which bits to ignore, says John Raven of the University of Dundee, UK. "To create a coherent hypothesis we have to say 'this bit of data doesn't fit, but we're going ahead anyway.'"[24]

This illustrates what is commonly seen with origin of life research—a certain degree of slack is granted to these speculations, as everyone realizes the topic is quite ambiguous and there is a huge problem extracting definitive information about these events. Thus, when brainstorming, sometimes you have to ignore some bit of data here and there, with the plan of returning to them once the original hypothesis is better worked out.

Origin-of-life research is a field of inquiry that lacks consensus, focuses on how things could have happened because such speculation itself is inherently worth contemplating, tolerates hypotheses that some experts might label as impossible, and entails a certain degree of subjectivity when focusing on the data. This is important to keep in mind as many expect a hypothesis of design to adhere to a much higher standard, insisting the initial design hypothesis have the properties of a mature scientific theory. Those who would follow the Rabbit need only follow the example scientists have laid down as they explore the origin of life.

So as we begin our journey, these lessons, coupled with all the lessons in these chapters, must be kept in mind. We are not engaging in a Duck Hunt; we are going to chase the Rabbit. So, do you see that rabbit hole over your shoulder? Yeah, that one. Wanna have some fun? Well, grab your Design Matrix, and follow that Rabbit.

References

1. "Using ID to Understand the Living World." http://www.idthink.net/ biot/proof/index.html. Also see "Proofreading and Deception?" http:// www.idthink.net/biot/proof2/index.html.
2. "Lagging Strand Synthesis from a Telic Perspective." http://www.idthink. net/biot/lag/index.html.
3. "Evolution's Design." http://www.idthink.net/biot/deam/index.html.
4. "Evolving the Bacterial Flagellum through Mutation and Cooption." http://www.idthink.net/biot/flag1/index.html.
5. "The Neglected Flagellum." http://www.idthink.net/biot/eflag/index. html. Also see "Assembling the Eukaryotic Flagellum: Another Example of IC?" http://www.idthink.net/biot/eflag2/index.html.
6. "A Teleological Hypothesis about a Machine." http://www.idthink.net/biot/ degrad/. Also see "Update on Degradosome Function: The Importance of Location." http://www.idthink.net/biot/degrad2/index.html.
7. "Spinning Wheels." http://www.idthink.net/biot/wheel/index.html.
8. There is much precedent for this type of scoring. For example, medical researchers commonly use scales to assess symptoms, environmental researchers use scales to assess the degree of pollution in a particular location, and teachers use rubrics to judge the performance of their students.
9. Of course, the score may differ depending on the particular car under consideration and the knowledge of engineering applied. Nevertheless, I am confident that when all aspects of any car are considered, the score would fall in the moderate to strong range.
10. Lindsay, J., 2005. "The Lack of Design in Nature?" http://www.jefflindsay.com/DesignFlaws.shtml; last accessed 11/17/04.
11. Fernald R.D., 2004. "Eyes: Variety, Development and Evolution." *Brain*

Behavior and Evolution, 64:141-147.

12. Glardon S., Holland L.Z., Gehring, W.J. and Holland, N.D., 1998. "Isolation and Developmental Expression of the Amphioxus Pax-6 Gene (AmphiPax-6): Insights into Eye and Photoreceptor Evolution." *Development*, 125:2701-2710.

13. Arendt, D., Tessmar-Raible, K., Snyman, H., Dorresteijn, A.W. and Wittbrodt, J., 2004. "Ciliary Photoreceptors with a Vertebrate-Type Opsin in an Invertebrate brain." *Science*, 306:869-871.

14. See Chapter 7.

15. Gehring, W.J., 2002. "The Genetic Control of Eye Development and Its Implications for the Evolution of the Various Eye-Types." *International Journal of Developmental Biology*, 46:65-73.

16. In this sense, it is interesting to ponder the ocular-centric nature of our thinking and whether it could have been front-loaded.

17. See Chapter 4.

18. Casti, J.L., 2001. *Five More Golden Rules: Knots, Codes, Chaos, and Other Great Theories of 20th-Century Mathematics*. Wiley, New York.

19. Gonzalez, D.L., 2004. "Can the Genetic Code Be Mathematically Described?" *Medical Science Monitor*, 10: HY11-17.

20. Karasev, V.A. and Stefanov, V.E., 2001. "Topological Nature of the Genetic Code." *Journal of Theoretical Biology*, 209: 303-317.

21. Freeland, S.J., Knight, R.D., Landweber, L.F. and Hurst, L.D., 2000. "Early Fixation of an Optimal Genetic Code." *Molecular Biology and Evolution*, 17:511-518.

22. McClellan, D.A., Whiting, D.G., Christensen, R. and Sailsbery, J., 2004. "Genetic Codes as Evolutionary Filters: Subtle Differences in the Structure of Genetic Codes Result in Significant Differences in the Pattern of Nucleotide Substitution." *Journal of Theoretical Biology*, 226: 393-400.

23. Martin, W. and Russell, M., 2002. "On the Origins of Cells: A Hypothesis for the Evolutionary Transitions from Abiotic Geochemistry to Chemoautotrophic Prokaryotes, and from Prokaryotes to Nucleated Cells." *Philosophical Transactions of the Royal Society of London*, 358:59-83.

24. Whitfield, J., 2002. "Mineral Cells Might Have Incubated First Living Things." http://www.nature.com/news/2002/021202/full/021202-2.html; last accessed 01/20/03.

INDEX

chance 8, 15, 19–20, 73–75, 115–116, 128, 131, 137, 142, 147, 153, 155, 164, 166, 170, 173, 175, 223–224, 226-228, 245, 259
Chandler, Daniel 125–126, 136
Chaos Theory 131
chaperones 40, 43, 91, 108
chaperonins 91
choanoflagellates 264–265
Cicero, Marcus 21
Clark, Mary Anne 72, 87
codon 68, 71–72, 74, 87, 174–175
coherence 253-254
Colwell, Rita 105
computer as design metaphor 39, 49–52, 59, 71, 74, 77, 79, 80, 103, 107, 144, 167, 171, 203–205, 259, 277
contingency 137–138, 142, 145, 159, 166, 169, 179
Conway-Morris, Simon 171, 187
cooption 170–171, 180–181, 226–231, 239, 289
  Cooption of Alternative Function 222–223, 227
  gradual cooption 229–235
  quantum cooption 229
Copley, Shelly D. 135, 162, 185, 198, 236
cost of complexity 169, 187
Creationism 28, 255
creationists 19, 20, 27–28
Crick, Francis 141, 182, 260–261, 266, 285
  central dogma 260–261
  frozen accident 73, 82, 260–262, 271, 281, 285
  Watson-Crick base pair 79
Cydonia 5–6
cytochromes 172–173
cytoplasm 13, 92, 108, 186
cytosine (C). See nucleotides: cytosine (C)

cytoskeleton 42, 151, 162

D

Darwin, Charles 11–12, 21, 22, 24–27, 36, 115–118, 128, 130, 141, 196, 208, 212, 215, 239, 279
  Gray, Asa, letter to 34, 36
  The Origin of Species 24
  Theory of Evolution 11, 22, 85, 128, 168
Darwinism / Darwinian evolution 22, 24–25, 85, 115–119, 129, 140, 142–145, 143, 179–181, 196, 215–219, 224, 227, 229, 230, 239, 258
databases
  Biological Abstracts 47, 57
  GeoRef 47, 57
  INSPEC 47, 57
  PubMed 59, 93, 199
Davies, Paul 47, 49, 62, 90, 107
Dawkins, Richard 8, 17, 117–118, 135, 181, 208, 212, 217–218, 238–239, 266, 277, 279
  abrupt precipice 217–218
  blind watchmaker 117–118, 211
  designoid 117–119
deamination 174–176, 178, 283
decomposition 247–252, 277
  functional decomposition 247–252, 277
  structural decomposition 247–252, 277
degradosomes 91
De Loof, Arnold 46, 62
Dembski, William 193, 236
Democritus 19
DeRosier, David 42, 61
design, inference of
  discontinuity 198–199, 214–217
  familiarity 9–10
  designer-centric approach 193–195

Q

Quake, Steve 106, 110
quantum mechanics 104
quantum physics 70, 104

R

rabbit 123, 127–131, 135, 146, 179,
    181, 260, 269, 271, 286,
    288–289
Ramasarma, T. 162–163, 185
Rational Design 182, 243, 248–250,
    254
rationality 85, 254, 258, 274, 281
Ratner, Daniel 210
Ratner, Mark 210
Raven, John 288
reducibly complex mousetrap.
    See McDonald, John: reducibly
    complex mousetrap
replication 23, 56, 78–79, 81, 83, 86,
    90, 94–95, 141–142, 150–151,
    205
replisome 90–91, 94
reproduction 23, 85, 106, 140–143,
    146, 263–264
ribosomes 72
RNA (ribonucleic acid) 50, 54, 56,
    62, 65–69, 71, 77, 81, 84–88,
    90–92, 94, 108, 141, 150–151,
    163, 178–179, 184, 186, 205,
    251, 252, 260
    messenger (mRNA) 69–70, 80, 84,
        94, 104, 221
    ribosomal RNA (rRNA) 69
    RNA polymerase 56, 68, 84–85, 94,
        152
    transfer RNA (tRNA) 69, 80, 87

S

Sagan, Carl 130–131, 136
Salmonella typhimurium 156
Sanchez, Deigo 170–171, 187

Schiaparelli, Giovanni 3
Scopes Trial 20
Scott, John D. 13, 18
Search for Extra-terrestrial Intelligence
    (SETI) 73, 194
Shanks, Niall 99, 109
Shannon information laws 73
Shapiro, James 50, 59, 62, 204–205,
    238
Shapiro, Lucy 13, 17, 107
Sidis, William James 25, 109
Smith, George 146, 182
Socrates 19–20, 279
Soup view of cell 12, 14–15
specificity 79, 145, 246, 252–254
Sphingomonas chlorophenolica 113,
    114–115
Spielberg, Stephen. *See* War of the
    Worlds
spliceosome 91
Stanciu, George 71, 87, 101–102, 109
Structural decomposition.
    See decomposition: structural
    decomposition
subfunctionalization 166, 167

T

tape-of-life 137
tape recorder (analogy) 49, 69
teleologists. *See* Aristotle;
    See Diogenes; *See* Paley,
    William; *See* Plato; *See* Socrates
teleology 22, 28, 34, 53, 96, 128, 137
theistic evolutionists 131
Thomas-Wohlever, J. 183
Thornhill, Richard 217–219, 239
thymine. *See* nucleotides: thymine
tinkerer, the. *See* Jacob, François:
    tinkerer, the
Tipler, Frank 20, 36
top-down processing 126
topoisomerases 91
Traditional Template 24, 26–27,
    29–31, 130, 181

Printed in the United States
104254LV00001B/18/A